PARADOXICAL FEMINISM

The Novels of Rebecca West

Ann V. Norton

International Scholars Publications
Lanham • New York • Oxford

Copyright 2000 by
International Scholars Publications
4720 Boston Way
Lanham, Maryland 20706

12 Hid's Copse Rd.
Cumnor Hill, Oxford OX2 9JJ

Library of Congress Cataloging-in-Publication Data

ISBN 1-57309-392-0 (cloth: alk. ppr.)

♾™ The paper used in this publication meets the minimum
requirements of American National Standard for Information
Sciences—Permanence of Paper for Printed Library Materials,
ANSI Z39.48—1984

For Kelly, Ella, Rebecca, and Tomi

Contents

Foreword

I first read Ann Norton's work on Rebecca West during research for a biography of Rebecca West. After reading feminist critics who seemed disappointed in West's career, and male critics who seemed far more taken with her nonfiction, Norton's resolute and perceptive probing of West's novels was bracing. Now that Norton has revised and updated her dissertation for book publication, she has enriched her readings of West's fiction by taking into account the most recent biographical and critical studies. No student of West or of her period can fail to profit from Norton's graceful and sensitive argument.

"Paradoxical feminism" seems precisely the right term for West. Norton never wavers in her view that West remained a feminist her entire life. Any number of quotations can be culled from West's body of work that attack patriarchy, that support the drive for women's rights, and that show how she expressed her solidarity with women. And yet West most often in her fiction seemed to succumb to the romance story of the all powerful male. Most disturbing perhaps is *The Judge,* in which the feisty Ellen Melville becomes caught up in love for a man who seems strong and yet is found to be hopelessly fixated on his mother. Therein lies the paradox: the idea of the powerful male, the king who sets the kingdom right, is appealing to West even as she exposes the fact that most men cannot sustain their pretensions to power. In the end, they fail their women, according to a bitterly disappointed West. Nevertheless, in her fiction, as in her life, she still sought her king.

Such a paradoxical feminist is off putting to programmatic feminists, who prefer the early, undaunted West, so much like the young and vigorous Ellen Melville. But West was honest about her weaknesses and about the weaknesses she saw in women. Some women, even strong women, yearn to be saved by a man. This does not seem a flaw in West's feminism so much as an acknowledgment of reality, of women like West, who portrayed women who felt they had to save themselves and wanted a savior nevertheless.

West's paradoxical feminism, it seems to me, is a very human contradiction that actually strengthens her fiction even if it does not issue marching orders to women in the war against patriarchy. I believe that West believed in D. H. Lawrence's sense of the novel as the "bright book of life." The novel had to encompass all contradictions; the novel did not simply present arguments for or against anything. In her fiction,

West courageously explored the psychology of herself and other women no matter what that meant for the positions she had taken as an essayist.

To put it another way, feminism as an ideology may require its adherents to present consistent, logical positions. But feminism, or any ism for that matter, is likely to look paradoxical when examined by a novelist working at full strength. Norton is not averse to claiming for West a measure of greatness as a novelist. I think Norton is right. While I still believe that *The Birds Fall Down* is West's best novel, her unfinished trilogy—perhaps because it is a ruin wrenched from her paradoxical life and art—represents a towering achievement, one that Ann Norton is the first to recognize and to illuminate.

CARL ROLLYSON

Baruch College, City University of New York

Foreword

Rebecca West, like most writers with strong views about the roles and relations of the sexes, has been more often judged than understood. In literary criticism, as in all other relationships between individuals, understanding is more important than approval, and Ann Norton is perhaps the first critic who has taken the trouble to listen to what Rebecca West had to say in her fiction, and the first critic to make sense of its complexities. Writing at a time in which West is little more than a famous name, Ann Norton makes clear why her books were once read not only by a mass audience but also by elite audiences of sophisticated and powerful readers through whom her work had an effect on both literary and political history.

West's career intriguingly mirrors that of the novelist she most admired, D.H. Lawrence. Both writers wrote fierce polemics on sexual and political subjects, although they professed opposite views on the proper status of the sexes. The views expressed in their polemics might be understood as their "official" positions: straightforward, assertive, and easily summarized. But both also wrote novels in which, without acknowledging that they were doing anything of the kind, they adopted what might be called their "unofficial" positions, in which they undermined and even reversed their official ones. In their expository prose, their self-presentations were uncomplicatedly heroic; in their fiction, complicatedly self-doubting and contradictory.

The swings in reputation suffered by many twentieth-century writers follow a consistent pattern, exemplified most clearly in D.H. Lawrence but also in T.S. Eliot. At first, these writers were honored as prophets and sages by a readership that read their imaginative works—their novels or poems—as statements of the official views in their expository prose. Then, when a new generation of readers began to piece together their unorthodox and unofficial views, and began to notice how different these were from the official ones, their reputations suffered a precipitous decline. But later still, a third generation, distant enough from the old polemical struggles to regard them as historically interesting rather than as occasions for new battles, discovered the complex humanity in these writers, and learned to sympathize with their divided motives without feeling the need to endorse or condemn them for their views. And their reputations slowly revived in a way that had seemed impossible only a few years earlier.

Ann Norton's book is a sign that the mature sympathy which readers have begun to offer Lawrence and Eliot may now also be granted to Rebecca West. Earlier critics chose to focus on either her official or unofficial position and responded to her with almost unequivocal praise or blame. Ann Norton perceives the shifting dialectic between the two positions, recognizes West's fiction as far more memorable and disturbing than her expository prose, and demonstrates that it deserves the close and intelligent attention that this book so persuasively and sympathetically offers.

EDWARD MENDELSON

Columbia University

Preface

In the last twenty years there has been an extraordinary revival of interest in non-canonical, "forgotten" female twentieth-century writers. This interest has included Rebecca West, who during and after her lifetime has been called "the world's number one woman writer," "the greatest woman since Elizabeth I," and "a strong contender for woman of the century."[1] Yet one is unlikely to read an article or book on West from the last twenty years that does not begin or end with the statement that she has been oddly neglected by scholars, critics, and common readers, and particularly by the feminists among them. Almost without fail, critics cite similar reasons for why West has not acquired a strong academic or popular status: her extraordinary tendency to write in different styles, genres, and voices; the fact that her published works span almost a century of incredible social, political, and literary changes; her eventually conservative stance, which included explosive anger toward Communists and homosexuals; and the fact that she does not inhabit a recognizably modernist or post-modernist space. Therefore, the scholar or critic may conclude, West must be viewed from outside the canon, as a powerful writer of unified themes if not recognizable forms, whose readership will inevitably be lessened by this disparate literary body. Indeed, West perpetuates this idea herself in *Black Lamb and Grey Falcon.* In an oft-quoted passage, she explains to a graduate student interested in writing her dissertation on West that she "was a writer wholly unsuitable for her purpose" since "the bulk" of her writing is "scattered through American and English periodicals." Her subjects "might severally play a part in theses on London or St. Augustine or the rich, but could not fuse to make a picture of a writer, since the interstices were too wide."[2]

If one clear impression of Rebecca West the artist and thinker remains in the public imagination one hundred years after her birth, it is that she was a feminist. Her career began in 1911 with suffrage-supporting articles in *The Freewoman,* and her 1983 *Newsweek* obituary was titled "Ninety Years of Ardent Feminism."[3] Yet the four

critical books on West that exist as I write in 1999 were all written by
men, who examine her entire canon according to genre or chronology.[4]
The authors concentrate on her rendering of meaty subjects like war,
espionage, European history, good and evil, the Augustinian doctrine of
original sin, justice and law, all the while admiring West's extraordinary
intellectual compass, astounding for any person, but especially for a
woman born in 1892. While each of these thorough monographs
discusses West's feminism, none focuses on it specifically, and each
(with the exception of Carl Rollyson's *The Literary Legacy of Rebecca
West)* specifically elevates her non-fiction over her fiction.

    Certain feminist critics have embraced West, and have tried to fuse
her wide interstices into some clear and positive picture of a twentieth-
century woman writer. Sandra Gilbert and Susan Gubar analyze her
"Indissoluble Matrimony," a Lawrence-influenced short story that
appeared in the first issue of *Blast*, as West's version of "the dis-ease of
no-manhood" that becomes "a basis for sexual battle."[5] Jane Marcus
edited West's early feminist and socialist articles for the collection *The
Young Rebecca: Writings of Rebecca West 1911-1917*, and has written
on *Harriet Hume* and *The Judge* as triumphant feminist modernist
literature.[6] There are perhaps a dozen scholarly articles on both her
journalism and fiction, most notably those by Margaret Diane Stetz,
who champions West as a feminist modernist who stressed "affiliation"
with artistic predecessors rather than the "dissociation and discontinuity"
that was the "favored aesthetic" of masculine modernists.[7] Loretta Stec
analyzes West's "contradictory career" as one that "approached, used, and
transformed dominant discourses" in twentieth-century England in ways
that gained her "authority and fame during her life," and that provide
feminists with "a rich set of texts in which conservative and radical
discourses intersect, diverge, and clash."[8] Bonnie Kime Scott includes
West in her pioneering anthology *The Gender of Modernism,* and as one
of three pivotal "women of 1928," along with Djuna Barnes and
Virginia Woolf, in her two-volume study *Refiguring Modernism.*[9]

    Yet other female critics have found reasons to question West's
feminist identity. Moira Ferguson writes that while West "never
foreswor[e] her early commitment to feminism (in the sense of an
ideology which practices as well as advocates the political equality of
women)," her

> feminist manicheanism. . .has tended to see history and human
> affairs less in a theoretical framework and more in terms of individual
> personalities. In this respect, she breaks ranks with those
> contemporary feminists who see the oppression of individual women
> as the result of institutionalized societal structure."[10]

Ferguson dislikes West's "stress on psychological rather than sociohistorical forces" (56) because she "never considers the contribution of *society* in bringing matters to this pitch, nor does she stress the need for collective as well as individual resistance" (59). She objects to West's self-congratulatory sense of herself "as an artist with special truths to offer the world" rather than as a feminist in solidarity with other feminists.

Gloria Fromm takes issue with the seemingly schizophrenic split between West's tough, excellent, "masculine" journalism and her "pulpy" fiction that celebrates traditional marriage. Fromm describes

> an attitude toward the sexes and the sex-relation that prevailed throughout Rebecca West's writing as well as her private life. Men, it seemed to her, were separate, other beings who, despite her feminist bravado, usually had the upper hand, which she deeply resented but at the same time had grown up accepting. And inclined as she always was to think in terms of antitheses. . .she put fiction, from the first, on the feminine or personal side of the ledger. One is almost tempted to say that she wrote fiction as a woman addressing women and nonfiction as a man speaking to men; and men were patently more important in her eyes than women, which means that fiction counted for less in the larger world of public affairs, the world inhabited by all the men who mattered to her.[11]

Even in the earliest days of feminist criticism West was used as a negative example. In Mary Ellmann's seminal 1968 work *Thinking About Women,* her exploration of female stereotypes includes "Balloonism," which is "the highest mental quirk. . .a conception of the woman's mind as light, fragile, drifting, and buoyant. In this guise, women are considered capable of pretty ascents, but they must be controlled by masculine Ballast if they are not to blow away."[12] According to Ellmann, West's travel and history book of Yugoslavia, *Black Lamb and Grey Falcon,* illustrates "balloonism."

> Miss West and her husband neatly divide their touristical duties. The Ballast [West's husband] thinks sound, solid, careful thoughts. . . Meanwhile, the Balloon [West] *appreciates*, her working day is given over to piercing perceptions and lightning intuitions. (114)

The balloon needs the "stability, good sense and practical resourcefulness of the Ballast" (115) if she is to understand her experiences fully; hence, says Ellmann, West deliberately feigns the centuries-old intellectual inferiority assigned to women even as she takes on the daunting task of explaining Yugoslavia's entire history and its relationship to the first and second world wars.

This criticism bothers Victoria Glendinning, West's first biographer, but she cannot flatly contradict it without being untruthful. "Although the Balloon and Ballast image does to some extent reflect the complementary qualities of Rebecca and Henry [her husband] in real life," she writes (eighteen years after Ellmann) in *Rebecca West: A Life*,

> and although she consulted the reference-library of his mind constantly and with gratitude, Rebecca was in fact both Balloon and Ballast, her thirst for information being equal to her capacity for intuitive insights. . . The division of labour between the author and "my husband" in the book is in part a structural device. . .if it also reflects. . .a desire for men to be men and women to be women, that was because she had reason to feel that the qualities traditionally ascribed to women were manifested in her own world by men, and vice versa.[13]

West did indeed want men to be men and women to be women; and for those who might ask, "What does that mean?" or, "What men, what women?" West tries to answer them all through *Black Lamb and Grey Falcon*. While watching "three men. . .contemplating the unfinished hull of a motorboat" in Dalmatia, she thinks

> Something has changed us. The life we lead does not suit us. [These men] were all three beautiful, with thick, straight, fair hair and bronze skins and high cheekbones pulling the flesh up from their large mouths, with broad chests and long legs springing from arched feet. These were men, they could beget children on women, they could shape certain kinds of materials for purposes that made them masters of their worlds. I thought of two kinds of men that the West produces: the cityish kind who wears spectacles without shame, as if they were the sign of quality and not a defect, who is overweight and puffy, who can drive a car but knows no other mastery over material, who presses buttons and turns switches without comprehending the result, who makes money when the market goes up and loses it when the market goes down; the high-nosed young man, who is somebody's secretary or is in the Foreign Office, who has a peevishly amusing voice and is very delicate, who knows a great deal but far from all there is to be known about French pictures. I understand why we cannot build, why we cannot govern, why we bear ourselves without pride in our international relations. . .It is strange, it is heartrending, to stray into a world where men are still men and women are still women. (208)

If it were not for the rich, distinctive prose of this passage, one could imagine it on the back cover of an airport romance novel, the front cover showing the requisite buxom beauty in ecstatic submission to a muscular man. It is perhaps unfair to mock West here; sexual appreciation of beautiful young men is hardly a declaration of anti-feminism, and many sections of *Black Lamb* laud the strength and intelligence of Yugoslavian women in the face of their men's violence and "lunacy." Yet a motif runs throughout: the men are *real* men because they rule politically and domestically, because they build things with their hands, because they are physically powerful; the women are *real* women because they keep an orderly household, because they are faithful wives and mothers, because they are beautiful. As the passage makes clear, West means this in deadly earnest: because men are no longer *men*—"no men," as Gilbert and Gubar would name them—nothing less than the decline of British civilization has resulted. Can this be the same Rebecca West who wrote in 1912, "Never will Woman be saved until she realises that it is a far, far better thing to keep a jolly public house really well than to produce a cathedral full of beautiful thoughts"? (*Young Rebecca,* 17).

The most telling (and some would say the most appalling) instance of West's odd belief in (or desire for) the propriety of male dominance is her unfinished novel *Sunflower,* published posthumously in 1986. Written in the mid-1920s, it is an "autobiographical" depiction of a beautiful actress having an affair with a famous statesman, obviously modeled on West and H.G. Wells, her lover of ten years and father of her only child, and her infatuation with a business tycoon, clearly Lord Beaverbrook, with whom West had an affair after her breakup with Wells. Reviewers were amused and aghast at this story of a "stupid" sex goddess who desires "an end to the fretfulness of using the will, passivity,"[14] and seems to find it with a short and ugly but sexually masculine man. Jane Marcus, who genuinely cares, worried in *The Nation* that "the publication of *Sunflower* has damaged [West's] reputation," seeing it as a "revenge fantasy. . .not so much written as spat upon the page" and obviously "not meant for publication."[15] As the editor of *The Young Rebecca* very well might be, she was amazed at Sunflower's "longing for passive dependence": "Did Rebecca West, arguably one of the best writers of the age, really feel this way? Are we to believe that her fiery feminism was rotten at the core with masochism and self-hate?" (438).

Whether or not one believes that a woman's longing for passive dependence on a man is masochistic and self-hating (and Sunflower's relationship with Essington, the Wells figure, is both), such a longing is certainly not ideologically the desire of a feminist; so Marcus asks a key question. Was West, the famous feminist, not really a feminist at all? Does this beautifully written but sometimes embarrassing manuscript from West's post-Wells, pre-marriage life indicate her "true" feelings? Or is this odd book just another attempt by West to get into a different voice, style, and mood? West was undergoing psychoanalysis while writing *Sunflower*, in an attempt to discover why all her sexual relationships failed. It is not hard to go one step further and say that this book is West's temporary backlash against temporary sexual loneliness; that Sunflower's exaggerated submission fantasies show how far a woman who is strong and successful as well as sexual could be pushed by male sexual rejections maybe caused by her strength and success. "Indissoluble Matrimony," from a different viewpoint and with very different characters, involves the same theme, defined by Gilbert and Gubar as "the connection between male sexual anxiety and women's entrance into the public sphere" (*Vol. I*, 98). Perhaps *Sunflower* is an exploration of that subject from a perspective deliberately opposite West's.

If *Sunflower* were the only work in West's canon to reveal a woman's desire for submission, it would be easy to dismiss its seeming anti-feminism with any of these explanations. (Certainly West herself never finished it or wanted it published, even after Wells and Beaverbrook were dead. She must have known that not only the autobiographical content was potentially damaging.) Yet there is that surprising insistence upon "true" gender roles in *Black Lamb and Grey Falcon*, in which men are the "masters." There is the "London fantasy" *Harriet Hume*, ostensibly a feminist novel about female artistry and autonomy, but one whose heroine cheerfully forgives her male murderer and then sets up eternal housekeeping for him. The marvelous young suffragist Ellen Melville in *The Judge* loses her initial autonomy when she follows a romantic hero to his doom. *The Harsh Voice*, a collection of four short novels set in the Depression-era U.S., describes a new economic equality between the sexes as essentially disastrous because it destroys the sexual balance in which men are ascendant. While *The Thinking Reed* is as much a satirical as a serious novel, its independently wealthy female protagonist solemnly concludes that she will endure her husband's potentially destructive domination rather than leave him. *The Birds Fall Down* is partly a lament for lost patriarchal strength and structures. And in the three novels of *Cousin Rosamund: A Saga of the Century,* the greatest artists and thinkers among the characters are, deliberately, men.

While Ellmann, Fromm, and Ferguson are only three voices among many who have commented on West's writing and politics, they strike at the heart of West's contradictory views on men and women, and perhaps explain why Rebecca West has not been a natural focus for feminist critical studies, in spite of her suffragist history, her visibility in the Anglo-American literary world of the twentieth century, her triumphs in male-dominated journalism, her acute interest in women, and the fact that she tirelessly recorded that interest in fiction and non-fiction. I suggest that the reason Rebecca West has received less attention than she might from women, considering her topicality and worth, is this attitude of near anti-feminism. A better term is "paradoxical feminism," for West never adopted a misogynous outlook or a stance against women's rights—quite the opposite. Yet her seeming belief in "natural" gender roles that have been somehow violated and confused in modern times allies her with the masculinist Lawrence, whom she called "passionately right," not the feminist icon Woolf, who advocated androgyny (and who takes a few good stabs at West in her diaries).[16] This makes her a problem for postmodern feminists, many of whom are convinced that gender is performative, acquired through nurture rather than nature. And though West continued to write disparagingly of Western patriarchal culture throughout her journalistic career, her novels show a surprising belief in and desire for male dominance that increased with time and culminates in *This Real Night* and the unfinished *Cousin Rosamund*. That is hardly the only idea these books promote. But West's interest in male and female natures is so insistent that her novels can be read like palimpsests on sexual roles over which a plot has been inscribed; and while the subject and tone of each is often superficially feminist, West undermines her own feminism with this theme of the legitimacy of male supremacy.

It is my intention in this study to explore the "paradoxical feminism" of Rebecca West's novels: her many and contradictory ideas about how women should live their lives, how they have lived their lives, and why.[17] It is the first book on West devoted solely to her fiction, and in fact to one particular aspect within that genre. Each chapter investigates different aspects of West's paradoxical feminism through close readings of the novels' characters, themes, and plots. These include her attitudes toward women as artists and professionals; women as subjects and objects in men's and women's narratives; women and men as parents; women and men in marriage; and the use of female "magic" as both a female language and a force for evil. I have concentrated most on the *Cousin Rosamund* trilogy, partly because it has received minimal critical attention, but largely because I believe this fascinating autobiographical *Kunstlerroman,* which aims to be no less than "a saga of the century," constitutes her greatest fiction.

West's most basic paradox is this: while she expresses tremendous anger toward men and many aspects of patriarchal structures, she creates simultaneously an elaborate, if at times cynical, rationalization for women's "appropriate" subordination to masculine frameworks and culture. She states, and implies, that men fail if women succeed, because men's ability to oppress women is an integral part of their overall incentive to work. West also implies that much of male sexual attraction to women is based on a traditional dominant/submissive dichotomy, and that if this dichotomy is removed, then so is the erotic desire. And to West, for a woman to live without sexual love is a tragedy greater than the waste of a woman's intellectual or artistic promise. This inspires her to subvert traditional female narratives in surprising ways: rather than going into marriages that prevent them from achieving artistic or professional selfhood, often her female characters choose marriages that diminish artistic or professional personas they have already worked hard to accomplish.

The germs for such ideas can be traced to West's own life, and to the twentieth century's fluctuating attitudes toward feminism, to which West was highly sensitive. Very successful in the male-dominated field of journalism from an early age, West believed that she intimidated men with her career, her brains, and her energy. Her affair with Wells never culminated in the marriage she desired; her strong attraction for Lord Beaverbrook was finally unrequited; her husband Henry Andrews stopped their sexual relations only five years into a thirty-eight year marriage. I believe that West used her fiction to assuage the feelings of guilt, anger, and confusion she had about her professional accomplishments and her private sexual dissatisfaction. She invents female characters who do what she never did: they relinquish their artistic, professional, and economic autonomy to men, and in so doing earn a peace they never achieve in independence. With these characters, West seems to apologize for her famous feminism and offers what would be thought—at least to the conservative majority, or maybe to the men she desired—a more sexually attractive and socially desirable vision. Moreover, West believes strongly that rituals and traditions exist as a way of making order out of chaos in a terrifyingly complex universe, and these include strong monogamous marriages in which men and women have gender-specific roles, and men are essentially ascendant.

West also demonstrates the feminine vulnerability patriarchal culture advocates by presenting female characters who cannot fully succeed without male custody. This is, again, partly a reliving of her own story: her father abandoned her family when she was eight, and West never recovered from the feeling that it was his moral and social duty to have supported his wife and daughters in spite of whatever personal unhappiness he may have suffered. She both punishes and forgives him, repeatedly, in her novels, creating male characters who do not live up to their part of the social gender bargain by "protecting" the women in their care. This is, to return to her contradictions, part of her way of undermining the male authority she simultaneously insists upon. Moreover, she blames insufficiently "masculine" men for aggressive or "unwomanly" women, and so turns the tables on male social and sexual censure of feminism. West's novels also contain tactics of female subversion of male hegemony even while they seem to uphold what Bonnie Kime Scott and Loretta Stec call West's "essentialism," which "divid[es] the functions of humanity into feminine nurture and masculine culture" (Scott, *Vol. 2*, 160). She deliberately presents women within traditional plots, and seems to indicate that such stories are somehow "correct" and even inevitable; yet within these narratives she exposes and deplores destructive cultural practices and attitudes that make these lives so often unhappy. It is finally difficult to define her feminism as anything but a paradox.

But as such, it is perhaps illustrative of (some) twentieth-century women's struggles to reconcile feminist beliefs with old structures and desires. The very fact that her ideas fight with one another is interesting and telling; her battles articulate and anticipate many of the problems contemporary women have in adjusting their new freedoms and responsibilities with the ancient roles of mother and wife, and the equally ancient role of woman as a mysterious, beautiful, fragile creature. It is also in line with the strategies of women writers who preceded her, who, as Susan Fraiman describes, "may all be said to 'argue in the same track as men,' reproducing many orthodoxies about middle-class female formation," but who "argue in other dissident tracks as well" as they attempt to achieve happiness and coherent selfhood.[18] There is a heavy irony in the fact that Rebecca West, the writer whose "great point" Virginia Woolf named as "her tenacious and muscular mind,"[19] whose largest worldly triumphs came from writing "masculine" journalism, would choose to support and praise male dominance in her fiction. But it conveys, more powerfully than direct statement would, the strength of the pressures she felt to conform to these ancient gender dichotomies. Even *A Room of One's Own*, Elaine Showalter claims in a controversial reading, illustrates that Woolf

> had taken to heart the cautionary tales to be found in the lives of earlier women writers. She had seen the punishment that society could inflict on women who made a nuisance of themselves by behaving in an uncivilized manner. It seems like a rationalization of her own fears that Woolf should have developed a literary theory that made anger and protest flaws in art. [20]

Something similar is at work in West when she writes of "real" men and women. To define a real woman as a nurturing saint was to be one; to declare that men should rule over women was to excuse her own authority.

Yet I wish to stress that my intention is *not* to reprove Rebecca West, an awe-inspiring woman born sixty-six years before me, for not being an "orthodox" feminist, if such a person exists or can even be defined. Instead, I want to look closely at one brilliant woman's struggle with the inevitable burdens of the twentieth century's changing social and sexual standards, granting her, as we grant all great writers, a license for genius, myopia, and obsessive desires—and understanding as well as I can from my late twentieth-century woman's life the social, cultural, and historical pressures that influenced West's choices and my own interpretations. Sandra Gilbert and Susan Gubar note at the start of their enormous study of twentieth-century women writers, *No Man's Land,* that

> [w]hat some feminists call 'positive role models' don't always make for great literature, and effective works of art don't always say what readers think they should. . .we are, we should stress, *de*scribing, not *pre*scribing, for our ultimate goal is to record and analyze the history that has made all of us who we are. (*Vol. I,* xiii)

I will dare to make the same claim in regard to this study of Rebecca West, a writer who wrote much literature that I would call great. I will also dare to hope that my readings inspire more critics to study this powerful, important writer, and, even better, more readers to read her.

Notes

1. See *Time* Magazine, 8 December, 1948; Bernard Levin, "The Light that Never Failed," *The Times,* 21 December, 1982; George Scialabba, "Woman of the Years," review of *Rebecca West: A Life* by Carl Rollyson, *Boston Globe* 17 November, 1996.
2. Rebecca West, *Black Lamb and Grey Falcon* (New York: The Viking Press, 1968): 1084. Further references will be to this edition, identified by page numbers in the text.
3. Peter S. Prescott with Edward Behr, "Ninety Years of Ardent Feminism," *Newsweek,* 28 March, 1983: 50.
4. Motley Deakin, *Rebecca West* (Boston: Twayne Publishers, 1980). Harold Orel, *The Literary Achievement of Rebecca West* (London: Macmillan, 1986). Carl Rollyson, *The Literary Legacy of Rebecca West* (San Francisco: International Scholars Publications, 1998). Peter Wolfe, *Rebecca West: Artist and Thinker* (Carbondale, Illinois: Southern Illinois University Press, 1971). Further references to each of these works will be identified by page numbers in the text.
5. Sandra M. Gilbert and Susan Gubar, *No Man's Land: The Place of the Woman Writer in the Twentieth Century.* 3 vols. (New Haven and London: Yale University Press, 1988-94). Further references will be to these editions, identified by volume and page number in the text.
6. Rebecca West, *The Young Rebecca: Writings of Rebecca West 1911-1917,* ed. Jane Marcus (New York: The Viking Press, 1982). Further references will be to this edition, identified by page numbers in the text. Jane Marcus, "A Wilderness of One's Own: Feminist Fantasy Novels of the

Twenties: Rebecca West and Sylvia Townsend Warner," in *Women Writers and the City: Essays in Feminist Literary Criticism*, ed. Susan Merrill Squier (Knoxville: The University of Tennessee Press, 1984): 134-160. Jane Marcus, introduction to *The Judge* by Rebecca West (New York: The Dial Press, 1980). Further references will be to this edition, identified by page numbers in the text.

7. Margaret Diane Stetz, "Rebecca West's Criticism: Alliance, Tradition, Modernism," in *Rereading Modernism: New Directions in Feminist Criticism*, ed. Lisa Rado (New York: Garland Publishing, Inc., 1994): 41-66.

8. Loretta Stec, "Writing Treason: Rebecca West's Contradictory Career" (Ph.D. diss., Rutgers, The State University of New Jersey, 1993): 11, 17. Further references will be identified by page numbers in the text.

9. *The Gender of Modernism*, ed. Bonnie Kime Scott (Bloomington: Indiana University Press, 1990). Bonnie Kime Scott, *Refiguring Modernism*, 2 vols. (Bloomington: Indiana University Press, 1995). Further references will be to these editions, identified by volume and page numbers in the text.

10. Moira Ferguson, "Feminist Manicheanism: Rebecca West's Unique Fusion," *Minnesota Review* 15 (1980): 53. Further references will be identified by page numbers in the text.

11. Gloria G. Fromm, "Rebecca West: The Fictions of Fact and the Facts of Fiction," *The New Criterion*, January 1991: 50.

12. Mary Ellmann, *Thinking About Women* (New York: Harcourt Brace Jovanovich, 1968): 113. Further references will be to this edition, identified by page numbers in the text.

13. Victoria Glendinning, *Rebecca West: A Life* (New York: Fawcett Columbine, 1987): 17. Further references will be to this edition, identified by page numbers in the text.

14. Rebecca West, *Sunflower* (New York: Penguin Books, 1986): 143. Further references will be to this edition, identified by page numbers in the text.

15. Jane Marcus, "Acting Out." Review of *Sunflower*, by Rebecca West, *The Nation*, 4 April 1987: 438. Further references will be identified by page numbers in the text.

16. West met D.H. Lawrence only once, but she revered him and his writing, and wrote an elegy on his death, reprinted in *Rebecca West: A Celebration*, ed. Samuel Hynes (New York: Penguin, 1978); she calls his life "a spiritual victory" (395). (Further references to *A Celebration* will be to this edition, identified by page numbers in the text.) Woolf, an acquaintance of West's, makes several references to her in the last four volumes of her diary. Some of them are admiring or grateful (West often praised Woolf in print), but many are definitely cutting, focusing on what Woolf considered West's crudeness and lack of upper class breeding versus her (eventual) material and literary success. Yet Woolf was also threatened by West's confident intellectual ability. See, for instance, Volume Four, Thursday June 27, 1935, where Woolf describes a dinner with West and her husband Henry Andrews. Virginia Woolf, *The Diary of Virginia Woolf,*

xxii   *Paradoxical Feminism*

Volume IV, 1931-1935, ed. Anne Olivier Bell assisted by Andrew McNeillie (New York: Harcourt Brace Jovanovich, 1982): 326-327.

17. There is one Rebecca West novel that I have not included in this study: *War Nurse: The True Story of a Woman Who Lived, Loved, and Suffered on the Western Front* (New York: Cosmopolitan Book Corporation, 1930). West ghost wrote this novel with a World War I nurse, whose memoirs furnished the story, for serialization in *Cosmopolitan.* According to Rollyson, West did it only for the money, and when it was published in book form, she had her name removed from it, calling it "hack work" (112). Very few libraries own this book, and it is the only one of her novels not to appear as a new edition in the last twenty years. *War Nurse* contains interesting observations about changing European and American sexual attitudes during the war and the post-war years, and it warrants study within that context. But it is obviously not a work into which West put her fullest effort or solely her own ideas; therefore, I do not believe it fits with the others in a serious analysis of her novels.

18. Susan Fraiman, *Unbecoming Women: British Women Writers and the Novel of Development* (New York: Columbia University Press, 1993): 31. Further references will be identified by page numbers in the text.

19. Quoted in Carl Rollyson, *Rebecca West: A Life* (New York: Scribner, 1996): 162. Further references will be to this edition, identified by page numbers in the text.

20. Elaine Showalter, *A Literature of Their Own: British Women Novelists From Bronte to Lessing* (Princeton: Princeton University Press, 1977), 288-9. Further references will be to this edition, identified by page numbers in the text.

Acknowledgments

A portion of Chapter Two appeared in *English Literature in Transition* 34: 3, Fall 1991.

I am grateful to my doctoral dissertation advisors at Columbia University: Ann Douglas, Jean Howard, Caroline Bynum, and especially Edward Mendelson, whose scholarship and encouragement I have greatly appreciated.

Carl Rollyson has been an invaluable source of information and support. His dedication to literature, his wide-ranging knowledge, and his industry have been inspirations to me.

I wish to thank several people at Saint Anselm College for their spirited friendship and help. My colleagues in the English department provided welcome sympathy and humor throughout the writing process. Jane Daly's secretarial support (and good cheer) made my work easier. Bruce Chakrin led me patiently through the labyrinth of computer formatting. Mark Purrington and Sue Gagnon in Interlibrary Loan worked tirelessly on my behalf.

Finally, I thank my husband Kelly and my daughters Ella and Rebecca for their generous love and patience.

Chapter 1

Money and Work

There are two kinds of imperialists - imperialists and bloody imperialists.
"The Position of Women in Indian Life"

Temperamentally I was born to acquiesce in patriarchy.
The Fountain Overflows

"The story of Rebecca West, who lived from 1892 to 1983, is the story of twentieth-century women. She was both an agent for change and a victim of change." So begins Victoria Glendinning's 1987 biography, and it is in many ways an apt prelude to the story of a woman who "was made anxious by her own comprehensiveness and nostalgic for some ideal simplicity" (xv). Such words as "agent for change" and "comprehensiveness" give the reader some sense of West's powerful intellect and influence, and Glendinning makes immediate reference to West's strong association with women's issues. But "victim," "anxious," "nostalgic," warn us that this story will contain strife connected to these same potencies; and Glendinning goes on to describe the heart of that strife. She cites West's very early article "Things Men Never Know," which explains that girls were reproached "for having weaker bodies, weaker brains, weaker wills, and weaker emotions than boys;" but if a girl then "decided to put this right, and to become strong and clever and brave then she was told she had lost her 'real' value and that no one would love her." Glendinning claims that "[t]his was the trap in which she herself felt caught," and that she "was thus fighting against herself a lot of the time" (xv). So, implies this introduction, do many women.

Carl Rollyson, whose biography was published nine years later, calls his first chapter "The Family Romance," and he also gets right to the heart of a personal battle that would inform West's public statements. He begins with a story of West's father rescuing her from the sea when she was two years old, and then ties it to a BBC radio interview in which West described this "physical maleness. . .a sort of thing that can save one physically, in a very simple way" as "what any child wants from a father" (17). Yet Rollyson aptly borrows phrases from West's 1925 article "I Regard Marriage with Fear and Horror" to describe the combination of brilliance and irresponsibility in West's father that she would then continue to see in most of the men she loved. "Set the house on fire, and he would put out the flames—but he could not be counted on to rebuild it" (19). Appropriately, Rollyson pinpoints from the start West's preoccupation with her father. She "would spend a lifetime" trying to "reclaim" him (26), and trying to understand both her father and mother as representative man and woman living in the world as parents, sexual beings, and artists and thinkers. This struggle, intimately connected to the "trap" of gender confusions that Glendinning names, underlies much of her work.

Cicely Isabel Fairfield, who was to become Dame Rebecca West, was born in London on December 21, 1892. Her Scottish mother Isabella Mackenzie was a brilliant pianist whose professional career was ultimately thwarted by poverty and the limitations imposed by her gender and her family responsibilities. Instead of performing, Isabella became a music governess. En route to Australia at her mother's request to check on the health of her consumptive brother, Isabella met her future husband and West's father the Anglo-Irishman Charles Fairfield, a strikingly handsome, charming man who had been a British soldier, and a businessman in America. Fairfield's interest in public finance and political systems, plus his remarkable talent as a polemical writer, led him to a career in journalism. But what success he enjoyed was marred by his irresponsibility. He was a gambler, a dilettante, and an adulterer. He lost jobs because of his controversial ideas and obstinate nature—he was conservative and elitist, against socialism and feminism and no great defender of democracy—which necessitated the family's many moves, and he speculated disastrously with what little money he made, with the result that insecurity and poverty became the Fairfields' way of life. When Cissie was eight, Charles left his wife and daughters for a job in West Africa, but soon returned to live alone in Liverpool. He never again saw his family, who stayed alive on an allowance from Isabella's ex-employers, and in five years he died penniless in a poor lodging house.

"Cissie," the youngest of three daughters, adored her exceptional but frustrated parents, and eulogized them decades later as Piers and Clare Aubrey in the unfinished tetralogy *Cousin Rosamund: A Saga of the Century*. Yet "Piers" is also the target of harsh criticism; as Rose says in the first novel, *The Fountain Overflows*, "I had a glorious father, I had no father at all."[1] This ambivalence about Charles Fairfield showed up in her autobiographical writing, and spilled over into her thinking and writing about all men as fathers and husbands. While West credits her father for teaching her about politics, philosophy, economics, and history (and her mother for introducing her to music and art), this early exposure to paternal failure left her forever convinced that men were economically and emotionally responsible for their family's well-being. And, as Rollyson points out, she and her two sisters "became suffragettes and socialists—repudiating their father's politics and resenting his treatment of their mother" (30).

Cicely Fairfield attended George Watson's Ladies' College and participated in suffrage demonstrations in Edinburgh, where the family moved after Charles's death. After attracting the attention of an acting teacher, she briefly attended the Royal Academy of Dramatic Arts in London. But the nineteen-year-old girl quickly became disillusioned with the theatre, believing that "only the beauties and the well-connected got jobs" (Rollyson 33), and found a more suitable vocation when she met Dora Marsden, editor of the feminist weekly *The Freewoman*. In its second issue Cissie wrote a review of a book about the position of women in Indian life, and her career as a writer was launched (and her formal education was over). She took the name "Rebecca West" after Ibsen's radical but tragic heroine in *Rosmersholm*, who is initially a triumphant feminist "free thinker," but who ultimately commits suicide over insinuations that her older married lover, and stepfather, may in fact be her father. This new name spoke volumes about the contradictions motivating the young Rebecca, although she later claimed that the name was chosen quickly and was not meant to be symbolic. As Bonnie Kime Scott says, "The young woman from Edinburgh remade Ibsen's suicidal character. . .into a feminist survivor" (*Vol. I*, 36), and certainly *The Freewoman* provided Cissie with a platform for her feminist anger, begun years earlier by her father's desertion and perpetuated by what she saw as women's tremendous social and economic disadvantages. Yet Ibsen's Rebecca West loses her initial power because of her vulnerability about a paternal relationship, as the woman who became Rebecca West was never free from the same vulnerability. Plus, Cicely Fairfield took a pseudonym chiefly to protect the reputation of her family, who would be hurt by association with an outspoken feminist. The cultural and familial nets enclosing the young woman were tight, no matter how she strained at the mesh.

Nevertheless, these early articles are brilliant and assured. West had a thorough knowledge of English law and politics, an irreverent humor, a rich metaphorical style, and a fearlessness that brought her to the attention of Shaw, Hardy, the Fabians, the Bloomsbury set, and H.G. Wells, among others. Whether she wrote on the failings of Lloyd George, the latest novel by Mrs. Humphry Ward, or the life of suffragist martyr Emily Davison, West expressed a unique viewpoint that startled and amused her readers. Jane Marcus introduces *The Young Rebecca* by quoting West's rebellious opposition to "the traditional lady with the lamp": "A strong hatred is the best lamp to bear in our hands as we go over the dark places of life, cutting away the dead things men tell us to revere" (3). A negative review West wrote of his novel *Marriage* so impressed Wells that he invited her to tea with his wife; and when the two fell in love, West found herself in the unexpected and undesired positions of mistress and unwed mother. This gave the young Rebecca more fuel for the fire of her anger against men, but less time and quite a bit less freedom in which to work. The issue, once again, was support from a man: this time emotional and monetary sustenance needed for an unmarried woman with a son whose father was usually absent.

Regardless of her childhood family experience, this was an ironic position for the young journalist. West at that time was a forceful opponent of the general social and economic reality in which women were supported by men (and the industrial system) to be, as she called some of them, "parasites," or house-bound paid and unpaid servants. She wrote thousands of words denouncing both the sterility of upper and middle-class "soft living" and the deadening effects of lower-class overwork.

> The parasite woman costs money. The nation is not wealthy enough to support a non-productive class. . .We practise the most determined concentration of wealth, one-tenth of the population own nine-tenths of the accumulated wealth, and one-fifth of the adults take to themselves two-thirds of the annual product and leave only a third to be shared by the four-fifths who are manual workers. Our poverty may be measured by reflecting how small a proportion of the nation is kept in comfort and how still a smaller proportion is kept in luxury by the poverty of these four-fifths who are never lifted clear of the subsistence level. It is not only a question of whether slaves will submit to supporting women, but whether women will submit to being supported by slaves. (*Young Rebecca,* 115)

West believed that women, as much as men, needed "to have a chance of being sifted clean through the sieve of work," and that "the monotony and squalor of domestic drudgery that men have thrust on the wife and mother" (*Young Rebecca,* 69) is an insufficient mode for such cleansing. Furthermore, unmarried women then had few choices of employment outside servant work or factories, and professional domestic service kept them from meeting eligible men, especially those provincial girls working in cities where they might have no friends. West asserts in a 1913 *Clarion* article that, thus, "they are bored and lonely and resentful at spending their lives in tending other people's homes and children" (*Young Rebecca*, 213).

As professional workers, of course, women generally received less pay than men for equal work. This was, according to West, not the case when British productivity was centered in agricultural life and men and women had separate but equal tasks in and outside the home. But the industrial revolution removed from women what had been traditionally female labor, such as baking bread, spinning wool and weaving cloth, preparation of preserved food, and doctoring the sick, and gave it to the factories, merchants, and professional men. So a British working woman of the early twentieth century, unable to afford housing and food on her pitiable wage, was left with the choice of marrying for support and being left "only the dish-washing and floor-scrubbing, which is now regarded as peculiarly feminine work" (*Young Rebecca*, 374); doing insular and unrewarding paid domestic service; or, what was more heinous if less crushing, becoming a parasite of her middle-class or upper-class husband, father, or other male relation.

Just before and during World War I, West's voice joined in the chorus of radical women who were fighting primarily for the vote, but also in protest against the network of laws and prejudices that entrapped women. As a feminist socialist in a capitalist country, West saw economic injustice perpetuated by a rigid patriarchal class system that forced these limited roles on women and thus ensured inequality between the sexes. West also blamed women themselves for many of their own problems, calling some "natural slaves" who "appeal for equal rights with men because of their weakness" (*Young Rebecca*, 28). West was therefore an ideal writer for Lady Rhondda's weekly feminist journal *Time and Tide,* established in 1920. *Time and Tide* tried not only to inspire women to organize independently of men, but also to make them aware of their own acquiescence in traditional but destructive ideas about women's "special sphere" that rationalized women's confinement to home and family.

Yet, with time, West's ideas about women in relation to employment and money changed. In both her early and late novels, she continues to abhor the facts of women's financial insecurity and their lesser artistic and professional opportunities. Nevertheless, she seems to advocate greater male responsibility rather than greater female independence as the answer to women's job limitations and poverty. Moreover, she shows the sexual problems caused by reversals in the traditional economic balance to be so bad as to offset any positive gains women have made toward financial and professional autonomy. And the female artists she creates may achieve economic power and aesthetic freedom, but they are socially isolated, and therefore often unhappy or insistently insular.

West's apparent change of heart can be related partly to the conflicted feminism of the 1920s, and beyond. The fierce fight for women's suffrage united most feminists, and it was at least partially won in 1918 when women aged thirty and over were granted the right to vote. But this was followed by a strong backlash, not unlike the one Susan Faludi described as following the social, economic, and political gains American women made in the 1970s.[2] Harold L. Smith explains that "[t]he First World War unleashed a powerful current of cultural conservatism. . .Alarm over the perceived wartime changes in sex roles strengthened the forces seeking to restore traditional roles."[3] As Loretta Stec argues, the pre-war West fits the description of an "equality feminist": one who urged for women opportunities equal to men's, and believed that men and women were more similar than different as human beings. Yet the post-war West, particularly from the 1930s on, more closely resembles the "new" feminists. They sought reforms that emphasized women's differences from men, particularly in their roles as mothers, and that rewarded them economically and politically for working within the home and family (for instance, with a "family allowance" paid by the government to mothers who raise children). In a discussion of *Sunflower,* Stec describes what she calls West's "split allegiance" to these doctrines, which "inscribes the poignant dilemma of a socialist-feminist writer 'caught' in the ideologies of her time" (72); and she speculates that West made a calculated move to support new feminism, since she knew that "women who remain passive, who desire the traditional roles of women, will gain certain rewards in a society such as England in the 1920s" (73), and after.

Moreover, as West's writing and speaking career developed during and after the First World War, she was struggling to raise her illegitimate son Anthony under the guise that she was his aunt. H.G. Wells provided only sporadic financial support; he was rarely present in Anthony's life, and certainly never shared in the daily care and nurturing of his son, which naturally fell to West and her servants. All the while she was suffering the emotional difficulty of being the mistress of a married man whose legal and domestic allegiances belonged to his wife. Furthermore, as West began the long and painful break with Wells, she believed that the men with whom she became involved refused emotional intimacy, and even suffered sexual impotence when with her. The list of her lovers in the years after Wells and before her marriage is impressive, as several were brilliant and often powerful men, like Wells: the newspaper magnate Lord (Max) Beaverbrook, the journalist John Gunther, the film genius Charlie Chaplin. Yet the famous Rebecca West, who triumphantly lectured in America on the modern novel and feminism, apparently frightened them enough that none made any lasting commitment to her. When she met the banker Henry

Andrews in 1929, an intelligent and erudite if slow and stolid man, he seemed the epitome of gentlemanly devotion and masculine solidity that she craved, and he seemed genuinely to adore her. She married him in 1930 at the age of thirty-seven. Both Rollyson and Glendinning mention that, as the couple departed from the ceremony, West's secretary June Head remarked that West was at last "going away with someone who will buy her railroad ticket. Hitherto, she has bought everyone else's" (Glendinning 144, Rollyson 148).

This comment obviously symbolized to both biographers the main reason why West married Andrews. Samuel Hynes calls it "the most surprising event in her whole life":

> In 1930, when it took place, she was world-famous as a journalist, socially in demand for her wit and beauty, and self-supporting on a fairly grand scale. She spent summers on the Riviera, wore elegant Paris clothes, and sent her son to a Public School. Yet she married Henry Andrews, who was as dull as an English summer, an unsuccessful banker whose strongest trait was his incompetence, a man who could do nothing right, not even sleep with his wife (he gave up after five years and turned to philandering). . .Evidently the condition of being married gave her something that she needed.[4]

Neither of West's biographers is so bluntly negative about Andrews; yet Hynes here captures what many of West's friends thought throughout her life about her husband. Most also realized that indeed West craved the stable structure of marriage around her after the long Wells affair and the disappointing sexual relationships that followed, and that she desired at least the appearance that she was being supported by a husband in traditional ways. However, both Andrews and West were having affairs by the mid 1930s, and in fact their sexual relationship essentially stopped at that time. Plus, as their married life continued past the Second World War, and they bought a country estate near London, West continued to write for money while Andrews "stayed home" and managed Ibstone House, sometimes with disastrous incompetence. Thus, their marriage was not the monogamous sexual unity West praises in fiction and non-fiction; nor was Henry a "real" man like those Dalmatian shipbuilders she admired in *Black Lamb and Grey Falcon*.

West's novels convey the struggles of these contradictory aspects of her life as a woman and a feminist, and clearly contain, like the works of countless writers, much wish-fulfillment. This chapter examines particularly the paradoxes of West's ideas about women, money, and work: both the injustices of patriarchal economic and professional structures, and the difficulties women (and men) face when those structures are altered.

West's first novel *The Return of the Soldier*, published in 1918, is in part a portrait of the British patriarchal structure, based on the economics of marriage and class, as it begins to suffer from the effects of World War I. It is also an exploration of the harmful gender roles, for women and men, that this structure engenders and maintains. Most critics have likened *The Return of the Soldier* to a Henry James novel. West published a short study of James two years before her novelistic debut, her first book and one of the first full-length studies of his entire career. His influence is obvious, though West emulates him in some surprising ways. In a James novel the narrator (first or third person) is usually a man, whose focus of interest is a woman experiencing changes or difficult challenges often related to her sexual roles or restrictions. Such a narrator is removed from the main action, and instead functions as the storyteller and psychological observer whose personal revelations shape the meaning of the drama he only witnesses. West follows that basic model, but switches the genders through her first-person narrator Jenny, a "spinster" living in the home of a male relative who supports her in upper-class English style, and who is now a soldier at the front. Her detachment from the main plot underscores her isolation from two "realities": war and work. As Peter Wolfe says, "What is fresh and new in this war novel is its viewpoint: rather than going to battle, the author shows us what war means to a woman who awaits the homecoming of a front-line soldier" (32). The difficult challenge facing Chris, Jenny's cousin and her focus of interest, is amnesia. The life he has forgotten is not only that of the battlefield; Chris has blocked out his entire adult existence. His reasons for doing so have to do with restrictions he faces as a man in world of parasitic women.

Born into wealth, Chris Baldry outwardly exemplifies, like Ford Madox Ford's Edward Ashburnham or Virginia Woolf's Jacob, the good soldier of the British empire. After a privileged youth and education, Chris takes over his father's business and supports his wife and relatives on the grand scale his economic class seems to require. When the war comes, he goes off to the front without complaint, his family fully expecting him to return to the business of their upkeep after his stint as a soldier fighting for their country. The novel opens with a conversation between his beautiful wife Kitty and his elegant cousin Jenny as they sit in a gorgeous room and anticipate his return. Kitty has no fear that Chris will not return; she does not worry that he has not written, boasting that "if he'd been anywhere interesting, anywhere where the fighting was really hot, he'd have found some way of telling me. . .He'll be all right."[5] Jenny muses on their past, thinking that she and Kitty "had made a fine place for Chris. . .had made happiness inevitable for him" (16).

The irony of their complacent delight in Chris and their home soon becomes apparent. A working class woman, Mrs. Margaret Grey, arrives to tell the startled and disbelieving Jenny and Kitty that Chris is in a hospital, and has written to her for help. Amazingly, he has not seen Margaret in fifteen years, but communicates with her as if they had recently been in touch, with an intimacy long past and by her maiden name. As the rich women study Margaret's poor appearance with distaste, they nevertheless realize she is telling the truth: that Chris has forgotten his wife and believes himself in love with Margaret. When he comes home, Chris wants only to see Margaret and amuse himself with boyhood games. He is uninterested in resuming his marriage or his business work: "All the inhabitants of this new tract of time were his enemies, all its circumstances his prison bars" (61-62). Kitty becomes "a little shrunk thing" whose one goal is to "cure" Chris of his amnesia, while Margaret takes on the implicit roles of mother, nurse, and lover to the shell-shocked soldier. Though Jenny realizes that Chris is happier in this dream-state than he would be in his "real" life, she too wants back the cousin she knew and with whom she is still fruitlessly in love.

Each of these characters represents a role in the British social edifice based on economics that West is analyzing and criticizing. Jenny and Kitty are classic parasites, though Kitty is the more contemptible of the two. She is both ignorant of money and as free with it as if it were air to breathe, stretching Chris's "conception of normal expenditure. . .as a woman stretches a new glove on her hand" (21). Jenny imagines that Kitty looks like a magazine cover with "a large '7d.' somewhere attached to her person" (11); when the calamity of Chris's rejection happens, she tries to take comfort in her beautiful silk underclothes, as if believing the mere possession of such luxury should ward off unhappiness. Her attempts to woo Chris back are all visual lures demonstrating her expensively maintained beauty and attire, or her mastery of the household arts appropriate to a rich married woman.

> Around her throat were her pearls, and her longer chain of diamonds dropped, looking cruelly bright, to her white breasts; because she held some needlework to her bosom I saw that her right hand was stiff with rings and her left hand bare save for her wedding-ring. With her lower lip thrust out, as if she were considering a menu, she lowered her head and looked down on herself. . .She looked cold as moonlight, as virginity, but precious; the falling candlelight struck her hair to bright, pure gold. So she waited for him. (56-7)

Jenny, less beautiful than Kitty but equally inured in the life of the gentry, does not take their wealth for granted. Rather she revels in the comfort and beauty of their home, wanting "to snatch. . .Christopher from the wars and seal him in this green pleasantness his wife and [she] now looked upon" (13), fully aware that she is benefiting from his ancestors' labor and trying to justify her own presence with devotion to Chris. But she too thinks of material beauty as the attraction of Baldry Court, sending her mind

> creeping from room to room like a purring cat, rubbing itself against all the brittle beautiful things that we had either recovered from antiquity or dug from the obscure pits of modern craftsmanship, basking in the colour that glowed from all our solemnly chosen fabrics with such pure intensity that it seemed to shed warmth like sunshine. Even now, when spending seemed a little disgraceful, I could think of that beauty with nothing but pride. I was sure that we were preserved from the reproach of luxury because we had made a fine place for Chris. . . (16)

This opulence that Kitty and Jenny share, however, does not change the fact that their lives are determined by an iron patriarchal tradition. The first chapter of *The Return of the Soldier*, as outwardly simple but dense with symbolism as one of Joyce's stories in *Dubliners*, introduces the theme of latent imprisonment as West undercuts Jenny's sensual descriptions with images of domination. While the women wait for news of the outside world via a letter from Chris, they sit in a nursery that emphasizes their relegation to the worlds of motherhood and the continuous "childhood" of a woman's life. The male child who lived there—Kitty's and Chris's son—died at age two, but his kingdom of toys is preserved like an emblem of expected masculine occupations. Jenny imagines the boy raising "a fat fist" to point out the rugs "patterned with strange beasts," the print of "the snarling tiger," and the stuffed animals "ready for play at their master's pleasure" (10-11). She sees outside the window trees "like darkness made palpable," their "minatory gauntness" (13) betokening the world and the war of which she knows so little, and the jail of her own dependence.

As a narrator, Jenny is no more direct or strictly truthful than *The Good Soldier's* John Dowell. Not only does she deconstruct this ostensibly peaceful scene with tropes of hunting and evil, but her description of Margaret, seemingly sympathetic, belies her own snobbish, slavish adherence to ideas of wealth and class. Imagining Margaret "repulsively furred with neglect and poverty, as. . .a good glove that has dropped down behind a bed in a hotel" (25), Jenny keeps staring at the poor woman's cheap and broken purse and thinking that "its emptiness had brought her to this humiliation" (31). In fact, the purse contains a telegram from Chris and is thus not empty at all, just as Margaret's life of poverty has not destroyed her essential superiority to Kitty and Jenny or her capacity for love.

Nevertheless, Margaret is, as surely as the shallow, vain Kitty or the unfulfilled Jenny, constrained and formed by her economic circumstances, and her relationship with Chris did and would reflect their financial inequality as his relationships with Kitty and Jenny reflect their dependence. She and Chris were lovers as teenagers, meeting at the Thameside inn her father owned and where she lived and worked far from Chris's aristocratic circles.[6] This sequestered atmosphere, romantically recounted to Jenny by the middle-aged Chris (in a chapter reminiscent of the "Ferdinand and Miranda" chapter in Meredith's *The Ordeal of Richard Feverel*, another ill-fated tale of rich boy loves poor girl), was convenient for secrecy. If Chris did not think of this specifically at the time, or about their difference in class, the reminders were there regardless. The Monkey Island Inn was built by a duke as a "folly," and Chris visits it like a young lord, ringing the bell for Margaret when he arrives as if she is his maid, accepting food and tea she makes when free from serving customers and her father. One time Chris decides to wait on customers himself, but the "great lark" turns sour when they offer him a tip: "he snarled absurdly, and ran back, miraculously relieved, to the bar-parlour" (82) where he is again the patrician with Margaret to minister to him. Their breakup comes from an argument started by Chris's unwarranted jealousy and concluded with Margaret's claim that he doesn't trust her "as he would trust a girl of his own class" (107). Even their love-making is shadowed by a cold mark of money. The happiest night Chris remembers took place in a small Greek temple the Duke built for his trysts with prostitutes. The most Margaret could hope for then, it seems, was to be Chris's servant or his whore; and now, as his lover, her main functions resemble those of nurse and mother.

The description of dreamy embraces in the Greek temple blends into a vision of trench warfare. It is not clear whether Jenny is imagining Chris's war ordeals, or if Chris has somehow regained a grisly part of his memory. But the connection that Chris makes, consciously or unconsciously, between the loss of Margaret and the experience of being a soldier is here suggested. As a young man of the upper class, Chris is not free, whether socially or emotionally, to love a working-class girl as an equal. Instead he conforms to the expectations of his rich family and marries Kitty, whose beauty is the prize for money and male economic incentive: her "civilizing mission" is "to flash the jewel of [her] beauty before all men, so that they shall desire it and work to get the wealth to buy it, and thus be seduced by a present appetite to a tilling of the earth that serves the future" (154). Nor is Chris free to live in the happy oblivion of his amnesia; he must go back to a family business "that was weighted by the needs of a mob of female relatives who were all useless in the old way with antimacassars or in the new

way with golf clubs" (20). But by regaining his identities as husband
and business director, he also recovers the nightmarish memory of
being a soldier. These three roles are conflated into the life that Chris
rejects but to which he must return as the good soldier of British life.
As unfortunate as Margaret may be, married to a dull, poor man after
losing her father and being forced to work as a "mother's help" in a
family that deserted her with wages unpaid; as unhappy as Jenny is in
her dependent, ineffectual life—Chris seems to fare the worst.

Faith Evans writes in the introduction to West's *Family Memories*
that "no man ever receives quite such bruising attention" as do West's
characters Gerda (from *Black Lamb and Grey Falcon*), Mary Ironside (of
Family Memories), and Cordelia (of the *Cousin Rosamund* trilogy).[7]
The same could be said for Jenny and Kitty in *The Return of the
Soldier*. Not only are they, and his "mob of female relatives," blamed
for Chris's desire to escape his real life; it is they who bring him back
to the tasks as soldier and provider he so hates by bringing in the
Freudian psychiatrist who "cures" him. Even Margaret, who is
genuinely "good" and not a "parasite," who represents the maternal,
positively feminine antithesis to the war's violent, masculine horror,
facilitates this process, realizing that a reminder of his dead son Oliver
will snap Chris back to the present. The irony of using the "new"
psychoanalysis, which purports to unlock the "truth" and thus seems to
promise new freedoms, is that it is used to maintain the old falsehoods,
to keep Chris in lockstep as the good soldier. But Freudian theory also
stresses a patriarchal view of men's roles as providers and women's roles
as nurturers. The fact that the boy died could imply that he too rejected
the male occupations, so amply symbolized in his nursery, that the
women had prepared for him. Margaret's son died at age two as well,
and she wonders how Oliver "could leave all this" wealth, imagining
that her son left "because [she] had so little to give him" (176). But she
also pictures Oliver, ironically, as "a man from the first" (177), just as
Jenny thinks Chris must regain his position as head of their family or
"not be quite a man" (183).

This is a puzzling conclusion to a novel in which the
destructiveness of traditional, economically-based gender roles has been
a keynote. That is not its only theme; many have analyzed *The Return
of the Soldier* as West's first testament to the importance of facing
"reality," or her attempt to explore the effects of shell-shock and the
possible benefits of Freudian psychoanalysis.[8] But certainly West's
obsessive interest in the opposing parts men and women play in life
shows up in this first novel, and in fact guides the narrator's growing
observations about herself and the people around her. The emotional and
intellectual climax of the book begins with Jenny's silent statement,
"This was the saddest spring" (a phrase that consciously allies *The*

i\eturn of the Soldier with *The Good Soldier,* another book in which women ultimately, and cruelly, control a man's life)[9], as she realizes that Chris's rejection of his family implies a discarding of the entire privileged world he supports, and that she agrees with his decision. "The whole truth about us lies in our material seeming," she thinks of herself and Kitty, and concludes that "no one weeps for this shattering of our world" (137) because it is contemptible. Yet it is at this point that she most desires the doctor to cure Chris; in spite of her epiphany, Jenny wants her world back. One of West's main messages, then, seems to be that the women are the ones who maintain this harmful cycle of overworked men and dependent women, but that somehow a man is not doing the right thing if he flees it.

While this seems a peculiar theme to come from a suffragist writer in 1918, it connects to an anxiety that Gilbert and Gubar describe as coming from both literary men and women during and after World War I.

> Can [it] be [that] the war. . .somehow threatened a female conquest of men? Because women were safe on the home front, is it possible that the war seemed in some peculiar sense their fault, a ritual of sacrifice to their victorious femininity?. . .Through a paradox that is at first almost incomprehensible, this war which has traditionally been defined as an apocalypse of masculinism seems here to have led to an apotheosis of femaleness, a triumph of women who feed on wounds and are fertilized by blood. (*Vol. 2,* 262)

The Return of the Soldier depicts such a "female conquest," and West abhors it here. But her distaste specifically targets Kitty's expectations of what constitutes "normal" life for a woman of her class; if this is what the men are fighting to maintain, West implies, then it is cruel and absurd to make them continue. Margaret, the lower-class heroine, is clearly the antidote to such bloodthirsty parasites as Kitty, and her reasons for wishing Chris to drink what Jenny calls "the wine of truth" and "celebrate communion with reality" are based on what she believes is best for him. Margaret wishes Chris to be sane so that he may be happy, whereas Kitty wants him to return to his life as her provider and publicly appropriate partner.[10] These two women could also represent West, as the loving Margaret, and Jane Wells, as the cold society woman. Rollyson describes West's belief that "Jane liked the good life H.G. provided," and that she "relied on his mistresses" to handle his "nervous breakdowns": West thought that "Jane actually cared very little for H.G. as a man—indeed, neglected his needs. . ." (89). West despised Jane's apparent ability to settle for only a part of H.G.'s life and heart, and disdained what she considered Jane's elevation of social position and financial comfort over fidelity, a sexual relationship grounded in monogamous marriage.

By the mid-1930s and the publication of *The Harsh Voice,* a collection of four short novels, and her fourth novel *The Thinking Reed*, West had been married for six years and was established as a writer of both journalism and fiction. Her fame, and the wealth she gained from writing, had provided her with far more exposure to the upper classes than she had had as Wells's lover; she also had experience as a wife. With this new knowledge, she revisited her preoccupation with the influence of money, and especially its bearing on gender roles and relations. According to Glendinning, West said that the two themes of *The Thinking Reed* were "the effect of riches on people, and the effect of men on women, both forms of slavery" (159). An expansion of this might be to say that the novel is about the effect of wealth on men's and women's treatments of each other, and the way possession of or desire for money makes both sexes into prostitutes, tyrants, victims, and profligates.

While *The Return of the Soldier* has a serious tone of psychological exploration, *The Thinking Reed* is heavily ironic as West satirizes the world of the ultra-rich in the 1920s. Isabelle Tarry, the protagonist, is a romance writer's dream heroine. Twenty-six years old and so "two years younger than the century," she is of noble descent, "beautiful. . .nearly exceedingly rich, [and]. . .tragically widowed."[11] The extreme physical luxury of her life and the lushness of her beauty are emphasized from the first page, but Isabelle sees herself as a *mind*. West borrows the novel's epigraph from Pascal; Isabelle is the thinking reed, more "noble" than the infinite universe who could "crush him," because "he knows that he dies and the advantage which the universe has over him; the universe knows nothing of this." West here goes back to one of her major criticism of James, which is that his heroines do not act as if they think in a way consistent with real women in the real world; the marriage of Isabel Archer to Gilbert Osmond, in *The Portrait of a Lady,* particularly demonstrates this, and West may have named her heroine after James's in a deliberate correction.[12] Yet while Isabelle is clearly intelligent and indeed analytical, West describes her with a mocking smile, pointing out the young widow's advantages and leisure.

> . . . her white skin never flushed, and her fine small features were as calmly gay as if she were a statue that had been carved looking like that [though] she was in motion all her waking hours. . .she rode horseback, she hunted the wild boar down in the Landes, sailed a boat at Cannes, played tennis with the aces. . .The game was too fast for her body, but her mind could always follow it. . .She would lie for hours on a chaise-longue. . .But even then her right hand moved ceaselessly, turning on her wrist as though it were throwing a

shuttle. There was indeed a shuttle at work, but it was behind her brows. Her competent steely mind never rested. . .So, between sport and pedantry, she was busy enough. (3-5)

Though Isabelle represents the upper-class parasite West denigrated earlier, she is not, unlike Jenny or Kitty, dependent upon a specific man for economic support or indulgence. An American in Paris, her fortune is based on an inheritance that grows with the wildly expanding stock market of the early twentieth century. Her first husband Roy was a daredevil aviator who died in a plane crash, and the implication is that Isabelle married an "exciting" man for love since she need not marry for money (though Roy was a Princeton man and probably no pauper). In her grief she has come to Paris for change, thinking of her life "as a room that had to be completely refurnished" (19), having the option as a woman of independent wealth to live anywhere she pleases without marrying or doing any sort of work. But her life, previously shattered by the loss of a man, is now in shambles because of another man, an aristocratic Frenchman named Andre de Verviers. Though the two are lovers, Isabelle hates Andre for his old-world attitudes toward women and sexual relations even as she revels in their sexual communion. Believing that the creation of petty quarrels excites desire, and having no interest in women in any way but as erotic objects to be manipulated for his enjoyment, Andre perpetuates discord, trapping Isabelle into the "scenes" she hates in her alleged love of rationality. But the way she imagines escaping Andre's sexual domination is through marriage to another man, an American who loves peace as Andre loves disharmony. Yet a third man wants Isabelle, a French industrial mogul whose working background and life she considers beneath her but whose astronomical wealth puts him in her social circles. He sends her absurdly extravagant gifts of flowers along with notes begging her hand in marriage; she sees him as a "terrier" to be petted but not taken seriously. In short, though Isabelle is rich and thus could escape male domination, and just about anything else, she still finds herself governed by her relationships with men.

These three suitors are tyrants, and thus typify many of West's male characters. In this case, all three men are rich, and West stresses their economic positions as the overriding influence in their behavior and choices. Each uses his moneyed position to bully inferiors or women, even if that bullying is more the product of innate decay than strength. Andre is a male parasite, the product of leisure and foolish indulgence afforded by inherited money. His love of deliberately evoked scenes stems from the realization that, as Isabelle thinks of herself, "the high degree of security [he] enjoyed thanks to [his] money" protected him from any "serious difficulties" (36); free from all danger, "he could play with danger to his heart's content. . .He loved what he feared, as spirits sapped with luxury always do" (37). Andre need not marry, work, or do anything other than play games of sexual politics, which European tradition has ensured he will win as an aristocrat and a male.

> Had he been a poor man, he would not have been free to spend his whole life proving a silly point about his power by leaving women who wanted him to stay with them and staying with women who wanted him to leave them. . .Andre was well aware that anything that threatened the existing conditions of society threatened him with extinction. (36)

Laurence Vernon, the American, stands for an agrarian ideal of peace and intellectuality—one that Isabelle craves after the daring, athletic Roy and the lazy, manipulative Andre—but he is essentially ineffective. Alone on his Southern plantation "Mount Iris," Laurence reads the classics and oversees his huge home, hoping to maintain his region's class-based agricultural life by fighting "every attempt to enslave the people by the same conscienceless industrialism as has made the Yankees the drab men-machines they were" (17). But his easily-maintained, inherited kingdom presents him with no serious challenges, and is of course upheld by slavery of a different kind: that of the poorly-paid farm laborer who has little chance of advancing to such a carefree scholar's existence. With unwitting irony, Isabelle imagines that Laurence is "what [she] would have been if [she] had been a man," though pleasurably anticipating the wifely role as her proper sphere.

> She could imagine herself sitting at dusk, in the hall, looking out at the white afterglow that was divided by the dark pillars of the colonnade, while Laurence walked up and down. . .He would be thinking over the material the day had brought him; he would be weaving an intellectual protection for him, for her, for their children, from the arrows that the passion-governed world shot so recklessly. (19)

Yet Isabelle loses this reason-governed but weak man through the violent action she reluctantly takes to rid herself of Andre. Realizing that only an extraordinary breach of public decorum will repulse Andre, Isabelle furiously, and publicly, tramples on his gift of roses, deliberately refuting social expectations of "ladylike" behavior. But Laurence witnesses it, and now considers her a "maenad." Frantically, Isabelle decides to accept the proposal of Marc Sallafranque, the French automobile maker she has previously scorned, rather than have Laurence think she wanted to marry him when it becomes clear that he will not ask. She imagines that Laurence "had brought this on her"—this marriage with a man she considers inferior to her or him—but as the marriage of Marc and Isabelle unfolds, it becomes clear that the industrialist is superior to either the European or the American aristocrat by virtue of (what West considers) his masculine authority. If Andre and Laurence have power or potency, it is only through money. Marc has genuine energy; the fact that he has had to work has made him morally and spiritually stronger than the other two. Isabelle is grateful to find herself falling in love with Marc, and settles easily into her role as wife of a millionaire, never seeming to realize her own incredible vanity in this instigation of a marriage to save sexual and social face.

Yet even Marc demonstrates poisonous qualities that are inevitably tied to his wealth. He feels free to kick a waiter's buttocks in the sheer joy following Isabelle's acceptance, knowing that he can pay for whatever damage his momentary indulgence might cause. Because he works so hard himself, he cannot understand that others do not wish to work as hard; he is insensitive to labor demands, and imagines that his workers are friendly to him because they like him, not because he is the boss. Worst of all, Marc is a gambler. Though it is his own money that he gains and loses at casinos, his employees are infuriated to imagine such individual wealth and waste when they are struggling by on wages. One man in particular is infuriated: Monsieur Campofiore, a government official who monitors Marc's gambling, and who is a symbol of the rising socialism in early twentieth-century Europe. While Marc believes that "a master must take more than his men, otherwise there wouldn't be any masters, and the industries would never get anywhere" (116), Campofiore despises economic inequality. Isabelle's beauty, refined through generations of beauties married to wealth and sustained by leisure and costly cosmetic procedures, enrages him; he appears in party scenes like an avenging angel, reminding Isabelle that she is of a privileged world envied and loathed by the masses. But Marc is still the more potent man, even if Campofiore can match him for energy and commitment, because of his wealth. In *The Thinking Reed*, money is power; and for the most part, the men have the money.

The pursuit of male money is therefore a pastime, and in some cases a profession, for the women in this world. As in most West novels, the "bad" female characters are more atrocious than the "bad" male characters; for all of the negative traits Isabelle exhibits, the women around her are worse. In some cases, their lesser wealth has made them envious or conniving, and in others, similar immense wealth has made them bored or insular. But the result is often the same: promiscuity, in and outside marriage, that borders on prostitution. Since one of *The Thinking Reed's* main themes is the virtue of marriage bound by sexual fidelity and mutual trust, the empty concupiscence shared by these rich world-travelers is related with disgust:

[A]ll their relationships were in a constant state of flux. . .[they] had
taken vows of wealth, unchastity, and disobedience to all standards. .
they lived in a sexual universe in which all frontiers had been broken
down, including those of time, and it was not less likely that people
would commit adultery on their honeymoon than at any other time
[since] unchastity was a far easier discipline to follow than
disobedience to all standards" (89-91).

"Poots," a casual acquaintance of the Sallafranques, is the most
abhorrent woman in the novel. Like her name that "doesn't mean
anything" (175), she is the mindless, selfish result of parasitic living
coupled with greed and dissatisfaction, a girl born with an aristocratic
name but not much money who seeks out rich men to seduce and then
subtly loot. Poots would never walk the streets picking up tricks, but
her desire for spending cash and social influence leads her to about the
same end. Interestingly, she is actually a business woman, running a
hat shop with another less-than-rich girl of the nobility. But Isabelle's
reflections on such hat shops indicate that this venture is a mere game
for a spoiled, ignorant child, not a well-run business like Marc's, or—in
a further implication—not one that a man would, and would have to,
manage efficiently.

One was forced to go there by an aunt of one of the noble milliners,
met at lunch, who insisted on taking one with a pertinacity which
would have seemed vulgar, had one not reflected that in her youth
there must have seemed so little need for her to push and cadge that
her preceptors might well have omitted to warn her against such
practices. . .One ordered a hat or two, but though one made a definite
appointment for the fitting, one had to go back several times,
because no note had been taken of it, and then the hats were never
delivered when they had been promised. . .The beautiful child's face
would go white with sullenness, her eyes would go blank as Poots's
eyes did. . .she would say obstinately, insolently, absurdly, "I really
can't tell you why they aren't ready. . ." (180-1)

If Poots is detestable in her choice to sleep with men for material
reward, Luba, the exiled Russian princess, is pathetic. A great beauty
who is now somewhat past her prime, she has gone from man to man
in a series of financially dependent relationships that constitute her
income. Like Poots and Isabelle, or Jenny and Kitty, nothing in her
upbringing prepared her to make a living, so the fading of her beauty is
the beginning of economic hardship. There is no question in Isabelle's
mind that the genuinely good Luba's true roles are those of wife and
mother (indeed, Isabelle believes that "there is no other way of living
for a woman" [158] but to be happily married); but the very rich man
Isabelle manipulates to fall in love with Luba is distracted by Poots.

The layers of irony here are thick: the respectable married woman attempts to marry off the whore-with-a-heart-of-gold, working with sly sexual and psychological stratagems that the wicked society harlot uses more successfully but with more selfish intentions. Even more ironically, Poots actually has both a husband and a job and so does not *need* support as Luba does. But, like Edith Wharton's Undine Spragg, Poots traffics in men, and she woos them or drops them like hot and cold stocks. The Russian princess Luba seems more a victim of what West calls in *The Court and the Castle* a monarchy's "temptation to hawk any young beauty in [its] brood" for the purpose of bonding with another royal family;[13] her semi-prostitution may have been forced on her by her looks and a mercenary society that sees and focuses on pulchritude as capital.

Harold Orel comments that all of West's stories "are, at least in part, social documents that illustrate modes of behaviour and codes understood and practised by a very limited number of people at a specific period of history" (124). *The Thinking Reed* is, obviously, an exploration of a small and specific world. Its 1928 setting (a date established early on the first page) gives the novel part of its ruthless air: the roles played by many of these people are created and maintained by their extreme financial worth, and the reader knows well that many of these tyrants, wastrels, sluts (to use a word West applies with peculiar frequency throughout her fiction and non-fiction), and parasites will get their comeuppance with a vengeance in just one year. Nevertheless, this novel well delineates West's hatred of these types of male and female lives, dominated and formed by money or its absence.

As in *The Return of the Soldier*, a woman's changing perceptions about her immediate universe mold and color the narration. Isabelle's main realization is that she wants her husband in spite of his tyranny and profligacy. This comes at the end of the novel, after she has miscarried Marc's child by a violent action she takes to save him from ruining his political and professional standing through gambling. She has turned down Alan, a painter who is still another would-be lover, in Marc's favor, seeing Alan not only as a bad artist, but as insufficiently masculine: "his gentleness could [not] fight the violence and disorder she hated" (404). Simply put, she suspends her own abhorrence of Marc's masculine violence and disorder so that he may be her master, as the oft-quoted last sentences make clear in a dominant/submissive sexual image.

> It struck her that the difference between men and women is the rock on which civilization will split before it can reach any goal that could justify its expenditure of effort. She knew also that her life would not be tolerable if he were not always there to crush gently her smooth hands with his strong short fingers. (431)

In the image of civilization "splitting" over the "rock" of sexual differences, West refers to the "sex antagonism" she wrote of as early as 1912. So much evidence of enmity and injustice exists, such as "the great economic grievance of women. . .that they are not given equal pay for equal work, and they are not allowed equal opportunities of education and profession," that it must have "a sound logical basis" (*Young Rebecca,* 101). Indeed, the fact that Isabelle must resort to deliberately feigned violence in order to achieve what she wants with both Andre and Marc—incidents that cost her enormously—shows West's pessimistic sense that men understand only force.

But West, two decades older here than when she first articulated the sex war, resigns Isabelle to losing it, or at least surrendering, in order that she may have love and, perhaps, children. This may reflect the powerfully influential discourses on sexuality following the prewar years that Susan Kingsley Kent describes in her essay "Gender Reconstruction After the First World War."[14] Such influential "sexologists" as Havelock Ellis "sought in the study of sexuality the solutions to the maintenance and salvation of civilization itself" (72), and insisted that sexuality be firmly rooted within marriage. They also strongly contradicted Victorian notions of women's "proper" lack of passion by emphasizing the importance of sexual pleasure for wives as well as husbands. Both Isabelle's hatred of promiscuity and her final truce with Mark could demonstrate what Kent calls "the metaphor [of] sexual peace, a model of marital accord achieved through mutual sexual enjoyment" (72). The sense of tragedy surrounding her miscarriage, and her willingness to try for another baby, also reflect the renewed importance British society was placing on motherhood in the 1930s, when, as Kent describes, "[d]omestic harmony, and thus social peace, appeared to Britons to depend upon a return to 'traditional' sex roles—to separate spheres of public and private" (73).

The marriage of Isabelle and Mark, however, does not reflect the reality of West's marriage to Andrews. Due to an ectopic pregnancy, in 1932 she underwent an abortion and a hysterectomy, but she never appeared to regret her inability to have another child.[15] In 1933 Andrews was fired from his German-based bank (for the admirable reason that he refused to cooperate with the Nazis' dismissal of a Jewish employee), and West was working long hours writing reviews and stories in order to earn extra money. Her letters at this time indicate fears that economic and political reversals might shatter the fragile peace she had found in marriage.[16] She was also aware that her husband's sexual desire for her was waning, and she foresaw a repeat of her problems with men in the 1920s: that her brilliance, strength, and professional success, which had initially attracted Henry, would now compel him to reject her.

Three of the four short novels collected in *The Harsh Voice* describe the effects on marriage of women's expanding professional and economic spheres. As in *The Thinking Reed,* West explores the destructive effects of money on human relations; its epigraph by "Richard Wynne Errington" (a second pseudonym for Cicely Fairfield Andrews) makes this clear: "Speaks the harsh voice/ We hear when money talks, or hate,/ Then comes the softest answer." But even more distinctly, she shows (especially in "Life Sentence" and "There is no Conversation") that upsetting the traditional economic balance whereby men earn the money and women manage the home is (for some) potentially calamitous. As Motley Deakin points out, here the women play masculine roles, the men feminine; these stories are about both "the irreconcilable differences between man and woman" (147) and the dangers of transcending those customary distinctions, especially as they relate to money, work, and power. Though West deplores the mental weakness in men that makes this role-switching a disaster, she nevertheless seems to suggest that women acquiesce in their own subordination.

A few years after the publication of *The Harsh Voice*, West recorded these thoughts about female dependence in *Black Lamb and Grey Falcon.* I quote her at length here because this surprising passage possibly articulates, in non-fiction form, a theme she rendered in her fiction, and particularly in *A Harsh Voice.* West watches a group of elderly Bosnian women in a Sarajevo market, none of whom can read, all of whom had to "take sound beatings every now and again, work till they drop[ped], even while child-bearing, and walk while their master rides"; yet they "do not look in the least oppressed" (327).

> I suspect that women such as these are not truly slaves, but have found a fraudulent method of persuading men to give them support and leave them their spiritual freedom. It is certain that men suffer from a certain timidity, a liability to discouragement which makes them reluctant to go on doing anything once it has been proved that women can do it as well. This was most painfully illustrated during the slump in both Europe and America, where wives found to their amazement that if they found jobs when their husbands lost theirs and took on the burden of keeping the family, they were in no luck at all. For their husbands became either their frenzied enemies or relapsed into an infantile state of dependence and never worked again. If women pretend that they are inferior to men and cannot do their work, and abase themselves by picturesque symbolic rites, such as giving men their food first and waiting on them while they eat, men will go on working and developing their powers to the utmost, and will not bother to interfere with what women are saying and thinking with their admittedly inferior powers.

It is an enormous risk to take. It makes marriage a gamble, since these symbols of abasement always include an abnegation of economic and civil rights, and while a genial husband takes no advantage of them - and that is to say the vast majority of husbands - a malign man will exploit them with the rapacity of the grave. It would also be a futile bargain to make in the modern industrialized world, for it can hold good only where there are no other factors except the equality of women threatening the self-confidence of men. In our own Western civilization man is devitalized by the insecurity of employment and its artificial nature, so he cannot be restored to primitive power by the withdrawal of female rivalry and the woman would not get any reward for her sacrifice. . .But the greatest objection to this artificial abjection is that it is a conscious fraud on the part of women, and life will never be easy until human beings can be honest with one another. Still, in this world of compromises, honour is due to one so far successful that it produces these grimly happy heroes, these women who stride and laugh, obeying the instructions of their own nature and not masculine prescription. (330)

In "Life Sentence," West seems strongly to advocate the "conscious fraud" in "a world of compromises." The American couple Josephine and Corrie (each of their names deliberately evocative of the sex they are not) begin their married life under the shadow of his sexual doubt: just before the ceremony, Corrie attempts to call off the wedding, claiming he doesn't care enough for Josie "in that way."[17] Before this statement, the reader has found out, through the third-person consciousness of her fiancee, that Josie is "far from pale" but that Corrie is "very pale," and that her "near goddess size" makes him feel "miserably at a disadvantage before her mere physical state" (11). The young woman likes "altering the look of things with her hands," and she—unlike Corrie, who is then hesitating—"would not have stopped at the foot of the stairs" (11) if she had important news. This verbal opposition of their qualities sets up an immediate sense of physical and emotional battle, and it is a battle in which Josie is clearly equipped to be the victor. Corrie thinks his news makes her face a "tragic mask," yet soon it seems more a cloak "not of tragedy but of command," with her "brows brought together in a straight line, her cheeks and her lips. . .as they always had been. . .It was as if her flesh had confidence that the order of things was not inimical to it, and refused to let the mind stampede it into panic" (13). They do marry, because Corrie is not strong enough, in the face of this girl who makes him "think of some great general scowling in a history book" (13), to go through with his desired withdrawal.

Corrie sees his wife as two women. One is the decisive, powerful Josephine of this first scene, who runs her house and cares for her family with military authority. The other is "the shrinking virginal

Josie," a woman of child-like timidity who seems to crave kindness as an antidote to sexual shyness. It is this second, yielding wife to whom Corrie is attracted; such a mood makes him the erotic conqueror, and his "kiss establishe[s] her a woman" (17). He chooses to believe that this shy woman is the real Josie, "just like a little girl inside, full of funny little feelings, wonderfully easily pleased, wonderfully easily hurt" (16). But this is Corrie's fantasy, as Josephine's business acumen soon illustrates. With a solid, though not magnificent, inheritance, Josie begins successfully investing in real estate, and her natural ambition and ability come easily to the fore. West makes explicit one of the story's main ideas in the description of Josie's new financial life, typically both praising male industry and deploring male control.

> . . .[this] happened just about the same time that the American woman began to discover herself as an amateur of business. Sitting back on the throne of prosperity her husband had built up for her, she could bide her time and pick her chances, and see her money increase in a way that seemed the happiest miracle to a sex which had been tied down since the beginning of time to fixed housekeeping allowances. (22)

Less explicit but equally deliberate is the symbolism of "Cherry-garden Bluff," the estate Josie wishes to buy and develop into separate, smaller homes. Corrie cherishes childhood memories of this Northeastern manor whose original Southern owner had there established a "plantation," replete with slave-style black servants, horses, and crops, and for thirty years "had set himself to play a game of pretending" (23). The lost and treasured patriarchy it represents to Corrie—in which everyone knew, and stayed in, his or her own place—corresponds with the lack in his marriage of the distinct, traditional gender roles he prefers. Just as Josephine's confidence undermines Corrie's masculine ego, her business sense wrecks an old dream of male-managed hierarchy; he cannot go on "pretending" that he, as husband, is the dominant partner any more than he can revisit the old gentleman's make-believe South.

Yet it is not fully accurate to say that Corrie is just another of West's characters who, in his refusal to be comfortable with Josie's assertiveness, does not face and accept the "reality" of women's new, and liberating, opportunities. Sister Mary Margarita Orlich asserts in a 1966 dissertation that Josie is the one who is, like the Southern gentleman, pretending, since she "narcissistically" encourages her masculine self to fulfill her self-esteem:

> For Josie Cherry-garden Bluff. . .is to be her bluff in yet another sense of the word - she seeks to find the sexual satisfaction she can

never allow herself in Corrie in a substitution of power. . .[which is]
the equivalent to her emasculation of Corrie and her assumption of
the male role.[18]

Orlich sees their marriage as a cycle of thwarted sexual intentions:
"Josie desires Corrie to prove his masculinity by dominating her"
because "it is only when he asserts himself that she fulfills the
feminine role," which is "[to rest] in the shadow of her husband's
strength and [respond] to him with feminine loveliness." That is the
way she should "[elicit] the masculine qualities in her husband and [be]
a source of fulfillment to his nature" (131), which is apparently Orlich's
idea of the wife's true purpose, and just what Josie does not do often
enough.

Writing more than thirty years ago from the perspective of a
Catholic nun, Orlich sets down such platitudes without a shred of
intentional irony. It is harder to pinpoint West's intended tone, partly
because the story is filtered through Corrie's fearful and perhaps self-
delusive consciousness. Does Josie really have this shy and "virginal"
aspect Corrie imagines? Or is this perhaps Josie's "fraudulent method,"
to go back to the *Black Lamb and Grey Falcon* passage, of pretending
to be inferior to her easily-threatened husband? The ambiguity is, in one
sense, deliberate: as most critics of *The Harsh Voice* have noted, the
general failure of human communication is a major motif in all four
stories, and Corrie's constant guesswork about his wife underscores
West's oft-emphasized belief that even the closest relationships suffer
misunderstandings.

But Orlich accurately analyzes the portrayal of Josie's and Corrie's
sexual struggle as a problem of gender expectations disappointed, and
she may be right, at least in her conjectures on West's intentions, to see
the fault as Josie's. On Josie's initiative they divorce, and each remarries
what each claims is a "real" representative of the opposite sex: in
Corrie's case, a woman whose proof of femininity is that she "can't
look after herself" (55), and in Josie's, a man who "doesn't just tag
around with" her (58). The final surprise of the story lies in its
revelation that in fact their love never died, and that their new partners,
despite the possessions of "appropriate" masculinity or femininity, are
much less desirable. So what should have been, as it were, a marriage
of true minds becomes instead a battle of the sexes. And though the
blame can be attributed to both, it seems that Josie is the real culprit
for taking on the male province of money-making and doing it better
than her husband without either safeguarding his male ego or deceiving
him about her true ability. Even if Josie's sexual reticence is a sham
intended for encouraging her husband, she should have continued the
pretense, in order to save what is apparently a good marriage.

Alexandra Pringle, in the introduction to a recent edition of *The Harsh Voice*, quotes part of an unpublished interview with Jill Craigie, a feminist scholar and a friend of West's. "She [Craigie] found that Rebecca West 'in conversation. . .gives the impression that she would prefer men to make good wives rather than women transmute themselves into good male company directors and politicians.'"[19] Such a statement could corroborate further West's intention to signify Josie's greater guilt. Corrie has the intuition usually ascribed to women, along with an empathy for laborers that indicates a maternal compassion and purpose: "[his job] was housing them and feeding them and clothing them and seeing they had the right sort of place to go nights to keep them sweet and efficient" (42). Conversely, Josie is out to make as much money as possible; she is the quintessential developer, and in her economic ambitions is the epitome of male "lunacy," which West describes in *Black Lamb and Grey Falcon* as "the male defect": "[men] are so obsessed by public affairs that they see the world as by moonlight, which shows the outlines of every object but not the details indicative of their nature" (3).

Nancy Sarle, the female focus of "There is no Conversation," is Josie taken farther down the path of this particular gender reversal, and her counterpart Etienne de Sevenac is a man who has picked up the least attractive of (ostensibly) feminine qualities. But the pursuit of money has made Nancy cheerfully masculine, "a helluva good fellow" (91), while the possession of money has made Etienne as vain as a courtesan, and in fact the epitome of "the female defect": "intent on their private lives, women follow their fate through a darkness deep as that cast by malformed cells in the brain" (3). In this story West again spotlights the results of sexual presumptions and gender postures turned upside down, though not so much for the purpose of getting across a "message" as to describe a possible clash of old and new.

As in *The Return of the Soldier*, a James-like first-person narrator, never named, intently observes these two main characters, and it is through her voice that we hear Etienne and Nancy tell contradictory stories about their disastrous affair. Etienne is a wealthy, aristocratic French dilettante who imagines he took pity on the American Nancy by showing her his usual brand of brief erotic attention.

> [S]he was not beautiful, not beautiful at all, and had a very bad figure, too broad, short but with shoulders like a man's, and was not at all elegant. And she was quite old. Forty-two. Forty-three. Perhaps forty-five! That is all right if a woman is elegant. But if she is not it is disgusting. I should have been warned by her lack of elegance! For a woman who does not care for that shows herself callous, cruel, vehement. . .It was pathetic to think of how little could have happened to her. She would have adored to be somebody, that little

thing! To have been elegant, to have had lovers, to have known passion and adventure in romantic surroundings, her heart was craving for it. (74-5)

Such statements are ironic not only in light of the story's ending, when it becomes clear that Nancy has been and is a "somebody" capable of destroying Etienne and his old world of smug, inherited male privilege. The narrator, before this conversation, has been pitying Etienne for an obsession with his own encroaching age and fading looks. The maintenance of his beauty has been Etienne's business; as a European nobleman, he considers any work the province of inferiors. Nancy, in her turn, cannot believe that he does nothing, and is as appalled by his lack of industry as he is by her inattention to personal appearance. She is the new American business woman while he is (very much like Andre de Verviers) a vainglorious sponge, and her eventual decision to bankrupt a company from which Etienne receives his income symbolizes the post World War I demise of unquestioned male (and European aristocratic) financial and mercantile supremacy.

Likewise, his supposition that Nancy's plain looks will mean her unhappiness is exposed for the foolishness it is, while emphasizing how unfairly and unnecessarily women have been judged by looks and relegated to the business of trying to be beautiful. His own desperate struggle to stay attractive points this out as well, though the parallel is lost on him. The "male" role of magnate suits Nancy better than the usually female role of beauty fits Etienne. West may be implying that the latter part is the tougher one, which is one reason Nancy wishes to join, in her straightforward attitude and dress, the "great safe army" (102) of men. In fact, she makes the decision to demolish the rival railway company because its owner, a "professional good woman" (120) whom Nancy's husband revered as representative of feminine "virtue," finally dies. Nancy's delayed revenge shows her desire to shed all adherence to women's habitual, and accepted, social customs; moreover, the woman's death symbolizes the demise of such rigidly followed conventions.

In the remaining two stories of *The Harsh Voice*, women are once again only wives, mothers, or mistresses, but they too are not entirely happy with those parts. Alice Pemberton of "The Salt of the Earth" (the only story set in England) releases pent-up organizational abilities by trying to run her relatives' lives. Having no children, she considers herself free to "do a whole lot of things for others," usually against their will; she imagines that she would have liked the nineteenth century better than "this horrid, hustling present day" (141), not realizing that she might perhaps be better off taking advantage of the working opportunities the present holds. Alice's meddling becomes so critical that her husband Jimmy, though he loves her, poisons her, and this murder could signify either the death of the "old-fashioned" (a description Alice proudly gives herself) woman's life or male resistance to female potency. Alice is a loathsome character whose homicide seems deserved, and "The Salt of the Earth" may be no more than a satisfying murder tale. Yet it fits into the general pattern of *The Harsh Voice* by having an aggressive female character; and since the other three stories have heavily ironic points of view, it is possible to assume that Alice's alleged satisfaction with her life, home, and husband is the opposite feeling (as her recurrent nightmares also indicate).[20]

"The Salt of the Earth" differs from "Life Sentence" and "There is no Conversation" in two ways: one, that the man is eventually triumphant over the woman, though Jimmy's victory will certainly mean the defeat of his own freedom; and two, that husband and wife fit (what was then) the conventional economic model of marriage. "The Abiding Vision" shares these differences and goes further: it is the only story in *The Harsh Voice* to depict a man who attracts and keeps beautiful women with money (certainly a subject known well in literature and life), and one who represents, in a deliberately common characterization, the good-old-boy network of masculine business. Sam Hartley's abiding erotic vision is of "a face unlined with care, smooth and shining flesh undepleted by self-sacrifice" (189). His ability to pay for young mistresses comes from his other abiding vision, male (and in this case American) entrepreneurship, a faith that is not broken by an indictment for illegal stock manipulation. Sam's once-beautiful wife Lulah and his lovely young paramour Lily are sustained by Sam's pre-1929 wealth. But both end the story drained by the self-sacrifices they have made in order to nurture him through, in Lulah's case, the social climb necessary for his business success, and in Lily's case, the sexual hunger which distracts him. Lulah's deathbed delirium indicates that she gave up her education to marry the young, ambitious Sam, while Lily has no job or marriage to depend upon once her beauty has faded.

Yet Sam continues to dream of young girls and new financial ventures, imagining that he is a "real" man, not a "college professor," as he disdainfully characterizes the lawyer cross-examining him about his stocks.

> This man was poison. Sam had heard he had been a college professor, and he had an air of being unfairly smart, of having stayed indoors and read books and got the low-down on things while decent male men would have felt an urge to go into the open and do real jobs and be sports. . .what he wanted to say was, "You poor white-face louse of a college professor, you wouldn't know what to do if you got among decent people, you wouldn't know what to do if you found yourself in bed with a woman. (236-8)

Sam manages to talk his way into an acquittal by appealing to the court
with, ironically, just this sort of reasoning, the all-too-familiar claim
that "real men," even businessmen, focus on the physical rather than
the intellectual. This feat, plus the fact that the story's last words are
again of his abiding vision of young flesh, indicate that West wished to
end this story, and perhaps *The Harsh Voice*, with a wry reaffirmation
of male economic and sexual conquest. Neither Sam Hartley nor his
actions are admirable, and West is obviously not sanctioning attitudes
as absurd as those that equate knowledge with sexual impotence. Still,
as Pringle suggests, Sam's "harsh voice" of money receives the "softest
answer" of Lily's love (xii); she and Lulah, in their nurturing loyalty
and selflessness, represent the positive side of woman as helpmeet in a
way that Alice, Josie, and Nancy do not. If they never develop talents
that might have enabled them to move beyond dependence on Sam
(Lily, for one, shows shrewd business smarts in her own right), each is
a kinder, more truthful human being than the women in the previous
stories.

The Harsh Voice presents, as Deakin names it, "an impression of a
society   moving   toward   androgynous   characteristics,   its   sexual
distinctions   in   flux"   (147).   The   stories   have   no   one   grievance   to
nourish or solution to advocate, but are instead representative of West's
major paradoxes. Women, she clearly thinks, have been forced for too
long into the narrow slots of homemaker, wife, mistress, and mother,
and their suppressed faculties spell problems for themselves, their
families, and society. But men, when threatened by new female
competitiveness and economic independence, lose the sense of
emotional and erotic mastery that West thinks feeds a healthy marriage
and keeps men from interfering with women's "spiritual freedom."
There seems little hope for compromise or flexibility in her own
abiding vision of a continuous power struggle between the genders, but
there is, I think, a judgment of degree: that the problems West would
consider ultimately worst occur when women assert their desires, not
when they subvert them.

Sunflower is in some ways a case in point. As previously noted,
this odd, unfinished manuscript published posthumously as a novel is a
fictional working out of the Freudian analysis West underwent in 1927
in an attempt to discover why all her relationships failed. (She even
took notes on her analysis on the back of the *Sunflower* manuscript.) In
particular, West's intense attraction for Lord "Max" Beaverbrook, the
influential Canadian newspaper magnate, had ended after several
disastrously incomplete sexual liaisons that devastated her. *Sunflower*
contains lyrical descriptions of powerful sexual passion for "Francis
Pitt," the Beaverbrook character, yet notably ends before Sybil and Pitt

make love. West outlined the next part of the novel to include Pitt's sexual rejection and Sybil's search for solace in humanitarian activities, yet she wanted to stress that Pitt does in fact love Sybil but is afraid of her.[21] While *Sunflower* presents the assertion of women's sexual desire rather than professional ambition in Sybil's infatuation with Francis Pitt, the fact that men fear women, even one who deliberately desires to be the subordinate in a sexual relationship, is one of its main points. The depiction of Sybil's relationship with Essington makes this point even more strongly. But both relationships show the difficulty men have in accepting a successful, and sexual, woman's desires, and how their failure to achieve proper "masculinity" results in women's failure to be properly "feminine."

Several years later West would object to Freud's ideas about women as "enigmas" and "riddles," and even here, Sybil's strong yearning for Pitt rejects Freud's insinuation that women are passive entities for whom "to be loved is a stronger need than to love" (Rollyson 161). Yet when West composed *Sunflower*, she earnestly tried to incorporate some Freudian theory into her understanding of her own sexual life. Sybil Fassendyll, like West's subsequent creation Harriet Hume, would seem to be all that is most appropriately feminine in Freudian terms. Her name gives clues to those traits, with its suggestions of the words "facile," "idyll," "idle," "sex," "fascinating," "fastened," and the mysterious "sibyl." She is matchlessly beautiful, always acquiescent, radiantly sexual, yet unabashedly maternal. Apparently "stupid," or at least far less educated or intellectual than the men in the book, Sybil allows Essington, her married lover (and a portrait of H.G. Wells), to rule her life, though he does not give her the two things she most wants: children, and a peaceful domestic existence in which she need not work outside the home. Essington's nickname for Sybil, "Sunflower," evokes the myth of Clytie, a nymph who was so obsessed by her love for Apollo that she did nothing but stare at the sun all day until she turned into a sunflower. Though Sybil has a busy and profitable career as an actress, she too spends most of her energy thinking about a man, and her existence reflects Essington's domination more than the personal or professional autonomy her success might entail. Her youthful beauty, but also poverty, catapulted her onto the stage; she became an actress by chance and necessity, not for need of an artistic outlet. Sybil is economically independent in a sense against her will, since Essington—a statesman and political thinker, the quintessential "great man"—supports his wife only.

Yet Essington is threatened by Sybil's work. His constant taunts about her lack of talent reinforce his supposed superiority and mask a larger fear of the sexual and emotional independence he knows she could achieve if she chose to leave him. Their relationship is posited upon her subordination, and she accepts as customary such abuse, even thinking that she deserves it. Sybil adores "strong" men; and though Essington's "strength" unfortunately contains this verbal tyranny (which she has the sense to despise), she imagines, forgiving as a mother, that "his soreness was sweetness tortured into the likeness of the opposite" (115). But the nature of these fears eventually unravels the master/subject fabric they have tenuously woven. When he accuses her of knowing about things she shouldn't know (such as the existence of homosexuals, or other men in general), he blames her "work" as "one of the chief difficulties of our relationship" (229), and tries to insist upon her (fantasized) role as servant by ordering her to make him food.

> This was a habit of his when he had risen to a certain pitch of rage against her. . .It was not such a bad thing as it seemed, for it was not a mere explosion of tyranny, it was more like a mechanical adjustment which made it possible for their relationship to run smoothly for a little while. . .It was perhaps the attempt. . .to make a relationship run right by forcing it into the groove along which such relationships traditionally ran. . .The imitation of it was so nearly right, was at any rate so allusive to rightness that it always felt sweet. But it was play-acting, it was pretence. . .(228-9)

The "pretence" of Essington's role as master ends, and with it their relationship, over such an argument about her career. When Essington begins his accusations about the sacrifices he makes because she is sometimes not there exactly when he wants her, she flashes back that she "had to have the money" because they "couldn't have had as comfortable a house if [she] hadn't worked" (231). The irony here is that Sybil would *rather* be supported; when she insists that now their connection is truly severed, Essington only makes himself absurd by shouting, "Yes, you can go to another paymaster!" (233). The main theme of *Sunflower* is signified and heightened when an actual physical battle almost occurs at the moment of their parting. Essington hits Sybil, but he cannot hurt her.

> This was the most horrible thing that had ever happened to her, that can have happened to anybody since the world began. . .He had not even made her sway on her feet. He was not as strong as she was. And that was shame, shame and ruin for them both. . .since indeed everything she felt about life depended on men being in some ways stronger than women. (233-4)

This portrait of a non-conventional non-marriage that goes wrong is obviously an exaggerated version of West's desires for male power and dominance and some ideal form of domestic happiness. I think it only fair to stress the fact that West never chose to publish or even to finish

Sunflower. But in its exaggeration it serves to clarify the strong influence West's Freudian analysis may have had upon this woman whose earlier ideas about women's lives and potential were very different, and whose own life was so different from Sybil's. Glendinning cites West's point that with Beaverbrook she wanted "a bond as between me and my father—purely sexual" (119), and much of her psychoanalysis centered on her thwarted desire for her father's love. But unlike the "normal" woman that Freud described, West never found in any man a substitute for her father, nor sought her life's meaning in motherhood. Sybil's insistence that her acting career was an economic necessity sounds like a version of West's almost apologetic declaration that journalism had been a mere drudgery she engaged in to support herself (Glendinning quotes West as saying, "I hate and loathe journalism" [540]), or her claim in *Black Lamb and Grey Falcon* that "trivial domestic rites" are delicious to "women like [herself], who have had to work at a specialized task all their lives" (945-6).

But while the reader can believe that Sybil may be as bad an actress as she says—since her "bad" acting indicates how poorly she is suited to the actress role, with the further implication that "acting" is what she does with Essington—certainly West was, and knew she was, a remarkably gifted writer. Loretta Stec, who analyzes the novel at length, points out that *Sunflower* can be read as West's attempt "to fictionalize her corresponding knowledge that women who remain passive, who desire the traditional roles of women, will gain certain rewards in a society such as England in the 1920s," but that "she could not fictionalize a happy ending to that quest, or draw an autobiographical portrait that did not incorporate some of her professional power" (73). Indeed, *Sunflower* is not an autobiographical portrait of West as reluctant artist. It is instead an acting-out of a female who is willing to adopt the Freudian paradigm of sexuality and love a dominant father figure, to be defeated in the battle of the sexes in a way that West probably never was. It seems logical to assume that her way of relieving self-blame following psychoanalysis was to concoct this earth mother/sex goddess who wants, "correctly," to channel her creative energies toward a man and children, and then to blame Sybil's inability to do this on a man's inadequate masculinity. Sybil thinks, as apparently West did at that time (and later), that this sexual sickness could be cured by a securely masculine man who would not allow her feminine energies to stray away from or overwhelm him.

West condemns not only Essington as ineffectively male. Strewn throughout *Sunflower* (and another unfinished novel, *Cousin Rosamund)* are bitter renunciations of a rampant homosexuality that implies female failure and disappointment at the hands of "not men," who enjoyed "adventures in which women had no part" (226). She contrasts them with the girls "who had rid themselves of all the traditional signs of womanhood," yet who remained "utterly women, with soft young faces that glowed in expectation of adventures the cause of which would be submission. . ." (227-8). West, like Freud and perhaps because of him, sees homosexuality as a perversion of the maturation process that can be overcome through conscious effort. If women can maintain their "intrinsic" heterosexuality in spite of the new, more androgynous world that followed World War I, West seems to wonder, why can't men? If Sybil's life as an actress so threatens Essington, why does he not relieve her, financially and emotionally, of the need to act? One of the attractions Francis Pitt has for Sybil is her fantasy of being a rich, pampered wife, a vision the younger Rebecca would have deplored. She believes that she would gladly trade her economic independence for complete immersion in marriage and motherhood.

Sybil would also happily renounce all claim to "artistic" work if it could mean an end to the claustrophobia and isolation of fame. Not only do Essington's jealousy and selfishness force her into an unnatural social quarantine; the visibility she endures because of her career compels her to shun ordinary public places or suffer what she considers a cruel singling-out. This understandable paranoia probably reflects West's hatred of the notoriety she gained as Wells's mistress, and may as well mirror the sense of personal vulnerability any polemical author might feel.

But it has another dimension: the mistrust and even scorn women who chose work over the home still endured. Though Sybil's career is one women have traditionally undertaken, and probably more often from desire than financial need, thirty years later West looks at women entering the tougher discipline of concert pianist in *The Fountain Overflows, This Real Night,* and *Cousin Rosamund;* in fact, West described the main subject of *The Fountain Overflows* as "the difficulty of leading an artist's life" (Rollyson 313). The social isolation that the twins Rose and Mary Aubrey face as girls dedicated to the grind of professional musical careers is stressed as an inevitable part of their choice. Rachel Blau DuPlessis claims that

[t]he figure of a female artist encodes the conflict between any empowered woman and the barriers to her achievement. Using the female artist as a literary motif dramatizes and heightens the already-present contradiction in bourgeois ideology between the ideals of striving, improvement, and visible public works, and the feminine version of that formula: passivity, "accomplishments," and invisible private acts.[22]

The three books of the *Cousin Rosamund* trilogy, which constitute West's autobiographical *Kunstlerroman,* illustrate exactly this point.

The rare talent Rose and Mary possess makes them avid pupils, but they are equally eager to gain, via artistic excellence, economic and personal independence. From the beginning of *The Fountain Overflows,* money—its lack or its availability—is associated with the cruelty or kindness of men. The women of the Aubrey family are continuously anxious that Piers, the father and husband whose small and unpredictable income supports them, will gamble away their tiny livelihood. Rose, the narrator of the Aubrey family saga and West's most autobiographical character, describes Piers's "lifelong wrestling match with money" as an erotic infatuation with "a gypsy mistress" whom he loves and hates: "he wanted hugely to possess it and then drove it away, so that he nearly perished of his need for it" (47). Rose's comparison of their monetary situation with illicit sex accentuates her unhappy sense of her father's wickedness, and in a sense equates financial solvency with fidelity in marriage. Piers is neither economically nor sexually faithful to his wife Clare; and though Rose and her sisters are at that time unaware of their father's affairs, they all acquire a desperate desire for the safety a steady income promises. Clare's musically brilliant but destructive cousin Jock, who makes plenty of money yet spends it on a sham study of popular parapsychology and not his family, reinforces the girls' impression of men as wasteful snares to be avoided.

Clare gave up a promising career as a concert pianist to marry for love, not for security or social acceptance or for lack of employment alternatives; her ability to earn a living had been proved, as various references to her past successes denote. But music continues to be her religion, and she raises the twins Rose and Mary to be as great or greater musicians, fully intending them to go as far as possible on the professional path she deserted. Clare's motivation is solely artistic: she sees the girls' potential, and believes it is her moral and aesthetic duty to encourage it. Yet Rose and Mary, as well as the untalented Cordelia, see concert careers as their way of escaping dependence upon capricious male support. None considers marriage a probability, even a possibility, since their lives have shown them the opposite of masculine stability.

Rose's first-person narrative consciousness makes this point repeatedly, since West wants to stress the Aubrey girls' deliberate deviation from the marriage plot. They never imagine that enticing a husband will be their paramount jobs in life, since they are rigorously training to be professional musicians. Nor do they believe that a man will bring them anything but anxiety and heartache. They do not even understand that their mother and father share a sexual love that exists outside their professions or their parenting; Rose repeatedly puzzles over why Clare seems to care so much for Piers when they are not actually related by blood. Although the girls adore their father to the point of worship, his unreliability convinces them that marriage would ruin their autonomy and self respect. When they worry that their music careers will fail, they imagine working in factories or the post office rather than marrying.

Clare worries about her daughters' unmarriageability, fearing that they "are not part of any world" (95) in their odd combination of poverty and erudition. But their treatment at school and in other public situations has taught them that they are even more scorned for their professional ambitions than for Piers's gambling and adultery, known to the Aubreys' neighbors and the children's peers. Rose thinks that she and her family live "in a more dangerous way than the children [she] knew at school and their fathers and mothers and teachers," imagining the Aubreys cling to "the edge of [an] abyss" (87). While their financial situation is less desperate after Piers's death, the older Rose of *This Real Night* is still socially alienated enough to see "going out into the adult world" as a chance to meet ordinary people who are "like the characters in books and plays" since "authors could not just have made them up out of nothing at all."[23]

Most galling is the lack of sexual attention she and Mary suffer as teenagers. One beautiful evening Rose sits near a young man, listening to her brother play the flute and wishing for an amorous exchange.

> But the young man did not speak or move. It was not to be expected that he should. That sort of young man would find his wife among the more prosperous families in Lovegrove, whose daughters stayed at home after they left school. I knew well that was the supreme attraction. It was no good at all for a girl to be clever, and not much being pretty; "staying at home" was what was irresistible. . .I was at a disadvantage compared to all the other girls sitting beside their partners in the warm moonlight, simply because I was known to be committed to a profession. (146-7)

Even the young male musical colleagues of Rose and Mary reject them, in spite of the genuine artistic respect the girls inspire: Rose complains that "people said how wonderful we were but they kept at a distance" (181).

The comprehensive inclusion their brother Richard Quin enjoys, juxtaposed with their feminine seclusion, emphasizes this conflict. Though he has had the same parents and upbringing as Rose and Mary, his sisters frequently marvel at the friends and places he has come to know through his extraordinary charm, but more importantly, through the freedom his gender affords. It is usually Richard Quin who explains tricky nuances of social situations, or who smoothes over difficult scenes with his greater worldly knowledge. Richard Quin is even a ticket to the outside world for his young female acquaintances, since he is willing to chaperone them to the ordinary sites of public discourse they cannot attend alone. Rose's adoration of her brother is in part a wistful longing for his male world, even a desire to be him, what Elaine Showalter calls "the wish-fulfillment in the feminine novel [that] comes from women wishing they were men, with the greater freedom and range masculinity confers" (136.)

> I wanted, so much that I wept at night, to be part of the general web, to be linked with boys and girls and men and women who were not yet what they would be in the end, and would disclose themselves in plays, and would let me act with them and find out what I was. But nobody wanted very much to be with any of us except Richard Quin, who constantly attached people of all ages to himself by simply meeting them, so that we were surprised. . .by the number of grown-ups who nodded and smiled at him, by the number of houses which were not just sealed boxes for him. . .It was not fair, this private golden age which had been given Richard Quin, where there were neither strangers nor trespassers, only friends and open doors. (142-3)

Even his musical universe is open in a way that the sisters' is not. Richard Quin tries all different instruments, gaining multiple skills that do not imply a dilettante's limitations, but a master's liberty. Unlike Rose and Mary, he need not focus intensely on one channel that leads one way because he has myriad employment opportunities. And, again unlike his sisters, Richard Quin's musical ability garners him admiration and invitations instead of mistrust and ostracism. Artistry sequesters Rose and Mary in a vacuum of unintended self-absorption; for Richard Quin, it means a license for communication. At this point of the *Cousin Rosamund* trilogy—about halfway through *This Real Night*—Rose wants only equality with her brother, and acceptance from the Edwardian middle-class world that shuns her for seeking that equality.

West created another female concert pianist in the 1929 novel *Harriet Hume*. While Harriet too experiences the isolation that comes with being a woman artist, hers is self-chosen: her beautiful garden and home in the middle of London are an oasis from the city that fosters a kind of female life she gently rejects.[22] Harriet is juxtaposed with Arnold Condorex, who represents a male public life defined and formed by specific social categories; her classlessness and freedom both attract and repel him, and she is arguably the victor in their struggle of opposing philosophies. But Harriet ultimately relinquishes her solitude and her art in order to live with Arnold for "eternity," as Rose will slow down her concert career once she marries (as a later chapter will discuss).

Such conclusions are common in West's fiction. Perhaps the most concrete element of her paradoxical feminism is this vision of female subordination in financial and professional realms, since so many of her plots and themes revolve around the problems of women's success in business or art. To claim that West believes women belong in the home only, or that they should never be artists or careerists, is too simple; her own life, and many passages of her writing, belie that idea. Yet the "admittedly inferior powers" for work she attributes to women in *Black Lamb and Grey Falcon* constantly show up in her novels as an almost grateful admission of male superiority. Gilbert and Gubar, in a discussion of Freud's "general analysis of what is normatively 'feminine,'" claim that "in constructing his theory of female psychosexual development he is not only describing but prescribing the one story about literary women that would be acceptable to their male contemporaries—the story of female defeat in the battle of the sexes" (*Vol. I*, 183). West prescribes this same story repeatedly in regard to almost any female endeavor, particularly in the novels she wrote during and after her psychoanalysis. It is somewhat obscured by the very real anger she displays toward economic inequality between the sexes and the social isolation women face when they attempt financial or artistic autonomy. Nevertheless, due to the complex forces of her own life, and the cultural pressures she could not avoid as a woman who was also a political journalist and novelist, the overriding vision she often chooses to present is an old one: men should work and create; women should serve and procreate.

Notes

1. Rebecca West, *The Fountain Overflows* (New York: The Viking Press, 1956): 218. Further references will be to this edition, identified by page numbers in the text.

2. Susan Faludi, *Backlash* (New York: Random House, 1991).

3. Harold L. Smith, "British Feminism in the 1920s," in *British Feminism in the Twentieth Century,* ed. Harold L. Smith (Amherst: University of Massachusetts Press, 1990): 47.

4. Samuel Hynes, review of *Rebecca West: A Life* by Victoria Glendinning, *The New Republic* 19 October, 1987: 47. Further references will be identified by page numbers in the text.

5. Rebecca West, *The Return of the Soldier* (New York: The Dial Press, 1980): 9. Further references will be to this edition, identified by page numbers in the text.

6. The favorite trysting place of Rebecca West and H.G. Wells was the tiny Monkey Island Inn on the Thames.

7. Rebecca West, *Family Memories*, ed. and introduced by Faith Evans (New York: Penguin, 1987): 5. Further references will be to this edition, identified by page numbers in the text.

8. Margaret Diane Stetz claims, "Clearly, the plot of *The Return of the Soldier* centers upon [a] change in the narrator's values and is, therefore, of a philosophical character," and that "some critics have been sidetracked by minor issues and. . .have missed grasping the work as a whole"(75). She emphasizes Jenny's acceptance of the necessity of Chris's "cure" - his need, and hers, to face "reality" - as the novel's main thrust. Margaret Diane Stetz, "Drinking 'The Wine of Truth': Philosophical Change in West's *The Return of the Soldier*," *Arizona Quarterly* 43.1 (1987): 63-78.

9. West considered *The Good Soldier* brilliant, "a much, much better book than any of us deserve," as she wrote in a London *Daily News* article published April 2, 1915. Her review pinpoints some of the subjects that so impressed her in Ford's novel, and were to show up three years later in *The Return of the Soldier*, such as "how the good soldier struggled from the mere clean innocence which was the most his class could expect from him to the knowledge of love. . ."(*Young Rebecca*, 299).

10. Gilbert and Gubar note several novels of this time period in which women act as nursemaids for wounded male soldiers, who see them as solace for and refuge from the war; they mention Margaret as one. See *Volume 2*, 287.

11. Rebecca West, *The Thinking Reed* (New York: The Viking Press, 1966): 3. Further references will be to this edition, identified by page numbers in the text.

12. "When we are told that Isabel married Osmond because 'there had been nothing very delicate in inheriting seventy thousand pounds, and she hoped he might use her fortune in a way that might make her think better of it and would rub off a certain grossness attaching to the good luck of an unexpected inheritance,' we feel that this is mere simpering. . .If their marriage was to be a reality it was to be a degradation of the will whose integrity the whole book is an invitation to admire; if it was to be a sham it was still a larger concession to society than should have been made by an honest woman." Rebecca West, *Henry James* (New York: Henry Holt and Company, 1916): 69-70. Rollyson notes this same passage, 61.

13. Rebecca West, *The Court and the Castle* (New Haven: Yale University Press, 1957): 21.

14. Susan Kingsley Kent, "Gender Reconstruction After the First World War," in *British Feminism in the Twentieth Century*. Further references will be identified by page numbers in the text.

15. See Rollyson, 153.

16. See Rollyson, 159.

17. Rebecca West, "Life Sentence," *The Harsh Voice* (Harmondsworth, Middlesex: Penguin Books, 1956): 12. Further references will be to this edition, including those to "There is No Conversation," "The Salt of the Earth," and "The Abiding Vision," identified by page numbers in the text.

18. Sister Mary Margarita Orlich, "The Novels of Rebecca West: A Complex Unity" (Ph.D. diss., University of Notre Dame, 1966): 9. Further references will be identified by page numbers in the text.

19. Alexandra Pringle, introduction to *The Harsh Voice,* by Rebecca West (New York: The Dial Press, 1981): x. Further references to Pringle's introduction will be from this edition, identified by page numbers in the text.

20. Nicola Beauman reads "The Salt of the Earth" in Freudian terms: "Clearly, Alice's conscious self prevents her from controlling her unconscious self, even though her dreams are showing her the way out." Nicola Beauman, *A Very Great Profession: The Women's Novel 1814-39* (London: Virago Press, 1983): 168. Further references will be identified by page numbers in the text.

21. See Rollyson, 117.

22. Rachel Blau DuPlessis, *Writing Beyond the Ending: Narrative Strategies of Twentieth-Century Women Writers* (Bloomington: Indiana University Press, 1985): 84. Further references will be identified by page numbers in the text.

23. Rebecca West, *This Real Night* (New York: Penguin Books, 1984): 17. Further references will be to this edition, identified by page numbers in the text.

24. For a discussion of *Harriet Hume* as "a female version of pastoral which posits chastity as freedom in a wilderness presided over by Artemis," see Jane Marcus, "A Wilderness of One's Own: Feminist Fantasy Novels of the Twenties: Rebecca West and Sylvia Townsend Warner," in *Women Writers and the City: Essays in Feminist Literary Criticism,* ed. Susan Merrill Squier (Knoxville: University of Tennessee Press, 1984): 134-60. Further references will be identified by page numbers in the text.

Chapter 2

Venus and Cinderella

Indeed, she contained within herself two of the great legendary figures that man has invented everywhere and in all times: Venus and Cinderella. And they were not - he bade her remember - invented idly. They fed desires that must be fed if man is not to lose heart and die. *Sunflower*

[Sarah Bernhardt's] impersonations were true impersonations, uncoloured by her personal desire to strike her audiences as any particular sort of woman. *Ending in Earnest*

In 1987, four years after her death, Rebecca West's *Family Memories* was published. For devoted readers of *The Fountain Overflows, This Real Night,* and *Cousin Rosamund,* this collection of "Parental Memoirs" (her original title) was a fascinating chance to learn more about the real-life Clare and Piers Aubrey, Isabella Mackenzie and Charles Fairfield. But these stories about the childhoods and courtship of West's mother and father are more than biography, and less; "illusion and reality join," Faith Evans writes, and "it is more like a sequence of inter-related novellas than a verifiable history. . .therefore, like so much of Rebecca West's work, [it] is only acceptable within its own terms" (3-4). West's "terms" include the inevitable, and fierce, presence of her major preoccupations—familial (and especially male) betrayal, women's personal and artistic sacrifices and the injustice of a social system that demands them, the forces of chance, male and female character, male responsibility—and the reader's ability to recognize that, as Evans observes, "she was caught in the historical bind of autonomy versus domestic respectability" (5). It is difficult, if not impossible, to know what is fact and what is fiction, since her memories are mostly culled from conversations with her parents (both of whom were dead before West was thirty, and these memoirs were written in the last two decades of her life), some of which can no longer be confirmed. But recording accurate history does not seem to have been West's primary intention. As in *Black Lamb and Grey Falcon* or *The Meaning of Treason,* she uses (purportedly) non-fiction narrative to express personal angers, beliefs, and impressions.

Not surprisingly, many of the women of *Family Memories* are victims. Much of the book is about the disintegration of Isabella Mackenzie's family, a destruction that West blames directly on her uncle Alick's "desertion" and its disastrous effect on the Mackenzie women, especially on her mother's life and musical career. But Alick, while based on the actual Sir Alexander Mackenzie, is more an abstraction than a person. He represents the quintessential Westian man: talented and practically capable, possibly beyond the range of (what West considers) feminine ability; ambitious, with early utopian goals eventually turned to less than honorable aims; able, but often unwilling, to love where it is deserved; ultimately false to the women who are dependent on him. His sister Isabella, perhaps the distillation of West's ideal woman, is his foil, since her sacrificial integrity accentuates Alick's familial dishonor. Moreover, the freedom he selfishly enjoys as the eldest male Mackenzie and a professional man directly contrasts the tight boundaries she endures as an unmarried woman, especially one living in a female-headed household within a self-righteously patriarchal society that perceives her situation as unsuitable and inferior. Quite bitterly, West compares the difference in their musical fortunes.

> My mother was a brilliant pianist, but she was denied by her sex the understanding of the whole field of music that her brothers had, for the reason that she could not play in an orchestra, or undergo any of the rough-and-tumble training that Alick had got for the asking between the ages of ten and eighteen. (31)

Just as Alick and Isabella are emblematic, in both character and fate, of Westian man and woman, so is the nineteenth-century Scottish community here portrayed a microcosm of the forces West blames for masculine advantage and feminine disadvantage. All of the female Mackenzies are acutely aware of men's (and society's) images of women, and realize that to show themselves in any way outside the stilted Scottish constructs of chaste, thrifty, subservient, obedient wife, daughter, and even mother, is to be alienated. Victory and survival depend upon how well each manipulates her carefully created reflection of customary womanhood. Isabella's cousin Elizabeth Campbell manages to elope successfully "because of the cynical use to which she put the tradition of female chastity" (37): leaving her aunt a mendacious note saying she had run off with a married actor "that she had for some time been meeting in secret," Elizabeth escapes unimpeded, calculating correctly that if the aunt "thought she had been a bad girl she would not trouble to search for her" (38). Isabella learns, as an impoverished, unmarried girl, "to make herself acceptable by limiting her conversation with men to petitions for enlightenment," since "any exchange of opinions was only permitted to married women, and the extent of female participation varied with rank and wealth" (113). The villainess of *Family Memories*, Mary Ironside, seduces Alick (and thus begins the cycle of family, and especially female, ruin) with great natural beauty and a feigned delicacy and moderation she rightly imagines appealing to masculine taste. She deliberately wears black, claiming mourning, but knowing it makes her look "not only a beautiful but also a serious young woman, and especially in need of consideration" (43). At table she expresses surprise at "lavish" helpings, "refusing an offer of wine with the Edinburgh idiom, a whispered exclamation, 'Oh no, I do not taste!'" (44).

Yet not all of West's women consciously create conventionally feminine faces to meet the masculine faces that they meet. Some are formed, or guided, or thwarted, or trapped by images men make of them that they cannot control: images that they project because the patterns exist in men's minds not only from communal culture, but also from art, myth, and literature. In *Family Memories* Isabella meets "a most beautiful girl" (164) whose voice the reader never hears directly, and who serves only to symbolize a sort of passive female victimization and unhappiness.

> The beauty of this girl was only just visible in the shadows. Through a break in the screens a ray of light had entered to discover her pale red-gold hair, her delicately blue closed eyelids, her high and fine cheekbones, fine as the bones in a small bird's wings, and the lovely curved melancholy of her mouth, that hallmark of Pre-Raphaelitism, which suggested that she realized how necessary it was for those about her to take some action regarding an element in their lives, but it was by now too late for the matter to be even named. . .[Isabella] wondered at the girl's extreme beauty and the meaning that seemed to lie behind it, though it gave no indications of intelligence, or any feeling but melancholy, and indeed hardly of life. The breath that shook the narrow and dark dress flickered like the flame of a taper, and no more. (164-5)

Norah O'Brien suffers from classic Victorian melancholia, but Charles Fairfield claims she will soon get over it, since "there was no reason why a woman as beautiful as she should not get what she wanted out of life" (181). Isabella counters that "we know what [her] beauty has got out of life, and that is Sam O'Brien [her husband]" (181); what she will probably get next, Isabella implies, is a child, "and she might well feel dissatisfied with that" (182). When Norah, Ophelia-like, is found drowned, the newly-wedded Fairfields feel a strangely potent sorrow that has not much to do with "the degree to which they had known her"; "it was more as if a famous picture had been destroyed" (185).

West's description of Norah, as her mention of Pre-Raphaelitism implies, seems deliberately romantic, and evocative of (among others) D.G. Rossetti's paintings of Elizabeth Siddal. Since the Fairfields were married in 1883, this particular depiction of a woman's style is appropriate (as many apparently feigned it), and in fact may be exactly as Isabella characterized her to young Cissie (West refers to Norah again as "the Pre-Raphaelite red-haired beauty"[172]). But why should this particular small incident have made its way into a memoir about West's family relations? One grants that the suicide of an extraordinarily beautiful and young person is an inherently interesting topic, but it is nevertheless telling that she should dwell on this young woman who played no part in the marriage of the Fairfields. In several of West's novels, a woman's loveliness works as a road to her entrapment in an erroneous life; the possession of feminine beauty can mean a tragic destiny, even for characters who seem to shun expected ways of emphasizing and exploiting personal attractiveness. The problem, as West sees it, is not only that beauty incites male desire and so invites male betrayal, but that the web of myths surrounding beautiful women is too strong for (some) individuals to escape. Norah's "narrow and dark dress" is symbolic of her constricted life (the details of which we can only guess), as her taper-like breath infers a funereal existence. Alive, she is more dead than Rossetti's blessed damozel; unlike the lonesome beauty of the poem, Norah lives, and with a man, but not in the "endless unity" Rossetti's angel imagines. West sets Norah's beauty against the backdrop of her unhappiness, and in so doing points out the ironic reality of this woman who, though stunning as Fairfield says, is not getting what she wants out of life. The Fairfields' sense of her as a portrait and not as a person is just West's point: Norah cannot be understood as the woman she is as long as her beauty unwittingly tells stories she cannot control.

This chapter explores the ways in which West portrays and criticizes, yet partly condones, several such artistic and social feminine images in her novels: images that steer and snare women in existing masculine plots, and all of which are loose variations on Venus, or women as "goddesses" of beauty and sexual love. One of the most interesting is that of the beauty who gets caught, willingly or unwillingly, in tragic, even Gothic, stories by the assumptions others make about her. Another is the pastoral nymph who represents a haven from male responsibility and symbolizes masculine fantasies both of uncomplicated, uncommitted sex and female virginal purity. The sexually triumphant female scoundrel is a third familiar type, and a fourth is the "stupid" woman who cannot comprehend important "male" topics like politics and business. A related topic is West's conflicted use of the equally omnipresent Cinderella myth: her insistence on the destructiveness, yet propriety, of women's dependence on men, and the ways in which unhappy children, thwarted by lack of choice and freedom, seem to work as metaphors for subordinate womanhood. In addition, one of her most dynamic female characters, Cordelia, adopts existing narratives about women and children, particularly Cinderella, for her own purposes, and thus demonstrates the fact that women can be complicit in creating their own limitations. As always, West's ideas present contradictions that come from her desire to rebel coupled with her desire to be loved and accepted within existing social and cultural structures.

In "*The Judge* Reexamined: Rebecca West's Underrated Gothic Romance," Philip E. Ray claims that this novel published in 1922, West's second, which "has been severely and consistently criticized" for "lapses in the handling of. . .subject, style, structure, and character," should be read differently.[1] He argues persuasively "that at least some of these 'lapses' are actually conventional features of Gothic fiction," and that "the standards appropriate to the discussion of the Gothic romance have the advantage of making *The Judge* appear to be a competently constructed work of literature" (297). Ray goes on to demonstrate how neatly this works, addressing in particular prior critics' complaints that the novel's two parts—Book I being mostly Ellen's story and set in Edinburgh, Book II mostly Marion's and in Yaverland's End—are too jarring to make for good fiction. It is just this contrast, Ray asserts, that gives *The Judge* its power as a Gothic tale: "such transitions from an orderly universe in which virtue and sanity prevail to a nightmare universe in which vice and madness undermine all order" are "primary characteristic[s] of Gothic fiction" (298).

An earlier critic, Motley Deakin, sees *The Judge* as a "sentimental" novel that should be "anathema" to feminists, since it "presents women as creatures subject to the tortures and tender worship that men could impose upon them" (139). He cites *Clarissa* as a precursor, and seems surprised that West, whose feminism he accepts as orthodox, would adopt such a fictional form.[2] Ray mentions Deakin only in his notes, coupling him with Jane Marcus as one of the critics who "apply the wrong standards" to *The Judge* (305).[3] Yet Ray, in his discussion of Gothic conventions, also points out the fact that Ellen is subject to tortures of a kind: "there must be a lord of the castle, usually male, and persons, predominantly female, owing him obedience" (298); Ellen is the "victimized heroine" (299). But that victimization, while beginning with Richard's changed attitude, becomes most acute because of the

Gothic "castle" that is Yaverland's End, and because of Richard's mother.

I would like to suggest that there is another dimension to the way in which West manipulates the conventions of Gothic fiction: a dimension that includes Deakin's acute if incompletely explored observation that *The Judge* is a sentimental novel whose heroine is an innocent seduced. Ellen Melville is a red-haired teenage beauty, but she sees herself as an intellectual and works for the suffrage movement in her native Edinburgh. Ellen's brain and body are continually contrasted, in her consciousness and in the minds of others who view her carnally or amusedly, and are at odds with one another. Similarly, this novel whose heroine wants to break out of her life as a "wee typist" and live freely and fully as men might is in many ways, as Ray claims, a traditionally Gothic novel that shows Ellen, the beautiful and frail protagonist, powerless against seduction and sophisticated villains. *The Judge* deliberately presents characters who imagine they are defying the black and white gender roles exaggerated in sentimental or Gothic novels while demonstrating how powerfully such sexual images do control and form their lives.

The first character trait emphasized about Ellen Melville is her strong sense of the world's physical beauty, and the way her powerful imagination colors it with visions of chivalrous romance. As she looks out the window of the drab office where she works, her imagination transforms Edinburgh into a glorified military spectacle, in language that crosses *Macbeth* with *Ivanhoe*.

> At this time all the town was ghostly, and she loved it so. She took her mind by the arm and marched it up and down among the sights of Edinburgh. . Now the Castle Esplanade, that all day had proudly supported the harsh, virile sounds and colours of the drilling regiments, would show to the slums its blank surface, bleached bone-white by the winds that raced above the city smoke. Now the Cowgate and the Canongate would be given over to the drama of the disorderly night; the slum-dwellers would foregather about the rotting doors of dead men's mansions and brawl among the not less brawling ghosts of a past that here never speaks of peace, but only of blood and argument. And Holyrood, under a black bank surmounted by a low bitten cliff, would lie like the camp of an invading and terrified army. . .She stopped and said, "Yon about Holyrood's a fine image for the institution of a monarchy."[4]

This last idea is as typical of Ellen as is a flight of reverie; she fights her illusion-making tendency with feminist and political ideas that are equally the products of her fine intelligence. Her ambitions—and the language in which they are couched—are hopelessly and ironically masculine, however, given her poverty and inexperience, and the

restrictions of her gender. Longing for adventure, she finds great
excitement in thoughts of sea journeys (hence her name "Melville") and
revolutions in exotic foreign lands rather than in thoughts of love,
while all around her see a ripe and gorgeous girl whose proper destiny is
to be the sexual property of a man.

Ellen's effect on various men is stressed. Her employers are a father
and son, both of whom are attracted to her, but in ways which reflect
their individual perceptions of women. Philip James, the son, wants to
subjugate this beautiful yet thinking girl into a "relationship [that] felt
absolutely right" by getting her to do "things that were all directed to
giving him comfort" (24). He finds Ellen's naturalness exciting, but for
the reason that it makes her vulnerable; since she "[does] anything for
itself, and not for its effect on the male," she must be incapable, and he
finds "incapacity in women exciting and endearing" (20). Philip's
visions of dominating Ellen are based in his repressed but ordinary
eroticism. Steeped in convention, he cannot imagine a woman so
young and lovely as his equal in intellect and energy without
transforming such an idea into fantasies of male physical advantage:
"He never could get over a feeling that to discover a woman excited
about an intellectual thing was like coming on her bathing; her cast-off
femininity affected him as a heap of her clothes on the beach might
have done" (24). Philip is, like West's earlier character George Silverton
in "Indissoluble Matrimony," a classic "no-man" who cannot in reality
dominate a woman, so instead imagines a violent conquering.[5] This
unspoken thought is given unmistakable reality by another man who
wolfishly follows Ellen and her mother on a deserted night street,
"savouring the women's terror under his tongue, sucking unimaginable
sweetness and refreshment from it" (11).

Mactavish James, middle-aged, kindly, and long married, does not
desire Ellen sadistically or feel the need to overpower her body and
subdue her intelligence. If Philip wishes to be a masculine threat to a
vulnerable maiden, then Mactavish wants to be the knight who rescues
the beauty from the dragons of poverty and would-be ravishers. But,
like his son, Mactavish views Ellen only as a stimulant for sweet
daydreams; she fits as nicely into his particular Cinderella fantasy as
into Philip's Zeus-like visions of rape.

> Age permitted him, in spite of his type, to delight in her. In his
> youth he had turned his back on romance, lest it should dictate
> conduct that led away from prosperity, or should alter him in some
> manner that would prevent him from attaining that ungymnastic
> dignity which makes the respected townsman. He had meant from the
> first to end with a paunch. But now wealth was inalienably his and
> Beauty could beckon him on no strange pilgrimages, his soul
> retraced its steps and contemplated this bright thing as an earth

creature might creep to the mouth of its lair and blink at the sun. And
he loved her. He had never had enough to do with pitiful things (his
wife Elizabeth had been a banker's daughter), and this child had come
to him, that day in June, so white, so weak, so chilled to the bone,
for all the summer heat, by her monstrous ill-usage. . .(14-15)

Mactavish takes pleasure in warning Ellen that "being seventeen [is] no
protection from a wicked world," and that "a good man" will be better
for her than to be his partner in law, as she claims she would be if she
were a man (15). Ellen's mental retort—"It was not a good man she
needed, of course, but nice men, nice women" (15)—shows her initial
intention not to play the sentimental heroine in need of rescue, or fall
into believing that marriage will satisfy her ambitious nature. More
importantly, her realization that both sexes fit into her hopes for a
better life indicates an ability to see beyond the romantic picture in
which the James men frame her. Ellen does not imagine her life in
constant relation to her beauty and gender, nor does she want to.

Of course, she does not know she is beautiful, unlike West's later
characters Mary Ironside, Cordelia Aubrey, or Susie Staunton, who
understand the range of male sexual imagination and the possibility of
manipulation their looks afford. Ellen *is* what these women pretend to
be: sincerely caring, deeply but innocently sensual, shy, and genuinely
untouched by sexual knowledge. In these aspects, and in her unprotected
and impoverished state, she is like a Gothic (or romance) heroine. And
Richard Yaverland, the man who sweeps into Ellen's life and carries her
away to a new world, is a decidedly Gothic hero. For Ellen, his initial
attraction is not sexual. He represents a life she wants to live, exactly
the adventurous, unfettered stream of discoveries Ellen fantasizes as
possible were she not a woman and poor. She admires his pirate-like
beauty and enormous size dispassionately; she is not looking for a lover
or a rescuer, only for evidence of excitement and liberty.

Ironically, Richard places her into the distressed damsel role as soon
as they meet. Walking into the James law offices, he interrupts Philip
"walking masterfully" toward an unsuspecting Ellen and literally
contemplating rape. Richard "saves" her then, though neither of them
knows it, and a recognizable pattern begins in which her beauty and
goodness become the prize for his strength and the salve for his
experience. He understands the conflict between her feminine body and
"masculine" mind, and is sensitive to "the woman question"—"her body
would imprison her in soft places: she would be allowed no adventures
other than love, no achievements other than births" (33)—yet
eventually he leads her into exactly this soft imprisonment, desirous, as
are Philip and Mactavish, of the woman he pities. Like Ellen, he is
aware of the problems of sexual stereotyping without being able to
transcend them, but his greater knowledge, freedom, and wealth indicate

that he could if he did not find women's secondariness convenient and exciting. Richard vacillates between thoughts of a "swaggering triumph" (61) over women and a seemingly genuine sympathy with their restrictions. But ultimately he is a masculinist who views them as "the devil" (70); he is not the chivalrous knight who wants to rescue the beautiful maiden any more than Ellen is really a helpless nymph. His reasons for loving her are based in misogyny and selfishness, along with Westian male "lunacy." Certainly his "scientific" work, which he finds so fulfilling, is in fact destructive: he sees the development of explosives as "a pretty piece of research" divorced from its consequences, and elevates "exquisitely consistent chemicals" over human beings (64).

[Women] were the clumsiest of biological devices, and as they handed on life they spoiled it. . .They served the seed of life, but to all the divine accretions that had gathered round it, the courage that adventures, the intellect that creates, the soul that questions how it came, they were hostile. . .and yet. . .Surely there was a woman somewhere who, if one loved her, would prove not a mere possession who would either bore one or go and get lost just when one had grown accustomed to it, but would be an endless research. A woman who would not be a mere film of graceful submissiveness but real as a chemical substance, so that one could observe her reactions and find out her properties; and like a chemical substance, irreducible to final terms, so that one never came to an end. (71)

Interestingly, Ellen has been playing a male role before Yaverland arrives. He imagines her "the princess that had no king for father" (106), but Ellen supports herself and her deserted mother. To Mrs. Melville, Ellen is like a son and husband combined who brings in money and news of the outside world, and protects her physically and emotionally. Richard sees Ellen's masculine side—he tells her, as she runs in the Pentlands in a decidedly unladylike fashion, that "in a way" she is "awfully like a boy" (105)—but he is determined to capture her for himself and develop her feminine sexuality, despite his thought that "real love was somehow a cruel thing for women; that the hour when she became his wife would be as illimitably tragic as it would be illimitably glorious" (117).

Nowhere is this tragedy more subtly yet powerfully presented than when they confess their love and become engaged. This scene is as sexually charged as any romance author could hope to make it, but the hints of disaster woven into the scene's rich passion subvert the reader's erotic satisfaction and foreshadow calamity. His first "I love you" makes her head droop; she tries to seize her "life's last chance at escape" (155), resisting, before allowing, his embrace.[6] Ellen's physical fragility coupled with Richard's height and strength indicate a bitter defeat instead of the usual mutually sweet yielding portrayed in conventional romance, and which is the basis of women's supposed submission fantasies. While love seems very much present, so does the "gentle tyranny" (156) Ellen feels in Richard's embrace. His kiss, which she prefigures as "romantic as music heard across moonlit water" (157), is actually pain, and a smothering sensation, but not pleasure. Then she feels bliss at the sacrifice of her life for him, since Richard definitely sees their union in a selfish light: "You are going to do such a lot for me!" (160). Only later does Ellen actually enjoy physical contact, but not because of her own desire; she likes him to like kissing her (171), and so picks up the traditionally ascribed feminine traits of vanity and submission while trying to appreciate their union from his side, missing her own experience. Though earlier Yaverland had deplored "the stupid sexual journey suggested by. . .vain, passive women" (61), he has unwittingly taught Ellen to use the power of her own beauty. And for Ellen to embrace her looks as a means of triumph subtracts from her earlier sincerity and integrity. Her face glitters with "a solemn and joyful rapacity" when "her unconscious being [divines] that there were before her many victories to be gained wholly without sweat of the will" (149).[7]

If Ellen is a woman in need of rescue, therefore, it is not from her poor flat, her tedious job, or her dependent mother; it is from her ostensible savior.[8] Richard, despite his selfishness, realizes this: "Alas, that it should turn out that he too was something from which her delicate little soul asked to be rescued!" (166). Still, he excuses his motives by citing the unavoidable influence Ellen's beauty must have on her life and him.

> But then, she was beautiful, not only lovely; destiny had marked her for a high career; to leave her as she was would be to miscast one who deserved to play the great tragic part, which cannot be played without the actress's heart beating at the prospect of so great a role. Oh, there was no going back! (166)

Richard misses the irony of his romantic vision: that to play a tragic part is not desirable at all; that despite his insistence that he loves Ellen's soul, it is her flesh that convinces him to marry.

Whether or not one believes that Ellen's fate will be tragic, as I do, certainly Mrs. Melville and Richard's mother Marion show what might await Ellen in thirty years. Both, like Ellen, were beauties, and both attracted unscrupulous men who did not maintain the sexual, emotional, or economic bonds their first erotic attachments promised. Ellen and Richard are each acutely aware of their mothers' physical ugliness, especially since it contrasts with former glory and seems a metaphor for the damage done by men. At Mrs. Melville's deathbed, her daughter thinks it "disastrous" that "beautiful women grow old and lose their beauty," and that "this had happened to one who did not deserve it" (189). Yet Marion's elegant clothes and meticulous self-maintenance offend Ellen as inappropriately dramatic "in an older woman"; the "suggestion of strong feeling" on Marion's face "was as unsuitable on cheeks so worn as paint would have been" (207). Marion, whose whole life was shaped by the fact that she was once an exotically lovely girl and attracted a rich man who gave her an illegitimate son, refuses to give up the illusion of being a dramatic heroine even when she is middle-aged and stagnant. When she gives up her erotic obsession with Harry Yaverland, Richard's father, she substitutes Richard so that she may go on being the exquisite and passionate lover. She consequently plays the great tragic part Richard believes so proper to a beautiful woman: committing suicide once her suitor-son has another woman to love, she has sacrificed her life to the continuation of romantic passion, even if not her own. Mrs. Melville, conversely, plays a tragic part without choosing it. Yet she too cherishes memories of her early brilliance, saving an old dress that is a "relique of the days when she was so beautiful that an artist, a professional, had wanted to paint her portrait" (188). The last words her mother hears from Ellen are a promise to go see this portrait in the New York museum where it hangs, and Mrs. Melville's reaction—"[she] pressed her daughter's hand more firmly than she had done for the last hour" (189)—shows how strongly the dying woman clings to a self-image of beauty.

I do not wish to reduce the complexity of *The Judge* to this minor theme of Mrs. Melville's and Marion Yaverland's lost beauty (after all, an unavoidable part of growing older), or Ellen's youthful beauty as the instigator of what may be her tragedy. But I do want to suggest that these three beautiful female characters from *The Judge* represent a constant motif in West's particular feminist vision: that of the beauty who, like countless mythological women human and semi-divine, attracts attention by her physical self and is then cut down to fit a male image of her, usually to the abandonment of her other strengths, or even to death. Richard forces Ellen into his Gothic melodrama and out of the story she might have composed alone; that is the tragedy of *The Judge*. Ellen appropriated male stories because they are full of freedom and excitement, and because she knew no female narratives so attractive. Having had no experience that tested her ability to exist in solitude or independence, Ellen is the proverbial blank slate. But that very blankness is what enables Richard to dictate her drama, and her beauty—a trait Ellen admirably, if ignorantly, has not capitalized on—is a story he uses for his own purposes. Jane Miller, in *Women Writing About Men,* puts it well:

[Ellen's] wonderfully frail energy and vision, her common sense and her political idealism, her intelligence and humor are roughly, arbitrarily, destroyed by her titanic hero and his inescapable charms. Her adventure has been eclipsed, merged into his. It is as if Rebecca West were begging Ellen, as a gloriously imagined incarnation of her younger self, to resist the blandishments of all striding giants, and then admitting exhausted defeat on her behalf.[9]

Ellen learns all too well the lesson that as a beautiful woman she must stay desirable in order to keep her man. Before Richard's climactic murder of Roger, she has a vision of her faded, plain mother that makes it clear "[ugliness] was what happened to women who allowed themselves to be disregarded; who allowed any other than themselves to dwell in their men's attention" (426). She then alerts the preoccupied Richard to the sexual insults Roger is aiming at them, and so unwittingly incites the event that exiles both her and Richard; because Richard has taught her to be vain and dependent, she destroys them both. She has become the tragic heroine he wanted her to be, the opposite of her early dreams; and though she thinks that staying by him is "choosing the side of victory" (430), the fact that pregnancy and separation from her lover await makes Ellen's repetition of Marion's and Mrs. Melville's fates certain. Her life—so promising when she was unaware of her beauty and the tragic narratives it potentially told—will fulfill the book's epigraph, a sentence that reduces a mother's life to an obsession with a man: "Every mother is a judge who sentences the children for the sins of the father." Like Tess, like Clarissa, like Meredith's Lucy in *The Ordeal of Richard Feverel* (to name only some of her numerous predecessors), Ellen is "rescued" from obscurity and poverty only to be wrecked by her rescuer.

The Judge is but one of several West novels to contain this theme of beauty as tragedy. Certainly Sybil Fassendyll's unhappy acting career and adulterous relationship were fomented by her extraordinary looks. Rosamund is wooed (and won, for reasons left maddeningly unclear in the unfinished *Cousin Rosamund* trilogy) by the detestable and pathetic but immensely wealthy Nestor Ganymedios because of her statuesque blonde beauty. Queenie's attractiveness gains her a rich husband, but he makes her miserable enough that she (almost) ruins her life by taking his.

Yet, like most of West's feminist complaints, this subject has its other side. Beauties may be the victims of masculine sexual quests that usurp feminine autonomy, but many women without beauty suffer unfulfilled lives. Miss Beevor and Aunt Lily of the *Cousin Rosamund* trilogy are graceless and plain yet kind and honorable women who spend most of their energy and thoughts on people not connected to their lives in any sexual sense: friends, pupils, siblings, in-laws. Critics have likened *The Fountain Overflows* and *This Real Night* to Dickens novels because of such distinct, humorously-drawn characters as Beatrice Beevor and Lily Moon. But these women stand for more than likable late-Victorian female eccentricity. They are, like Woolf's pathetic Miss Kilman, women utterly without conventional physical attractiveness and so, also because of poverty, utterly without social safety nets.

Ironically, and comically, both Lily and Miss Beevor feign ornately feminine styles of appearance that cruelly accentuate the women's plainness. Aunt Lily is a camel-faced Stella Dallas, hatted and furred and bangled in garish, clashing colors, her attire lovingly chosen and proudly worn though it makes others cringe. Beatrice Beevor ("Bee-ah-tree-chay" is her preferred pronunciation, since she likes to think of herself as akin to Dante's unsurpassable female saint) wears "artistic" clothes that show only a complete lack of aesthetic understanding, while they are meant to convey both the sense and possession of romantic beauty. West's point in these characterizations, I believe, is to show that all women think they must try to look beautiful in romantic ways even when they are not remotely "pretty," and that this was particularly obvious in Victorian times, when the heavy, intricate clothing was so obviously a costume designed for some imagined (and absurd) feminine standard.

West's third novel *Harriet Hume,* published seven years after *The Judge* in 1929, satirizes this absurdity. Throughout the novel the reader listens to Arnold's mind watch and think about Harriet, who is both physically and mentally, as Victoria Glendinning remarks, "the essence of femininity" to this consciously masculine man.[10] He imagines her, within the first five pages, as an angel, "a bird-woman built by a magician expert in fine jeweller's work and ornithology" (11), "a long scarf of spirit," and "the most ethereal" woman he has ever known (11). Harriet's beauty, grace, and slight, fine build fascinate him; he sees her every move as a tableau signifying classic feminine delicacy.

> . . .she whisked her skirts towards the mantelpiece, where there were still two tall vases of the flowers that had been given to her at her last concert, took out a rosebud, ran to him, snapped the long stalk and set it in his buttonhole, and went back and found another for her bosom. And there at the hearth she came to rest, her rose-coloured nail toying with the nail-coloured rose, the involved wrist as finely tuned as one would have been led to suppose from the carriage of her head (which supported a Grecian knot as hardly another head in a million), and the stance of her feet (of which one was turned out as far as could be, while the other rested behind it on the very point of the toe, as if she were a little girl at her dancing-class), while her other arm lay like a rod of spirally rounded ivory along the mantelpiece. (12)

Harriet's isolated garden home is a place where Arnold may escape the Parliamentary ambitions and anxiety about his social standing that obsess him, and wallow in the reality of Harriet's sexuality (they are lovers) and his dream of her feminine innocence (based largely on his belief in her ignorance); she is for him both whore and madonna, the ultimate fantasy woman. He compares his time with her to childhood times with his uncle, a man who represented a consummate fantasy man:

> Do you know, Harriet, I have never been so sorry to leave anybody in my life, since I was a little boy and used to go spend the afternoon with my old uncle who had been a soldier and fought with Roberts at Kandahar, and I would kick and scream and blubber when my mother came to tea to end our talks of bloodshed and rifles and Ashantis. (48)

Harriet Hume is about the way people see the world in pairs of opposites—male/female, artist/politician, private life/public life—and Arnold thinks of men and women in broad, dualistic stereotypes. But it is to mock just such thinking that West grants Harriet the power to read Arnold's mind. It becomes Harriet's mission to save Arnold from the consequences of his destructive "masculine" ideals of political and social power and to instruct him about her true self, and in so doing erase his ingrained images of what men and women should or should not be.

One of the most specific ways in which Arnold envisions Harriet is as a pastoral nymph. She often dresses as a Dresden china shepherdess, with simple "parchment-coloured" gowns that are tight at the waist but flow in pleats around her lower body, and sometimes with a "peasantish broad straw hat" (75) hung across her back. With sandals on her tiny feet and a rose at her throat, she serves Arnold with little gifts of tea and food and stories as if he is the master visiting one of his more charming country serfs. Their relationship is, in Arnold's mind's eye, as heavily symbolic as a Pre-Raphaelite painting; she is a "sylph" (34), but also a "doll" with "qualities above the ruck of dolls" (35).

Harriet emphasizes this image of herself as a pastoral nymph by reciting part of Andrew Marvell's poem "The Nymph Complaining for the Death of Her Fawn" when Arnold "begs" her to tell him how she reads his mind.

> I have a garden of my own,
> But so with roses overgrown
> And lilies, that you would it guess
> To be a little wilderness;
> And all the springtime of the year. . .(33)

By choosing this poem, Harriet shows that she understands how Arnold makes her into a symbol of mysterious and beautiful womanhood. But there is a bite to her message. In Marvell's poem, the nymph is complaining about two things: the fact that "wanton troopers riding by/ Have shot [her] fawn, and it will die," but also that the lover who gave her the fawn proved "unconstant" and "counterfeit." Her recitation foreshadows Arnold's own inconstancy, and intimates that the gifts he gives her—sexual pleasure, affection, intellectual stimulation—are easily killed by the cruelty of his masculine ambition. Her answer to this cruelty is to stress, like Marvell's nymph, that she has a garden of her own, literally and figuratively, which represents the autonomy and artistry which uphold her; she gently shows him that she has an identity outside his romantic image of her, one that is a "wilderness" of rich growths and that will survive his desertion. As she speaks, the keys of the piano begin to vibrate hard enough to create a tone, as if to make unmistakable her feminine voice, powerful enough to express her own thoughts and not merely reiterate men's ideas. Arnold's reaction to this magically produced sound seems representative of male anxiety over burgeoning twentieth-century female artistic accomplishment, as if women refused any longer to be the pianos on which men played.

> Rather was it as if some inhabiting spirit of the instrument had resolved no longer to tolerate the age-old conditions by which human virtuosity steals all the credit of its tunefulness, and was essaying to make its music by itself, and found its new art difficult. But that it made a sound could not be gainsaid. [Arnold] made an uneasy exclamation. (34)

Arnold is not very interested in Harriet as concert pianist, except to be jealous that she has a power he cannot control or understand. In fact, the reader never witnesses a scene in which Harriet seriously plays; she frequently refers to her vocation, and both Arnold and the reader are aware that she is a dedicated musician, but her beauty and clairvoyance are Arnold's central concerns, and so become the reader's. Although Harriet eloquently voices her thoughts, the reader has direct access only to Arnold's consciousness throughout *Harriet Hume*. West deliberately makes Arnold the purveyor of information about Harriet in order to emphasize his (often erroneous) assumptions about her, and one of his strongest mistakes is not to understand, and to underestimate, her artistry. Instead, he focuses on what she can tell him about himself, and what pleasure she can give him sexually and visually. As Harriet recites (or reveals her art), he misses the irony and the message of her poem (or women's art) as he thinks of her looks and his prestige.

The moment provided a triple occupation for Arnold Condorex; for
he was delirious at having the extremes of love and strangeness
revealed to him in an afternoon with such heavenly lightness and
benignity; and he was reflecting how remarkable it was that her
skin, the billows of her skirt, and the glossy varnished wall behind
her, were within a tone or two of each other in colour, yet presented a
spectacle in which the eye could dwell with a sense of the most
abundant variousness; and he was embarrassed as he always was when
he heard anyone repeating poetry, since his lack of memory for
words prevented him from ever recognising it, and his pride made
him itch to say he did. (34)

Arnold misses the point of Harriet's story about the Three Graces as
well. While there are several possible interpretations of this myth-fairy
tale with which Harriet amuses Arnold, two points of it seem clear: that
men do not understand the women to whom they are attracted and with
whom they live; and that contact with men, or that living in a man's
world, can destroy women's autonomy and silence women's voices. The
Ladies Frances, Georgina, and Arabella Dudley are even more
obviously, and absurdly, representative of male feminine fantasies than
Harriet is, since they exist literally as icons of "grace" in a painting by
Sir Joshua Reynolds called "The Three Graces Decorating a Statue of
Hymen" (38): the three sister goddesses who presided over pleasure,
charm, elegance, and beauty. Like the seven sisters of West's 1959
short story "Parthenope," these three embody a romantic vision of the
young, beautiful, ethereal maiden taken to an extreme, comically
wearing garlands of flowers at all times (as the seven sisters liked to
wear their medieval-damsel gowns).[11] They attract husbands, aided by
parents and society, by the picture they present rather than by the
human beings they are.

Three young noblemen of immense estates met the three girls at a
garden fete in Wales where under the directions of an eccentric
landowner enamoured of the romantic movement they were able to
traipse about among brand-new Gothic ruins from dawn to dusk. (42)

Of course, the marriages are disasters: when the girls are forced to
give up their ornamental flowers, they lose their beauty (their image of
mysterious feminine otherness) and their happiness (their choice to be
always together and garlanded with flowers, a state which for them
signifies freedom and integrity). "They were still handsome; but they
were not, as they had often seemed when they trod the sward of parks in
their floral panoply, immortal goddesses" (43). The sisters eventually
flee their husbands, encountering on the way a band of "Mohocks"
intent on raping and robbing them; to escape, they become trees (in
what will be Harriet's garden) in a re-enactment of Daphne's

metamorphosis. Whether the husbands or the Mohocks would be the worse fate is unclear, but the sisters' need for escape from a world that views their choices as inappropriate is certain. Arnold calls this a "happy ending," claiming that he would like to be a tree in Harriet's garden: "I would. . .never make a fool of myself or get into mischief again" (48). He cannot envision the women's tragedy inherent in this fantasy, for he immediately turns the story to his own use.

Jane Marcus writes that this myth has a "moral": "women turn into trees to escape male violence, and men kick the trees. Marriage. . destroys sisterhood and art for women. They are possible only in death" (147). West also implies that men, in marriage, destroy what they seek: the dream-like maiden inevitably loses her freshness, charm, and mystery when she gives up self-government to a husband, who then realizes he has married a woman and not a nymph. Harriet lives with Arnold only after he has effectively lost all vestiges of his imperialist attitudes and privileges, including his once-primary vision of her as a dainty sylph. But this is also, either literally or symbolically, after both have died (it is difficult to know whether Arnold's suicide and murder of Harriet are fantasy or reality), so West's hopes seem slim for such a union of people who see each other for who they really are. As she does in *The Judge,* West cedes the victory to patriarchy. But not without showing, again, that male images of women can be destructive to both sexes.

J.R. Hammond points out that *Harriet Hume* embodies "many of the themes and tensions implicit in [West's] relationship with Wells."[12] Like Harriet with Arnold, West saw herself as all that Wells had rejected, particularly in her tendency to celebrate the personal and situational over the abstract, and in her abhorrence of his ability to separate sexual desire from the rest of his life. The novel was in fact written after their breakup and following her infatuation with Beaverbrook, like Wells a public figure who would seem to embody the same masculine force and blindness that Arnold does, and also a man to whom West was ultimately unsuited. Its lighthearted tone, unusual in West's canon, reflects West's desire for some positive marriage of male and female, one that she in fact hoped to accomplish by marrying Andrews a year after its publication. Yet Wells, after reading the novel, commented that West should now read Jung since she was "driving at the same thing in the love-antagonism of Harriet and Arnold. . she is Arnold's anima" (Rollyson, 138). Certainly Arnold resists any sense of himself as feminine, and pushes Harriet away angrily when she tries to make him see beyond his political calculations and connect to the positive life-force she represents. But he nevertheless desires Harriet as the archetype of desirable woman, and the fact that he can hate her as well as love her illustrates West's Freudian belief that men are overpowered by the death-instinct rather than love of life.

West deplores an archetype opposite to Harriet Hume ten years later. In *Black Lamb and Grey Falcon,* West calls Louis XIV's acquaintance Madame de Maintenon (a woman who had "inflamed" the king with "Pro-Jesuit passion") a "supreme type of the she-alligator whom men often like and admire" (238). She created several "she-alligators" in her fiction, usually to show just how much men like and admire these "bitch-goddesses" (so familiar to twentieth-century readers, film-viewers, and television-watchers) and how their approval perpetuates both the image and the behavior of sexually and economically unscrupulous women. Most commonly it is beauty that inspires and enables a woman to become the callous heartbreaker, the casual thief of their admirers' money and other women's loves. But it is more than just good looks that instigates she-alligator behavior, since several of West's most praiseworthy fictional women are beautiful (Rosamund, Laura Rowan, Ellen Melville). It is the knowledge that they can get away with it precisely because they are women; it is behavior sanctioned and even adored by some men, especially those with power and wealth.

The Thinking Reed, almost a study of money's corrupting influence on both sexes, contains one of West's most vehemently disapproving portraits in "Poots." This young, aristocratic (though not wealthy) Englishwoman infuriates Marc and Isabelle with her unpunctuality and deceit, her hypocritical conventionality, and her vicious, self-serving search for rich suitors. West aims a stinging attack as well on the Midwestern, immensely rich Mr. Pillans by showing the absurdity of his attractions for first Luba and then Poots, which are based on his belief that both are "cruel" women who go from man to man and whim to whim without a thought for other people. The fact that this is true for detestable Poots but not true for kindly Luba is what gives Poots the initial edge in the women's race for Pillans's millions. Luba, a verifiable princess and a famous beauty, has at first the advantage of an established reputation for high living and high-powered lovers. Pillans remembers happily that at their previous meeting, "she was with a big, tall chap they said was a very rich man who was crazy about her," and he actually takes pleasure in the idea that she will not remember his name, since "beautiful women are very cruel" (196).

Although Luba's apparent innocence and kindness please him too, Poots presents herself to him in a way that she understands will be titillating. Pillans "[sits] and [worships] her while she put[s] a wall of scarlet paint on her lips. . .just putting up an advertisement of her whorishness" (203). He comes when she beckons with her "blood-tipped forefinger" (208); in order to invite him to a party, she puts on an expression "that [makes] her face look like an unmade bed" (205).

Poots wants money from Pillans, nothing more; but what he wants
from her is more complicated. She represents for him a fantasy of
woman as an indulged, spoiled, beautiful child who will use her
sexuality to get what she wants, and who cares for nothing but her
present pleasure. In Pillans's dream—and, so it seems, in the ruthless
world of the rich—she is the ultimate luxury pet for men with the
money and the worldly (or sexual) power to leash her for a time.
Isabelle sees this easily.

> It was apparent that nobody could cure him of his infatuation for
> Poots by giving him proofs that she was mercenary and treacherous,
> since these emetic qualities affected his perverse soul as
> aphrodisiacs. . ."You think Madame Renart very chic, don't you?"
> "Why, yes," said Mr. Pillans timidly. . ."I think she's lovely. She
> may be a little playful, and apt to walk out on people if they aren't
> giving her a good time, but that's only natural. She's young, and so
> very attractive that she's used to having things her way."
> "But you think she's wicked, don't you?" Isabelle pressed him.
> "Wicked, I mean, in little exciting ways, like being unfaithful to her
> lovers, and getting what she can out of them, and throwing them
> over before they have stopped caring for her. You see she's full of
> that, don't you?"
> His eyes glistened, he smiled bashfully, as if he were a boy owning
> to some precocious appetite. "I guess all the most attractive women
> are like that," he said. "They get spoiled with all of us men running
> after them." (295-296)

Isabelle manages to get Pillans's interest in Luba revived by
exploiting his imbecile attitude, claiming that Poots's amours are petty
compared with Luba's "grand manner" affairs, that Luba is consistently
"triumphant and pitiless." "[Luba] breaks faith, is exigent, cruel, and
lascivious. Takes men away from women for other reasons than that
she cares for them, leaves those men for other reasons than that she
wants to give them back to [their] women. . ." (298). Desperate to
secure Luba's future, Isabelle goes so far as to claim that Marc is in
love with the princess, which does the trick of gaining back Pillans's
interest. But Isabelle cannot help voicing her disgust for his belief that
"women like that own the world. . .that they have an innate right of
precedence over the women who are simple and faithful and loving,"
and for "his enjoyment of his past experience of being robbed,
cuckolded, and deserted, and in his sure and certain hope of being so
again" (300-1).

The Thinking Reed contains West's fullest and most articulate
denunciation of the "worship" men feel for beautiful women as
scoundrels out to gouge men and to defeat sexual rivals. (Later
incarnations include Susie Staunton in *The Birds Fall Down*, and

various aristocratic society beauties in *Cousin Rosamund,* particularly Lady Mortlake.) As Isabelle later thinks, such an attitude serves the pursuit of death, not life, the basic Westian premise for most of the unpleasantness human beings cause. Contemporary soap operas specialize in characters (mostly female, though some are male) like Poots. Clearly this type still appeals to a mass market, and its perpetuation has grown stronger with the proliferation of advertisements that show beautiful but malevolent-looking women as men's prizes for drinking the right beer or driving the right car. Such images, West emphasizes, surely harm not only the men who embrace selfishness and cruelty as an attractive woman's justified behavior; they encourage women to emulate this apparently seductive conduct.

West also debunks the popular myth that women are bound to lack intelligence in proportion to the degree that they possess good looks. Two of West's most beautiful characters, Sybil and Rosamund, are called "stupid" repeatedly. In fact, in each case West's narrators are so insistent about these women's stupidity that some critics have been irked. Jane Marcus, in her general condemnation of the appearance of *Sunflower,* claims West "would surely never have published a book in which her characters think beyond themselves so blatantly. . .a whole novel in which 'stupid' Sybil (and we are ordered to think of her as stupid) thinks bright thoughts?" (438). "Rosamund's characterization," writes Peter Wolfe, "if intellectually pleasing, is artistically ragged. Statuesque and slow moving, she comes close to immobility, and her excellence is nearly equated with blankness" (108). These criticisms are not inaccurate if the reader takes West's narration at its word and believes Sybil and Rosamund to be stupid. Rosamund's density (her "blankness") in particular seems suspicious, given the fact that she inspires her brilliant, accomplished cousins Rose and Mary to near worship; and Marcus is right about the purportedly dim Sybil's unmistakably keen mind.

Yet once again West could be showing how powerfully effective are certain social and artistic clichés about beautiful women. Sybil and Rosamund (and, to some extent, the characters around them) think that they are stupid when there is strong evidence to the contrary. We are all as familiar with the modern "bimbo," whose voluptuousness automatically denotes her shallow, weak mind, as we are with the shark-like beauty who lies and cheats to gain sexual and economic power. While such stereotypes existed less obviously in the early twentieth century than in the late, Sybil is as unable to escape the fact of her beauty (and its display and care) as were legendary screen beauties like Marilyn Monroe or Rita Hayworth. Gloria Steinem recounts the histories of sexual abuse suffered from childhood by legendary screen beauties who were unable to escape, at least initially, the unwanted and cruel attention from fathers, managers, and husbands (to name a few) that their extraordinary looks attracted.[13]

Sybil's sense of her conspicuous body saturates her conscious mind. One horrendous image describes her unhappy fantasy of herself as

> a vast naked torso, but not of stone, of living, flushing flesh, fallen helpless on its side in some public place of ruins like the Forum in Rome, with ant-droves of tourists passing incessantly round her quickly, inquisitively, too close. (13)

She imagines them touching her in a dry, dusty wind, grotesquely putting up "their sweaty hands to experience her texture and [stroking] the grit into her flesh" (13), or pricking her flanks with the spokes of their umbrellas when it rained. But Sybil is also haunted by her own ostensible intellectual and artistic limitations, a feeling made acute by her association with the blatantly brainy Essington and her unwanted stage career. Over and over he tells her, or the reviewers tell her, that her beauty is her sole appeal; Sybil's age of thirty is thematically important, since (according to the usual lore) her gorgeousness will now inevitably deteriorate and soon cease to be a meal ticket and an automatic exemption from ordinary life. She clings to a dream of "primal" existence, in which she need not exhibit any "beastly dreams of the world as [people] would have liked it to be. . .pretend[ing] that they were real things that happened to real people" (11), or worry that she cannot "confine the great bull life in her minute and brittle mind" as Essington can, whose mind is "as large as life" (15).

Yet the profundity of her visions and ideas points to a very different Sybil than the one who insists, in the book's opening line, that "she never could understand machinery." Likewise, the expert way that Rosamund plays chess with the brilliant Piers indicates that she understands complicated thought in a way that her "stupidity" should not allow. Rosamund's physical presence is so striking that Rose, the narrator, feels compelled to describe her repeatedly: her hair consists of heavy sugar-barley curls, her face has "a golden heaviness. . .to look on it [is] like watching honey drop slowly from a spoon" *(Fountain Overflows,* 106), she is all that is luminous and richly pleasing. Piers is astonished by Rosamund's beauty at their first meeting, claiming that she "is amazing" and she "should make a great marriage" (131). But ultimately it is her skill at chess that he appreciates and desires, especially since none of the others, not even Richard Quin, has this ability. Piers exclaims that she is "a very clever girl"; and when Rosamund, as is her wont, looks "blind" and stammers a denial, that this is all she can do, he rejoinders that "that is a very great deal. . .you can play the most intricate game in the world, and if you can do that, then you can do a great many other things as well" (138).

Rosamund, as the central symbol of the trilogy named for her, represents a myriad of interconnecting themes and ideas (several of which will be examined in later chapters); that she is not "stupid," despite the repetition of that word in relation to her, becomes as obvious as the fact of Clare's wisdom. But her physical presence, in the world's eye, seems to override her intelligence (as Harriet's loveliness, not her talent, dominates Arnold's idea of her). Nestor Ganymedios is proud of her beauty and seems uninterested in (or unaware of) her saint-like acumen, and Rosamund appears trapped, like Ellen Melville, into a marriage that emphasizes her ornamental qualities, which is a tragic reduction. When a woman looks like Venus, it is hard for her to act as Minerva or Diana, and that is unfair: this, it appears, is West's message about feminine beauty.

Or is it? Once again I turn to *Black Lamb and Grey Falcon* for partial enlightenment. In the village of Gruda in Dalmatia, West and her husband encounter "one of those strange pockets" that are "scattered here and there at vast intervals in the universe, where beauty is the common lot" (262). Seeing three young girls "as lovely as primroses in a wood" who are lightheartedly begging for pennies, West and Andrews, moved by their exquisite looks, wish to give them three tenpenny pieces. Their Yugoslavian chauffeur objects, saying that this is too much money, and that besides, "begging is disgraceful." West agrees that "there was much to be said for his point of view" (263) and that in fact he was right and they—West, Andrews, and the girls—were wrong.

> But they were so beautiful, and in spite of their beauty they would be poor all their lives long, and that is an injustice I can never bear. It is the flat violation of a promise. Women are told from the day they are born that they must be beautiful, and if they are ugly everything is withheld from them, and the reason scarcely disguised. It follows therefore that women who are beautiful should want for nothing. (263)

The violation of promises that men make to women is at the heart of West's paradoxical attitudes toward feminism. If, as this statement from the late thirties attests, she changed (or added to) her view of beauties as frequent victims of masculine plots to beauties as justified victors in a man's world, it was part of her way of turning the tables of feminist thought to blame men for insufficiently adhering to the gender rules they set up. "This is what you say you want," she seems to pronounce, "so do what you say." If beautiful women are the pinnacle of feminine worth, then reward them consistently; if women are in need of masculine rule and support, then rule and support them responsibly. West's vocal support in 1963 for the prostitutes in the Profumo Scandal expresses this same challenge: "Here were a number of girls whose beauty ought to have aroused tenderness and sweetness who were used by men only to be beaten. . ." (Rollyson, 346).

West's oddly antagonistic outlook on childhood might be explained as her objection to an inadequate support system for women. Samuel Hynes says in his introduction to *A Celebration* that *The Fountain Overflows* "is about the condition of childhood, as *Black Lamb* is about the condition of Serbs and Croats—that is, childhood is a metaphor for a view of the world" (xvi). I suggest that childhood also works as a metaphor for womanhood in *The Judge* and *The Birds Fall Down*, and especially in the three books of the *Cousin Rosamund* trilogy. Female children see themselves as prisoners who must endure an unnatural state of unfulfillment before beginning the lives they already feel equipped to handle. Martin Pargiter, in Virginia Woolf's *The Years,* has a memory that convinces him that children lead "awful lives": "he saw Rose sitting there at the tea table with her fist still clenched. . .very red in the face, with her lips tight shut. . .She had wanted him to do something. And he had crumpled a ball of paper in his hand and shied it at her."[14] That vision typifies West's; it is particularly apt because it is Rose who is frustrated, and Martin who is doing the frustrating. Women, like children, are always wanting something they cannot get because of the subordinate state men (or parents, or society) have insisted they inhabit, and often because of the deliberately perverse actions men (or parents, or society) take to thwart women's happiness. But, unlike Woolf's, West's ultimate vision is not of women living lives independent of men's approval or support, as Rose Pargiter will, but of women finding men who play their traditional dominant roles without complaint or negligence.

Just how strongly West felt about the rightness of male and parental protection for women can be seen in her essay "Charlotte Bronte." Claiming that Bronte's subject matter "is, under one disguise or another, the Cinderella theme which is the stand-by of the sub-artist in fiction and the theatre," West explains that Bronte subverts the standard story by making the heroine the ugly instead of the beautiful sister, "though possessed of an invisible talisman of spiritual quality which wholly annuls that disadvantage." In so doing, Bronte "sets out not to explore reality, but to nourish the neurotic fantasies with which feebler brains defend themselves from reality" (*Celebration,* 429). Nevertheless, West defends Bronte from her own accusation of "infantilism" by calling Bronte's work "as powerful an analysis of the working of the sense of inferiority and its part in creating romanticism as the mind of man has ever made" (431). Although Bronte committed the most heinous of literary crimes, "sentimental writing," this "was not due to an innate inaptitude for the artistic process, but to the pressure of external circumstance," which was

> her specially acute need to make, by separate and violent acts of the will, the place in the world for herself and her two younger sisters which should have been made for them by their elders. Her realization of this need must have been panic-stricken and desperate, for the whole of her life was ravaged by a series of progressively bitter disappointments in the protection which children expect from adults and which women expect from men . (431)

West clearly considered herself ravaged by a series of similar disappointments. Not only did her father, H.G. Wells, and Henry Andrews fail to "protect" her in a way she apparently craved, but the bitterness of women and children unprotected by husbands and parents, particularly fathers, is a constant in her own fiction. West writes, "It is confessed honestly and radiantly in Charlotte Bronte's books how she craved for the support that the child-bearing faculty of woman logically entitles her to expect from man" (432). Though it is not only women's anatomy that entitles them to that support in West's novels, she is equally vocal, if not perhaps as honest or radiant, about her craving for such support.

A reader could accuse West of inventing her own versions of the Cinderella story, though without clearly happy or sad endings, through Ellen Melville, Laura Rowan, and most significantly the Aubrey sisters. Generally these Cinderellas are attractive adolescent girls or young women who possess, like Bronte's heroines, a keen intelligence or tremendous talent. Their brains and sensitivity set them apart from other girls of their age, but their poverty (in some cases) and their inattentive fathers (in all) put them in the equivalent of Cinderella's corner by the fire: without opportunity to shine in or even cope with social situations, without emotional and economic backing, without the normalcy that would allow them the carefree existence supposedly allotted to a child. They see the states of childhood and adolescence as smothering cocoons from which only the coming of age will free them. Their fairy godmother's gift, as they initially imagine it, would not be a chance to meet and captivate Prince Charming—indeed, they want no tie with men, whom they see as irrational jailers—but a free rein with his coach and four and a portion of his kingdom. In this they are like frustrated women of a patriarchal culture who wish to be free of male control.

West wrote a review of Violet Hunt's *Their Lives,* which she calls "the account of an adolescent of genius, who is so consumed by the will to power that immaturity and exclusion from adult experience is a torment. Childhood is like a deformity, girlhood is impatiently endured as the last traces of a lingering disease" (*Young Rebecca,* 337). Although Rose Aubrey eventually comes to revere the memory of her childhood, this 1917 passage anticipates the story of her young life as Rose tells it herself. Part of West's technique in the *Cousin Rosamund* trilogy is to make Rose a very deliberate and conscious narrator, one who understands, explains, and then rejects the various plots available to her, especially those concerning women. Rose wants not to be an unconscious victim of plots outside her control, but rather a willing player in a play of her choosing.[15] Elaine Showalter describes both Virginia Woolf and Katherine Mansfield's women characters "as artists whose creative energy has gone chiefly into the maintenance of myths about themselves and about those they love. To become aware of the creation of a myth is to lose faith in it" (247). Rose as narrator wants the reader to know that she is aware of the myths, and that she has never had faith in them.

This not only applies to the marriage plot all the sisters reject, as discussed in the first chapter, but also to the ideal of childhood presented in Victorian and Edwardian culture. Rose considers it a matter of honor to despise the state of childhood, and to describe fully the insecurity she and her sisters suffered when the world might have imagined them safe and happy. Any child worthy of Rose's friendship understands that children are as smart as adults, but also knows that most grown-ups like to pretend that children are ignorant and unaware and prefer those who go along with the charade. Rose's first impression of Rosamund, her idol, was not only that she was extremely "handsome," but that

[s]he did not look at all silly, as grown-ups like children to be. She had a deeply indented upper lip, there was a faint cleft in her chin, and I knew from everything about her that she was in the same case as myself, as every child I liked, she found childhood an embarrassing state. We did not like wearing ridiculous clothes, and being ordered about by people whom we often recognized as stupid and horrid, and we could not earn our own livings or, because of our ignorance, draw fully on our own powers. (*Fountain Overflows,* 77)

It does not stretch the imagination much to see this passage as a feminist complaint only slightly in disguise, especially since Rose remarks throughout *The Fountain Overflows* and *This Real Night* on the ponderous and preposterous clothes women wore in Victorian and Edwardian England. (She does contradict herself, however, in the beginning of *Cousin Rosamund,* saying that when she "first grew up clothes were quite beautiful, though they were nearly always too bulky," and going on to deride Chanel's "hideous uniform" [2] of the straight shift with a wide belt. This is perhaps evidence of Rose's switch, which happens in *Cousin Rosamund,* from thinking her childhood an escaped prison to believing it an enchanted season.) Likewise, this description of Cousin Jock's behavior when Rose knowledgeably runs her hand over the treble keys of a piano to see if the keyboard, strings, or hammer were damaged seems to indicate an anger that goes beyond that of a child toward an adult to that of a woman toward a man.

> . . .Cousin Jock took my wrist and put my arm down by my side. It was a gentle movement yet extremely brutal. It told me that I had no rights, that I was a child, and children are slaves, and that I was a fool besides; I knew that I hated him and would hate him all my life. I also knew that he had wanted me to hate him, and had cleverly made it worse for me by seeing to it that I could never feel easy in hating him, because he had been so rude to me that I must always suspect my hatred of springing from hurt vanity. (*Fountain Overflows,* 84-5)

The "hurt vanity" Rose fears to show, and that Jock knows she fears to show, aligns her with Milton's Eve, whose initial mistake was to love herself first and not her intended husband. Jock is clever enough to imply that Rose harbors women's most commonly named vice, and to know that she strives not to be what he nastily imagines women to be.

Cordelia is vain, however, and her attitudes toward music and performance are the opposite of Rose's, Mary's, and Clare's. Rather than attempting to wring the greatest possible beauty out of works of genius by tremendous, unselfish effort, as a true artist would, Cordelia wants to be a spectacle of pretty girlhood making sentimental music; she wants to be for adult audiences what she thinks they want, "mindless and will-less as grown-ups like pretty little girls to be" (*Fountain Overflows,* 105). What most infuriates Rose and Mary about Cordelia, for all their lives, is Cordelia's successful imitation of stereotypes, and her impersonation of an "innocent" and vulnerable young girl is the most exasperating: "a remote and dreaming child, unaware of her own loveliness, and terrified lest someone should be unkind to her, since, as far as she knew, she had no claim on the world's kindness" (*This Real Night,* 48). Cordelia is in fact strong—"sturdy" is the adjective Rose most uses—but this performance is convincing, and so helps to perpetuate a false vision against which Rose feels herself judged.

Rose hates the fact that these are popular images of childhood, and her fierce honesty compels her to insist that she, and by extension many others, do not fit those pictures. Nancy Phillips has lived, apparently, the kind of life Cordelia thinks young girls ought to live: wearing properly delicate clothing, knowing nothing of money troubles, having parents of social and financial ambition. She does in fact seem to be mindless and will-less, and she is certainly vulnerable. But the paucity of Nancy's resources stuns even Cordelia. Nancy's tragedy is not only that her mother murders her father, but that this rich Edwardian child has been taught nothing of self-sufficiency; the Aubreys are amazed at her idleness, and at the contrast between her expensive, "frivolous" clothes and her "pale and reticent and even resentful" face (*Fountain Overflows,* 138), as if she is a puppet dressed up and then abandoned by her master. Nancy's only "occupation" that she "seemed to think legitimate was what she called her 'work': a linen nightdress stamped on one side with a trivial design of trailing flowers, which she was outlining in the simplest possible embroidery stitch" (187). The contrast of Nancy with the four lively and accomplished Aubrey children highlights the difference between her conventional, and thus empty, "real" childhood and their difficult upbringing, which lacks iron patriarchal support but is ultimately rewarding. Rose is frustrated by childhood (and by extension womanhood) because she wishes to live the financially and intellectually independent life for which her mother's training prepares her. Nancy's unhappy childhood is in part caused by the idle parasitism her parents teach her.

Yet one could say that both women are "rescued" from their unhappiness, their Cinderella state, by marriage, and that several of West's female characters are "saved" through marriages that rob them of unique distinctions but result in a good that, as West presents it, is unmistakable. Clare and Constance, the matriarchs of the *Cousin Rosamund* trilogy, submerge their talents in marriages that demand they cope constantly with capricious, often disastrous husbands, but they find the justification for these unions in the children they raise to go beyond their own limitations. Rose's stepdaughter-type status, by the time of *Cousin Rosamund,* is no longer a result of her social and economic deficiencies, because she has made money and respectability for herself. Rather she is held back by the difficulty men have in accepting her as a brilliant musician, as a woman who is a master. She and Mary agree that men propose to them "angrily," as if the sisters "had stolen something from them and this was the only way they could get it back" (14). But when Rose does love a man and is loved by him, he is someone capable of greater achievement in music: a composer, not an interpreter. Similarly, Nancy loves a man who can "teach" her, Queenie loves a man who can dominate her mentally and sexually, Rosamund marries a man of incredible wealth. Ellen Melville, of course, is conquered by a dashing hero, and Isabelle Sallafranque allies herself with one of the richest and most powerful industrialists in France. All, even taking into consideration their multiple thematic purposes (some of which will be explored in later chapters), could be seen as variations on Cinderella marrying the prince.

Still, the hatred West shows for the overt Cinderella theme in "Charlotte Bronte" shows up in the *Cousin Rosamund* trilogy in a surprising way through the character of Cordelia. Cordelia is based on West's older sister Letitia, "Lettie," with whom West was in competition from infancy; her fictional portraits also include Alice in "The Salt of the Earth," and the self-righteous elder sister of her unpublished story "The Short Life of a Saint."[16] Lettie Fairfield was as ambitious and energetic as Cecily, becoming a Fabian socialist and a suffragette before going to medical school on a scholarship. Never married, Lettie converted to Catholicism in her thirties and attended law school even as she did medical work, and throughout her adult life she was active as a religious writer and thinker. Like West, she was not a conventional woman who focused her interests on home and family.

From what autobiographical and biographical sources exist, it is difficult to know whether Lettie was as hateful to West as she claimed both in letters and through these fictional characters, since some family members have loving memories of Lettie and are more inclined to believe that West's paranoid imagination reconfigured the actual woman and her actions.[17] Few of Lettie's clearly positive qualities show up in West's portrayals, though she does grant her energy and drive. Instead she focuses on Lettie's constant chastisement and disapproval, her need to punish West for continuous and even unspecified wrongdoing, an attitude that apparently flourished in spite of and perhaps because of West's enormous success as a writer. The underlying reasons for such animosity are complex, but related always to their particular family romance. West came to believe that Lettie was jealous and resentful of her as an infant. Her niece Alison MacLeod, West's sister Winnie's daughter, once reported to West that Lettie remembered Charles Fairfield beating her about the time of West's birth, and that she must have connected the two events, which was the reason for her resentment.[18] West saw this as an admission for life-long hostility. Conversely, Bonnie Kime Scott points out that the eight-years-older Lettie "had years longer to be a favorite with their father," which must have been a "lasting source of envy" for West (*Vol. I,* 13).

Whatever the truth of these particular claims, clearly envy was at the heart of the sisters' feud. Ann and Barry Ulanov, in *Cinderella and Her Sisters: The Envied and the Envying,* call the story of Cinderella "the story of envy," and claim that the emphasis in the Cinderella story is on "envy between women."[19] Cordelia imagines herself as Cinderella the rejected daughter and the "good" person, like the daughter of King Lear for whom she is (ironically) named. Rose derides Cordelia's need to imagine herself as the righteous truth-seeker, the only person in the family who understands the ways of the world and just how the Aubreys fail to live up to them. Cordelia's constant performance disgusts Rose, since she melodramatically plays parts in stories that fit her particular egotistical needs: for instance, after a violin performance, when Cordelia "impersonat[es] a genius exhausted by having given her all" for her unconvinced siblings (*Fountain Overflows,* 229). Clare and her other children see Cordelia as a tragic figure because she lacks the musical talent they have, and that is necessary to satisfy her devouring ambition to be a professional musician. They discourage her attempts to play the violin because, as true musicians, they can clearly perceive her lack of ability. But Cordelia interprets this as an unjust rejection of her right to exercise autonomy and express herself, as their need to keep her in the cinders and away from the prince they themselves seek through music. The prince she wishes to gain in this case is not only successful artistic expression, but also, perhaps more intensely, independence from the insecurity Piers has forced his family to endure. In this Rose sympathizes with her.

Nevertheless, Cordelia's strongest motivation is the wild hurt she feels from her own inability to be a genius in this family of geniuses. This too has a practical side: only a genius could thrive in this unconventional family that feeds on art and ideas. Her psychological defense is to turn the rest of her family into the ones who are lacking, in the worldly virtues of common sense, seriousness, and comprehension of "reality." She sees her siblings and her parents only in reference to her own need to defend herself against the pain of not belonging. Melanie Klein, in *Envy and Gratitude,* essentially claims that the envier wishes to spoil the goodness of the envied one; this is exactly what Cordelia attempts throughout the *Cousin Rosamund* trilogy.[20] In her self-image as Cinderella, she ironically treats her siblings as the wicked stepsisters treat Cinderella, forcing them to perpetuate their dislike of her, which then enforces her sense of isolation. Rose suffers badly the effects of being envied throughout the *Cousin Rosamund* trilogy. Cordelia nullifies Rose's real self, and, as the Ulanovs describe the experience of being envied, "[h]er reality as a person is obliterated. Her hurt, her anger, or her shock in response to envious assault seems not to matter at all to the envier" (17). Rose repeatedly describes her fury at Cordelia's continuing disapproval, which belies the reality of Rose's (and Mary's) success.

Yet Cordelia sees herself as the envied, as does her infatuated violin teacher Miss Beevor, who blames Clare's failure to see Cordelia as an exceptional person on implicit envy. The mother dominates in the Cinderella story, as she dominates *The Fountain Overflows* and *This Real Night,* because the father is chronically absent. Of course Piers is largely to blame for Cordelia's desperate desire to make money playing the violin. Yet Cordelia erroneously focuses on her mother as the bad mother. Miss Beevor becomes the good mother, not only the lost birth mother who would understand her daughter's true worth and love her, but also the fairy godmother who will deliver her into the destiny that is rightfully hers: marriage with the prince, which ironically, given Cordelia's conventionality, is not marriage, but a professional music career. This will deliver her to audiences who will recognize her true self, as the prince recognizes Cinderella, to the shunning of all other women, especially the stepsisters who try desperately to trick him into believing they are the desirable ones—in this case, Rose and Mary, whom Clare treats as the true musicians.

Still more irony surrounds this situation: Clare in fact loves Cordelia, and by discouraging Cordelia's public violin performances tries to protect her against just the brutal rejection she eventually suffers from a world-class violin teacher. But Cordelia chooses to see Clare as one who fails to promote her daughter's life in the world, who does not engineer her success at the ball and so fails in her rightful role as mother. In her blind envy of Clare's (and by extension Rose and Mary's) genius, she misreads her mother's motives. Klein claims that envy seeks to "put badness. . .into the mother. . .in order to spoil and destroy her. In the deepest sense this means destroying her creativeness" (7). Cordelia wants to destroy her mother's (and by extension her sisters') creativity because she does not have it herself. She does not recognize, as Rose, Mary, and Richard Quin do, that Clare is brilliantly equipping them for their proper destinies: for the first three, the lives of artists. The purity of Clare's vision, of her dedication to music, is stressed by her different approach to Cordelia. To the siblings, Cordelia is "a complicated problem"; to Clare, the problem is "simple": "Cordelia was someone who could not play the violin and who insisted on doing so" (*Fountain Overflows,* 55).

Clare's single-mindedness, however, also illustrates that Cordelia has a point about her mother's admirable but eccentric lack of attention to practical considerations, especially her children's fit within a social network. She does fret some over the lack of suitable mates available to her children, but this has never been her highest priority for any of them. Rose and Mary "thought it not bad at all. How. . .did they think we could run a big house and look after a husband and children and travel all over the world giving concerts?" (*Fountain Overflows,* 228). When the siblings realize that in fact Cordelia might marry, it is a revelation, and its revelatory quality is stressed again to point out the fact that these daughters have not been raised to follow traditional plots or think in conventional ways about women's lives. For instance, Rose often mentions Cordelia's prettiness, usually as a deceptive contrast to her hard nature, but only as the children get older does it occur to them that her beauty might trick some gullible man into taking her off their hands. As they watch her play at a charity concert, Mary imagines with wild hope that "some stranger will see Cordelia in the street. . .and there we are, she will be happy, and there will be no more nonsense about playing the violin" (*Fountain Overflows,* 228). Cordelia settles for marriage since she cannot be an artist, and it is a consolation prize for her rather than a chance to express deep truths, as art is for the others and marriage becomes for Rose. Yet while marriage almost tames Cordelia's nasty critical temperament, since now she has her husband and home to occupy her, she continues to see herself, and be seen by her siblings, as the stepchild, "that stranger," as Rose names her near the end of *Cousin Rosamund* (261).

There are several reasons why West might have reconfigured the Cinderella myth to encompass Cordelia, and by extension Lettie Fairfield. On a simple level, degrading Lettie in fiction is revenge for Lettie's apparent disapproval. On a less simple level, West deliberately robs Lettie of her intellectual power through the insulting portrait of Cordelia, and makes her the lesser artist, the impostor to West's genuine artist and thinker, and thus she wins in fiction the contest waged by the sisters throughout their lives. In fact, West's cruel portrayals of Lettie constitute one of her least attractive qualities as a fiction writer. They illustrate only too well the unmistakable paranoia she frequently manifested and that worsened after her stance as an anti-Communist and her feud with Anthony became so public.[21] West often named ill treatment from her family and friends as the source of her worst problems; this explains, in part, her fascination with betrayal at the state level, which she was exploring in such nonfiction works as *The Meaning of Treason* and *A Train of Powder* at the same time she was writing *The Fountain Overflows* and its sequels.

Yet conversely, West could be blaming the Cinderella myth—or rather the cultural expectations that account for its perpetuation—for the envy and competitiveness that so undeniably exist between women. If in fact this theme comes across without West's conscious effort, that makes it all the more effective; and, as usual with West, it is more complex than it at first appears. Both Cecily and Letitia Fairfield were deliberate players in fields dominated by men; one could say that they disputed which of the two was the most able to succeed like a man in the man's world that they credited as the "real" one, the important one. Such an argument harks back to Gloria Fromm's complaint that West wrote like a man to men in her journalism, and like a woman to women in her fiction.

On another level, however, West shows how women might utilize the Cinderella myth to justify their own cowardice, and the ways in which the Cinderella myth can be used to excuse the pain of facing "reality," and the necessity of hard work to achieve goodness: in art, in morality, in life. Women can avoid blaming themselves for their own lack of success by blaming others, by seeing themselves as the rejected Cinderella. They can also avoid the harder work of achieving authentic selfhood through work; according to this attitude, marriage is a last resort rather than a primary goal. Here West seems to embrace Simone de Beauvoir's explanation of why the Cinderella myth has such endurance.

> Everything still encourages the young girls to expect fortune and happiness from some Prince Charming rather than to attempt by herself their difficult and uncertain conquest. In particular she can hope to rise, thanks to him, into a caste superior to her own, a miracle that could not be bought by the labor of her lifetime. But such a hope is a thing of evil because it divides her strength and her interests; this division is perhaps woman's greatest handicap. . .the result is that she is often less specially trained, less solidly grounded than her brothers, she is less deeply involved in her profession. In this way she dooms herself to remain in its lower levels, to be inferior; and the vicious circle is formed: this professional inferiority reinforces her desire to find a husband.[22]

Yet West ultimately does not elevate careers for women over marriage in her fiction, as other chapters in this book discuss. Instead, West's attitudes toward both the Venus and Cinderella myths showcase her paradoxes. Rebecca West explored these old narratives with a vengeance, showing how cultural and artistic stereotypes perpetuated themselves in life because of the omnipresence of their images, and deploring the unhappiness they could cause for men and women. She sometimes seems to agree with postmodern feminists that gender is culturally rather than biologically constructed, and with the many feminists who have written about the need for women, and men, to find new narratives, fresh stories, about female lives.[23]

But her reasons for despising these narratives do not necessarily support women's equality and independence. Men's worship of Venus limits women to a life that their looks rather than their minds and souls create; yet she believes that women's beauty entitles them to love and support in a world inevitably dominated by men. She is not only angry that the Cinderella myth teaches women that marriage should be their ultimate goal, but she blames Cinderella's existence on men's inadequate support systems for the women whose dependence they create. One could say that she agrees with Judith Butler's overall assertion that we cannot escape the "cultural locus of gender meanings" or "find the body that preexists its cultural interpretation."[24] But rather than advocate as Butler does a kind of subversive free play within these cultural norms in order ultimately to wear them down, West wants to settle into these norms as they are—as if they could be—ideally lived. Her method of accepting these apparently inevitable norms is to wish them consistently and justly enforced, and then to blame men for not following their own rules.

As usual, West's paradoxes illustrate the complexity of wishing for genuine gender equality within an overwhelmingly unequal world, and the variety of strategies that women utilize in their search for a satisfactory identity within it. Her contradictions, however we may not like them, are ones that many women experience. As such, these fictional portrayals are valuable.

Notes

1. Philip E. Ray, "*The Judge* Reexamined: Rebecca West's Underrated Gothic Romance," *English Literature in Transition* 31.3 (1988): 297. Further references to this article will be identified by page numbers in the text.

2. Deakin recognizes that West is rehearsing the plot of a "conventional" sentimental or Gothic novel, but he does not attempt to explain why. "From Richardson's Clarissa to Hardy's Tess, literary heroines had suffered and died within this convention. In [*The Judge*] Rebecca West hardly moves beyond it" (139).

3. Jane Marcus introduces the reprint of *The Judge* by the Dial Press, 1980. She emphasizes its feminist themes, not its Gothic elements.

4. *The Judge* (New York: The Dial Press, 1980): 9-10. Further references will be to this edition, identified by page numbers in the text.

5. "For feminist modernists 'Indissoluble Matrimony' might have functioned as a witty exploration of the dynamics of sex-antagonism, a paradigmatic (female) joke about the neurotic never-never land inhabited by the lost boys who became the early twentieth century's no-men. For. . .West sees the dis-ease of no-manhood as a basis for sexual battle." Sandra M. Gilbert and Susan Gubar, *Vol. I,* 97.

6. Peter Wolfe writes that Ellen is "not womanly enough to see that she has moved Yaverland sexually," and so instead "tries to win him intellectually." He sees her progress into a relationship with Richard as "the steps by which a girl becomes a woman," and her revelations as "a true understanding of the woman's lot" (36-37). I agree with Wolfe that "Ellen's ordeal will probably be worse than Marion's," but I do not think that immaturity is what makes Ellen initially resist Richard. She opposes instinctively the "woman's lot" of submission and self-effacement that Richard represents, not the sexuality he arouses.

7. Sue Thomas reads this scene very differently, seeing Ellen's reaction as evidence of West's "Romantic vitalist feminism": "As the vital, natural sexual energy of Ellen was earthed like lightning, she became the drowning woman sinking 'confused,' not rationally, into the 'darkness,' the mysterious otherness of Richard. West's metaphor of drowning insisted implicitly that Ellen's submission was not a sign of the fixity or stillness she associated in 'The World's Worst Failure' with culturally conditioned

passive sexuality, and that Richard's vital, natural sexuality was fluid rather than monolithic." *Genders,* Vol. 13, Spring 1992: 90-107.

8. Harold Orel recognizes Ellen's tragedy. "We have exchanged the Ellen of Book I - for all her faults, an adolescent dreamer capable of becoming a strong, mature, and attractive woman, a leader of fashion, a wife who may not be destroyed by lesser temperaments - for a mess of pottage" (131).

9. Jane Miller, *Women Writing About Men* (New York: Pantheon Books, 1986): 99.

10. Victoria Glendinning, introduction to *Harriet Hume* by Rebecca West (New York: Dial Press, 1980): 3. Further references to *Harriet Hume* will be to this edition, identified by page numbers in the text.

11. Rebecca West, "Parthenope," reprinted in *A Celebration:* 469-96.

12. J.R. Hammond, *H.G. Wells and Rebecca West* (New York: St. Martin's Press, 1991): 169.

13. Gloria Steinem, "Women in the Dark: Of Sex Goddesses, Abuse and Dreams," *Ms.,* January/February 1991: 35-37. Steinem also discusses Lana Turner, Hedy Lamarr, Dorothy Dandridge, and Kim Novak.

14. Virginia Woolf, *The Years* (New York: Harcourt Brace Jovanovich, 1965): 159.

15. Susan Fraiman studies "the divergent narrative, the rival ideologies" within women's texts as women "unbecoming women," and shows the ways they "tell this story - alongside conventional stories - in. . .a spirit of protest, challenging the myth of courtship as education, railing against the belittlement of women, willing to hazard the distasteful and indecorous" (xi). Rose Aubrey's story, and narration, fit this description.

16. See Rollyson, 309.

17. See Rollyson, 400-1. At Lettie's deathbed, West noticed the family's affection for her, and their nephew Norman Macleod said that "everyone loved Lettie." West believed that Lettie was merely deceiving everyone about her true nature, but Macleod was astonished that West saw Lettie as "a fool and a bore," when he and his own children adored her.

18. See Rollyson, 402.

19. Ann and Barry Ulanov, *Cinderella and Her Sisters: The Envied and the Envying* (Philadelphia: The Westminster Press, 1983): 14-5. Further references will be identified by page numbers in the text.

20. See Melanie Klein, *Envy and Gratitude: A Study of Unconscious Sources* (New York: Basic Books, Inc., 1957). Klein sees envy developing from an infant's relation to her mother's breast, from the "earliest object relations and internalization process that is rooted in orality. . .It could be said that the envious person is insatiable, he can never be satisfied because his envy stems from within and therefore always finds an object to focus on." Klein draws distinctions between envy and jealousy, saying that Othello's famous words about jealousy, "the green-eyed monster which doth mock/The meat if feeds on," apply better to envy. "One is reminded of the saying 'to bite the hand which feeds one,' which is almost synonymous with biting, destroying, and spoiling the breast" (8-9). Further references will be identified by page numbers in the text.

21. For instance, in March 1962, Mary McCarthy met West on board a ship as West sailed home from a trip to the U.S. Rollyson reports that

McCarthy "paid tribute to Rebecca's sparkling conversation but thought her 'cracked. . .she imagines that various authors are alluding to her and all her relations under disguises in their books'" (343).

22. Simone de Beauvoir, *The Second Sex,* trans. and ed. H.M. Parshley (New York: Alfred A. Knopf, 1971): 136-7.

23. See, for instance, *Feminists Theorize the Political,* ed. Judith Butler and Joan W. Scott (New York: Routledge, 1992), and Carolyn Heilbrun, *Writing a Woman's Life* (New York: Norton, 1988).

24. Judith Butler, "Variations on Sex and Gender: Beauvoir, Wittig and Foucault," in *Modern Literary Theory,* ed. Philip Rice and Patricia Waugh (New York: Routledge, 1996): 145.

Chapter 3

Mothers and Fathers

Laura said to the crucifix, "You created Kamensky, and someone had to do something. And if Chubinov and I did the wrong thing, remember You created us too." *The Birds Fall Down*

I did not want to grow up. I could not face the task of being a human being, because I did not fully exist. It was my father and mother who existed. *The Fountain Overflows*

Carol Gilligan, in her 1982 study *In a Different Voice: Psychological Theory and Women's Development*, argues that theories of human progress toward maturity and moral understanding have been based almost exclusively on observations of men's lives, and that if we are to understand the way women develop, their "different voice" must be heard in a different theoretical context.[1] Taking from Freud, Erikson, Jean Piaget, Lawrence Kohlberg, and others, she shows that (mostly male) psychologists have seen the process of "healthy" maturation as a progressive separation from others toward autonomy and independence—conclusions reached through studies of boys and men—and that women's failure to follow this pattern has resulted in declarations of female inferiority. Gilligan's own research demonstrates that women battle more intensely and for much longer than men the problem of balancing commitment to the self with responsibility to others. They see morality as a matter of care; men see it as a matter of impartial justice that stresses individual rights. Moreover, women are much more likely than men to see moral problems contextually, solving dilemmas according to the specific circumstances and people involved instead of looking, as men do, to absolute rules or laws to settle a debate.

These theories of male and female psychologies correspond closely to those of Rebecca West, who decided long before the publication of Gilligan's cogent book that women think of human beings when making moral decisions and that men think of the rules constituting ideologies.[2] Gilligan writes, "Hypothetical dilemmas, in the abstraction of their presentation, divest moral actors from the history and psychology of their individual lives and separate the moral problem from the social contingencies of its possible occurrence" (100). West writes, to quote again this statement from *Black Lamb and Grey Falcon*, that "lunatic" men "are so obsessed by public affairs that they see the world as by moonlight, which shows the outlines of every object but not the details indicative of their nature" (3). Although she counters this with criticism of "idiotic" women's obsession with their "private lives," which makes them "follow their fate through a darkness deep as that cast by malformed cells in the brain" (3), West champions, in her fiction and non-fiction, women's nurturing tendencies and despises men's detachment from the feelings and lives of the people supposedly closest to them.

Most specifically, she attacks fathers and venerates mothers. By "fathers," I mean not only men who beget and raise children, but also the male leaders who have formed and ruled religions, governments, societies, and businesses. These assaults are present in the criticisms of powerful historical "fathers" in her political writing and in the specific indictments of her male fictional fathers. By "mothers," I mean mostly the mothers of daughters and sons whom she creates in her novels. West's fathers are blind to the particulars of their ideas and ideologies; they fail to see the consequences of their "hypothetical" thinking when taken to action, and so hurt people when they think they are helping. West's mothers are much more likely to follow Gilligan's model for female thought; they reconstruct dilemmas, hypothetical or actual, "in terms of the real," and "request or. . .supply missing information about the nature of the people and the places where they live, shift[ing] their judgment away from the hierarchical ordering of principles and the formal procedures of decision making" (101). Thus they give to their children, or to the people who know them, love and care dictated by need and worth, whereas fathers fail to (or do not want to) see, in their mature "separation" from others, what is desired of them, and so they neglect their personal relationships. This neglect shows in the patriarchal structure itself. Male religious and political leaders follow stubbornly the rules they have devised without caring for their impact on individual lives, and so perpetuate human, and particularly female, unhappiness. Mothers represent an antidote to this rigidity, but they cannot override the immense, far-reaching power structures based on such rule-bound thinking.

West would call Communism the most extreme example of this, and her vocal anti-Communism cost her readers and supporters both in the 1950s, when she supported Joseph McCarthy's cause, and now, when McCarthy and the House Committee on Un-American activities have come to symbolize the worst of political repression and conformity. Loretta Stec points out that

> West's turn to the right politically was not unique in England during and after the war. . .[Her] postwar writing was part of a larger ideological shift in attitude among the British intelligentsia in the middle of this century away from the Left and especially from Communism. (138)

But West stressed always that she was not backing McCarthy the individual, whom she called a man "who has not the faintest idea how to use his gifts in harmony with the established practices of civilization. . ." (Rollyson, 288). Rather she believed that what mistakes he made in pursuing Communist sympathizers were minimal compared to the justice of his fight to squelch Stalinist crimes, and that those who quarreled with McCarthy's tactics were thinking more of abstract rights to privacy than the suffering of human beings embroiled in Communist states. West also deplored the Communist (or any) revolutionary insistence upon destruction of the old to make way for the new, again believing that it ignored the reality of the human beings involved. Rollyson succinctly summarizes her attitude in a discussion of her essay "The Revolutionary," about William Joyce, the "Lord Haw Haw" who broadcast fascist propaganda from Germany to Britain during World War II: "One cannot murder society in order to save it" (243).

By 1966 and the publication of *The Birds Fall Down*—the last major work to come out in her lifetime—West had published a biography of Saint Augustine, *Black Lamb and Grey Falcon*, and three books that are essentially studies of treachery: *The Meaning of Treason, A Train of Powder*, and *The New Meaning of Treason*. As Moira Ferguson points out, West tended in these books to seek for explanations of individual psyches that influenced the many, rather than giant forces composed of numerous factors, as shapers of history. This connects her to *In a Different Voice* again, not only in subject matter but in the negative reception both writers have eventually received. Gilligan's book has been one of the most influential studies of gender in the second half of the twentieth century. Yet many feminists believe that her conclusions only reinforce and validate existing male and female stereotypes, and Gilligan's "different voice" has often been abjured as one that will perpetuate women's relegation to secondary social, cultural, and political status.[3] Gilligan's contention that women look to individual people and situations rather than to a more abstract understanding would seem to support ideas of women's intellectual inferiority, their inability to see past the particular at the universal.

Ferguson is one of several critics to note West's interest in individual rights over communitarian values. Stec sees West's post

World War II reportage works on betrayal as evidence of "the distance
West had come since her early days as a socialist-feminist writer" (134).
In particular Stec notices that West's "socialist thinking usually
emphasized the importance of society meeting the needs of the
individual above the attempt to achieve some communal goal or
organization" (137). West, who had a profound knowledge of history
and politics, certainly places her subjects within social and historical
structures. But, like her fictional mothers, she illustrates Gilligan's
claim for a woman's "different voice": she brings the universal down to
the particular in many cases, and looks closely at individual lives for
the explication of even the most momentous events. The "absent"
moral center that Moira Ferguson notices in West's men is often due to
their inability to see the particular for obsession with the universal.[4]

West's attitude toward Christianity demonstrates this hatred for the
"male" will run amok in actions motivated by beliefs based on a set of
theories. Born of Protestant parents, she outwardly followed the
Anglican church for most of her life. But readers will find no Christian
piety in her work, even if they frequently discover Christianity as overt
and covert subject, and though she professed her belief in the human
need for religion (manifested most clearly in the *Cousin Rosamund*
trilogy). In *Black Lamb and Grey Falcon* (and in other works), an
admiring West describes in detail many rituals of the Orthodox faith,
openly fascinated by and attracted to their mysterious, "magical"
elements and the positive emotional response they generated in people
she respected. But she rejects, in more fiction and non-fiction passages
than it is sensible to cite, the basic premise of Christianity's eastern and
western sects: the Atonement. Glendinning says, "The core of *Black
Lamb and Grey Falcon* is about this problem" of "the savage
irrationality of the crucifixion" (222), and it seems a good place to go
for an illustration of this basic Westian philosophy.

West sees the logic behind the crucifixion (or rather its illogic) as
representative not only of a colossal misunderstanding by Christians,
but of humanity's worst psychological error. Her magnum opus gets its
title from two things: an old Yugoslavian poem featuring a grey falcon
who advocates sacrificing earthly happiness for the hope of a heavenly
kingdom, a poem that "celebrate[s an] appetite for self-immolation"
(1145); and a Muslim fertility rite she witnessed in Macedonia in which
black lambs and cocks are sacrificed on a rock and their blood is smeared
on children to ensure the future conception of their mothers. Borrowing
an image from "The Waste Land," West, in the emotional and
intellectual climax of *Black Lamb*, excoriates what she sees as the
useless butchery of this ancient ceremony and all it symbolizes.

> I knew this rock well. I had lived under the shadow of it all my life.
> All our Western thought is founded on this repulsive pretence that

pain is the proper price of any good thing. Here it could be seen how the meaning of the Crucifixion had been hidden from us, though it was written clear. A supremely good man was born on earth, a man who was without cruelty, who could have taught mankind to live in perpetual happiness; and because we are infatuated with this idea of sacrifice, of shedding innocent blood to secure innocent advantages, we found nothing better to do with this passport to deliverance than to destroy him. . .The cruel spirit which informed [the crucifixion] saved itself by a ruse, a theological ruse. So successful has this ruse been that the rock disgusted me with the added loathsomeness of familiarity. . .Its rite, under various disguises, had been recommended to me since my infancy by various religious bodies, by Roman Catholicism, by Anglicanism, by Methodism, by the Salvation Army. Since its earliest days Christianity has been compelled to seem its opposite. This stone, the knife, the filth, the blood, is what many people desire beyond anything else, and they fight to obtain it. (827)

West continues with specific examples of those who have fought to obtain "the knife, the filth, the blood." St. Paul, whom she calls only "Saul of Tarsus," "an enemy of love and Christ," could not bear the image of the crucifixion, and so studied the gospel "till [he] found a way of making it appear as if cruelty was the way of salvation." His "monstrous theory" is

that God was angry with man for his sins and that He wanted to punish him for these, not in any way that might lead to his reformation, but simply by inflicting pain on him; and that He allowed Christ to suffer this pain instead of man and thereafter was willing on certain terms to treat man as if he had not committed these sins. (828)

West then throws St. Paul, and by extension centuries of believers, to the lions. "This theory flouts reason at all points, for it is not possible that a just God should forgive people who are wicked because another person who was good endured agony by being nailed to a cross" (828).

Augustine, "so curiously called a saint," also embraces cruelty, and so tries to find logic enough in St. Paul's doctrine to support it. But Augustine's "logic" seems to West just as arbitrary, since "he adopted a theory that the Devil had acquired a rightful power over man because of his sins, and lost it because he forfeited all rights by crucifying Christ, who was sinless." This shows the universe "to be as nonsensical as the devotees of the rock wished it to be," presenting us with a Devil "who was apparently to a certain degree respectable, at least respectable enough to be allowed by God to exercise his legal rights in the universe, until he killed Christ." Man's sins, therefore, seem "not so bad, just what you might expect from the subjects of a disorderly native prince" (828-9). Luther does not even get the respect of having his religious tenets briefly explained; West devotes most of a paragraph to comparing him with a hog who "howled against man's gift of reason" (829). Even Shakespeare yields to the "authority" of the rock, though he was fully aware of its "horror": "His respect for the rock forced him to write *King Lear* and take up all lambs of the herd one by one and draw his knife across their throat" (830).

What Jane Marcus calls West's "voice of authority," a voice of "historical necessity and urgency,"[5] could not be more evident than in these passages from *Black Lamb*. In criticizing such "great" men as Augustine, Luther, Saint Paul, Shakespeare, and Tolstoy (against whom she showers frequent invectives),[6] West dares to rebel, in the full confidence of her own intellect, against mighty "fathers." She sees many of their elaborate theological, philosophical, and political systems as absurd justifications for getting their own way regardless of consequences to others, and so sets out to illustrate just how ridiculous (she thinks) the effects of their reasoning can be. The rage she expresses toward the world-ruling male psyche, however, is so strong that it must come from, as Ferguson claims, a subjective as well as objective anger at men. It is powerful enough that she takes Freud's thanatos and eros principles literally, and works them into most of her writing as the dualism of male and female. Men embrace aggression and death, she says directly and implies repeatedly, while women, if not exempt from error, seek life and pleasure.

Her insistence upon the personal and psychological seems an attempt to bring "great" men and "historic" situations into a recognizable (or female and thus implicitly more rational) sphere and to divorce from them their inherited (male) sense of logical inevitability. West, who was no "idiot" in her own formulation, knew enough of politics, history, philosophy, and religion to criticize thinkers who broke or formed molds—Paul, Augustine, Luther, Shakespeare—and at least attempt to bring them from the historicity of their influence to the "real" history of their lives. As a Freudian (surely the undeniable Freudian elements of *The Return of the Soldier, The Judge, St. Augustine*, the treason books, *Black Lamb,* and others justify the giving of that title), West looked to mothers and fathers as the key to a human soul. As a feminist (problematic as that title is), she blamed men and the patriarchal structure of society—or fathers—for human unhappiness. But as Rebecca West, a woman haunted by the specter of the missing father in her writing and in her life, she sees the treachery of familial and cultural fathers as the epitome of human failure.

It is not surprising that she takes on such eminent father figures in her non-fiction when one considers the fury with which she portrays

most fathers in her fiction. All of the fathers in *The Judge* are
contemptible: Harry Yaverland, in his complacent role as the noble
entitled to a youthful sowing of uncommitted oats, is absent from his
son's life; the never-seen Mr. Melville abandoned his wife and daughter
in poverty; Peacey is a liar and a rapist and a physically brutal parent;
Richard, it seems, will conceive a child whom he cannot care for or
support. The novel's subtitle warns of sinning fathers, angry mothers,
doomed children. Marc Sallafranque, in *The Thinking Reed*, indirectly
causes his wife's miscarriage when he becomes abusively drunk and
gambles in a way dangerous to his present and future family. Most
obviously, there is Piers Aubrey, also a gambler, the fictional
presentation of West's own father Charles Fairfield and a man who
embodies the male drive toward pain and death that West sees
represented in the Atonement.

Glendinning reports that "much of the vivid material uncovered
during [West's] sessions with [Freudian analyst Mary] Wilshere related
to Rebecca's original and inconclusive romance with her father" (119).
"Inconclusive" seems an appropriate word, since West's feelings toward
Fairfield (and Rose's toward Piers) swing from a fury nearly hatred to a
wistful admiration and love. In the short chapter "My Father" in *Family
Memories*, West alternates terse condemnation with sympathy.[7]

> The detachment of my father from the consequences of his actions
> was almost a cause, like his anti-socialism. The whole strength of
> his being was turned in a direction which led him away from his wife
> and children. He admired my mother and was quite proud of all three
> of his daughters, but he felt no desire to keep us or assist us in any
> way. . .Looking back on my father, it seems to me that he had many
> Slav characteristics: no sense of time, a gift for warm immediate
> intimacy which might suddenly change to self-cloistering
> melancholy; subtlety in everything except the business of
> conciliating his fellow men to whom he explained his motives only
> rarely, and then in terms he did not trouble to make acceptable any
> more than the Tsarist Empire or the Soviet Union. (203-4)

Included in this same chapter is a description of an unnamed young
doctor who attended West's sister Winnie when she had meningitis.
West remembers her early crush on him, based on her sense that he
"was a protector, and a source of happiness" (206); as such, he serves as
a contrast with her father, and his memory brings West to a bitter
conclusion about her relationships with men.

> If I had ever known a man who looked like my doctor and had been
> my contemporary, then I would have loved him. But I never did. A
> sound and logical judgment, 'this is what I would be safe with,'
> tethered me to a man who, as far as I know, never existed. (206)

To discuss West's criticisms of death-desiring "fathers" with her desire for fatherly protection and attention serves to point out again the major factor, and paradox, of West's thinking on sex roles. Although she delights in ripping apart aspects of the patriarchy, she craves its support and in fact desires its continuance, though in altered form. She despises certain male systems of religion and politics as icons of the death wish, but she does not imagine a new order so much as she desires to patch up the old one with better, stronger, more fatherly men who connect with their children and subordinates in a way that women can and do. It seems she projects both her wish to punish men and her wish to build them up simultaneously; she wants to rewrite God and fathers into a patriarchy without thanatos and aggression, without arbitrary systems of faith and state that support illogical and cruel behavior. (The myth of Manicheanism appeals to her perhaps because it is so clearly dualistic, as is her own thinking, and because it lacks the complicated, human-modeled Trinity.) But she never actually gets that far. Instead she dissects, over and over, the decaying male world, and illustrates the frustration of its daughters, who are stuck in dependent roles with undependable supporters.

Against this paternal disintegration she posits maternal sanity and unity as an origin of strength for women and some men. Yet West's mothers can also be a source of artistic or sexual anxiety for their children. And motherhood is usually catastrophic for her women even while it proves their goodness. They sacrifice their own happiness for the sake of their children or husbands—a sacrifice that was once considered a woman's proper life—and so live out the glorified victimization she deplores. Though West seems to advocate such female altruism, the undeniable rage she shows toward fathers who take advantage of mothers and who do not then pay their share of the price undercuts her seeming support for maternity as unselfishness. Still, she concludes often that maternity is, if not more, at least as important as autonomy for women. This chapter describes some of the mothers and fathers of West's novels, and the ways in which they illustrate her desire for nurturing but even stronger fathers, her worship of but pity for the mother, and the problems she sees in time-honored parental roles.

The Birds Fall Down, the last of her novels to be published in West's lifetime, is a spy mystery and a thriller, usually likened to *The Secret Agent*, *Under Western Eyes*, and *The Princess Cassamassima*. Carl Rollyson and Samuel Hynes both call it her finest novel, in Hynes's words "excellent enough to bear comparison with the great political novels."[8] Peter Wolfe, critical of *The Fountain Overflows*, admires it; Motley Deakin, who believes that "not all of Rebecca West's fiction will endure" (164), believes *The Birds Fall Down* will, since it is the prime example of "the kind of fiction she writes well," "a careful construct made from an accumulation of research and thoughtful consideration" (165). Only Harold Orel, of West's recent male critics, likes it less than *The Fountain Overflows*, claiming (I think justifiably) that it is too long. Interestingly, few women have written on *The Birds Fall Down*, which may mean that its categorization as a "spy novel" has disguised what I see as its strong emphasis on gender roles, particularly in the context of family relations.[9]

Its protagonist, Laura Rowan, is the archetypal Westian woman bashing her head against the male absorption in public affairs that masks a death wish: the daughter furious at her father while she longs for his love and protection. Laura is surrounded by presumed father-figures entrusted with her care, yet none understands her true situation, at the novel's beginning or its end, or credits her actual ability to observe, comprehend, and act upon the conditions that surround her. She is to them a beautiful and aristocratic young British girl who will naturally be cloistered from governmental involvement or decisions, and whose proper concerns should be stereotypically feminine: her beauty, her marriage prospects, clothes, light literature. Laura's indifference to these supposed interests never penetrates their set perceptions. Throughout the novel men mouth platitudes at her about her looks and the chivalrous feelings she provokes that only point up the irony of her predicament: that the adults apparently consigned to her care are incapable of it; that she is the intended victim of a political murder; and that the masculine systems of protection supposedly in place to safeguard her will not or cannot. Laura learns fast how to take care of herself, but only after she has lost faith in all her alleged protectors and everything they believe in, leaving her with all familiar structures shattered and only her "will-to-live" intact as a guide. Most importantly, she discards any possible belief she might have had in numerous male-formed ideological systems: Orthodox Christianity, Tsarist Russia, the behavior of English "gentlemen," Marxist revolutionaries, Hegelian philosophy, and a father's right to govern a daughter.

The book opens onto a family scene in London. We meet eighteen-year-old Laura "embroidering a handkerchief. . .[at] her father's house" in "an early summer of this century," and her father Edward grumbling at a chair that does not "comply with his high standards of comfort."[10] Laura hopes to avoid him, since his criticism is not "urgent," but is nevertheless "continuous." These are signals to us that this is a story of the time when girls did needlework and fathers ruled the roost—that here is a traditional family of daughterly submission and paternal authority—but also that this is a difficult father and that there is something wrong in this house, an impression further strengthened by

Edward's negative attitude toward Laura's mother Tania. Like the half child, half adult that she is, Laura comments to herself on the broken social promise represented by her parents' argument. "It's no use pretending that they're fond of each other anymore. They were, but they aren't. Is that unusual, I wonder? Are other people's parents happy together? They all pretend to be, of course. But is it true?" (10).

Outwardly, Edward Rowan is a popular young MP with a beautiful Russian wife, two sons at Eton, and a lovely daughter. But Laura knows that the secret existence he lives as the lover of Tania's ex-friend Susie Staunton is more important to him than his family, knowledge that taunts her as proof that nothing is as it seems. Sadly remembering the Rowan home before it was "forbidding like barracks full of troops divided against themselves," she ruminates on Edward's entrenched position in British society versus his illicit liaison.

> Laura knew that husbands could do several sorts of things which angered their wives. . .[but] she could not imagine her father doing any of them. Such husbands "ran away." Her father could not have moved an inch from where he was. His friends had all sprung up around him in a crowd, at Eton, at New College, in the Commons. When he travelled he was invited to stay with people he knew; his appropriate hosts had scattered themselves everywhere. The house in Radnage Square had been built for his father, and he could walk about it in the dark without bumping into anything. . .her father, though not dull, had committed himself to dullness for life and liked it; he enjoyed blue books, general elections, questions in the House, Ministerial posts. (15-16)

Laura's imagination is, at this point, limited to what she has been taught to expect; while she can see that social structures, such as the family, can be stretched to include the unexpected, she still believes that they will stand. The crux of *The Birds Fall Down* is her realization that they may not, and the plot development is framed and given meaning by her psychological journey to this point.

Count Nikolai Nikolaievitch Diakonov, Laura's grandfather, is almost a caricature of one who believes in absolute, unquestionable structures. He is the culmination of patriarchal attitudes and achievements in the most patriarchal of states: Russia before the Revolution. A devout Orthodox Christian, a wealthy aristocrat and a firm upholder of the feudal class system, a man who prides himself on having helped to close schools for women doctors, he is also a political exile in Paris, having been wrongly accused of negligence that resulted in the assassination of several tsarist officials. Nevertheless, Nikolai defends the tsar who banished him, believing Nicholas II to be a divine instrument of the Orthodox Christian God with whom the old count is obsessed. Laura loves her grandfather, admiring his size, strength, and knowledge—he is a "man's man," and Laura has been taught to respect that—but she recognizes elements of his philosophies as self-serving and absurd and is willing to argue with him, unlike his obedient daughter Tania and dutiful wife Sofia. The loosening of ancient strictures is evident in Laura's doubt about the old man's rigid, painstakingly expounded theology, and in her unwillingness to go along with his ideas of her aristocratic but passive future.

The fact that Nikolai is her grandfather and not her father is significant. Literally "grand," in its sense of noble and dramatic, the old count is a sort of super-father figure who has created a state in miniature of which he is king. Laura sees him "like someone in the Bible," a man "out of the Old Testament" (48). His wife Sofia married him when she was eighteen and he a middle-aged man, and though Laura thinks of her grandmother as remarkably strong, Sofia has always consigned herself to Nikolai's will and so now is as "poisoned" by his grief as he. The servants are emotionally and economically dependent upon him and also share his religion and attitudes. Nikolai's strongest image of God is that He is above all a father, an emphasis he constantly tries to impress upon his daughter and granddaughter: "The Trinity is the means taken by God to enable man to comprehend Him, for it is the image of the family, it shows God as the Father" (63).

But Nikolai is also not Laura's father; he is a generational step removed from that authority over her, and by extension the world she will live in as an adult. Moreover, the power he wields in his own house is lessening with his increasing infirmity, and the servants and even his wife are often merely humoring him when they seem to bend to his will. Laura imagines that "he might belong to a different species, and one generally supposed to be extinct. If there had been men at the same time there were mastodons and dinosaurs, he might have been one of them" (48). And Nikolai's trust in a patriarchy that starts with God and trickles down through human fathers is almost laughable to Laura and Tania, given Edward's behavior. "Think of your own father. All the essence of his being is confined to his family. . .Love flows from him to you, unfailingly" (63).

Kamensky, Nikolai's personal secretary, is conversely, in Laura's mind, someone out of the New Testament.[11] An outwardly gentle and self-effacing man, he is Nikolai's apparent foil, bourgeois rather than noble, small rather than large, down-to-earth instead of heaven-haunted. The combined Diakonov and Rowan families think of him as "the excellent little Kamensky" who arranges dates and train tickets, escorts the ladies when they need male chaperonage, caters to the count's needs, and generally acts as butler/brother/counselor, the ideal man about the house. The perfect convention of Kamensky's impersonation shields the

truths of his triple identity: though he acts indeed as Kamensky, the
secretary, he is also Kaspar the tsarist police agent, and Gorin the leader
of revolutionary espionage and terrorism. He alone sees Laura for who
she is, a skeptical and intelligent girl who "has an eye for little things"
(32) that her grandfather does not. She discovers by accident that
Kamensky's eyeglasses are clear glass, though he feigns acute myopia,
and so early on the two of them are set up as mutual but antagonistic
observers of the person behind the mask and the reason behind events;
they alone can see beyond the strictly-followed structures in the
Diakanov household, and thus are capable of acting outside them.
Kamensky also represents, as past and potential murderer, the male
physical threat to women and to the world, which makes doubly ironic
the fact that he is considered the only man capable of properly tending
to Sofia, Tania, and Laura.

The train ride that Laura and Nikolai take with the aristocrat-turned-
revolutionary Chubinov (which takes up a full quarter of the book)
almost completes the process of Laura's unwitting education in
hypocrisy and her mental exile from the family fold. Initially a docile
Laura sits with the magazines *pour les jeunes filles* that Kamensky
bought for her and tries to act as she imagines her mother or father
would, though she is really ruminating on the fact that she does not
want a husband, since "men are not interesting in themselves" (90).
This dislike for men grows stronger as she listens to Chubinov and her
grandfather. Although Chubinov is acting from noble impulses when
he warns Nikolai of Kamensky's treachery—he wants to save the count
further humiliation from the Tsar and even murder at Kamensky's
hands—he clings to the belief that his cause is great and that
revolutionaries are therefore justified in committing murder, just as
Nikolai will accept his own undeserved exile as martyrdom for Tsar and
God. Chubinov insists to Nikolai that "it's you, not we, who are the
murderers. We are the instruments of justice. No guilt rests on us.
There is blood on our hands, but it is turned to glory by the rectitude of
our cause." He adds that is "strange. . .that one of us two should have
lived a life which is like a noble poem and the other a life which is that
poem's ignoble parody" (185). Snapping back, "One day you'll learn
which side it was that produced the parody," Nikolai voices his own
twisted rationalization. "If the Tsar wishes me to return to Russia in
order to humiliate me and accuse me of a crime I have not committed,
and insult me by pardoning my innocence, then to Russia I must go"
(185). When Laura asks if he cannot think of her grandmother, his wife,
Nikolai ignores the question as irrelevant in the greater scheme of his
own self-important life. Though Laura loves her grandfather and
recognizes kindness in Chubinov, she despises them for "behaving as
women would never dare to behave. . .They never need have started this

stupid game, and they could have stopped it at any moment they chose" (188-9).

The one woman in *The Birds Fall Down* who plays "games" to her own advantage is Susie Staunton, who comes to Laura's mind every time she has an angry thought about men's inconsistencies. The lovely blonde Susie feigns looks of wonder at the Rowans' wealth, acting shy and humble as if she "hunger[s] after plenty" (189), an act she apparently thinks will gain her affection, and that in fact succeeds in seducing Laura's father. Oddly, Susie is quite rich; Laura wonders "why she did not settle down to spending her huge income joyously" (188). Susie's hypocrisy parallels Edward's, Nikolai's, Chubinov's, and Kamensky's; she uses social conventions to hide motivations and actions contrary to those customs. But she is also an example of a person preferring the bad to the good, death to life, and in this she is specifically "like a man" (190): "She had great possessions, she had this hair, but she was racked, as if she were wandering waterless in the desert, by this phantom yet unassuageable need" (73). Susie must be attractive to Edward Rowan because of this negativity, for though she is golden and beautiful, the life-affirming Tania is even more so. The abandoned Mrs. Rowan despairs over this preference as a breached male pledge.

> What's unbearable to me is that I'm still beautiful. If I were old and ugly, then what's happened would be natural. . .But I'm beautiful and if he leaves me now, and our life is nothing but a form of desertion in which he both deserts me and is at my side to see how much I'm hurt at being deserted, then it means that he's rejecting my beauty, and my beauty is me, and I'm being rejected. But I can't say that, it sounds like vanity. That shows how impossible it is to be a woman. One's whole life depends on one's looks, but one mayn't speak of one's own beauty and one mayn't say either that it's specially galling if one's husband leaves one for a woman who isn't as nice as one is oneself. That would be counted as vanity too. (355-6)

Laura is also beautiful, but her conspicuous looks are a disadvantage in her precarious position, a fact partly comprehended by Madame Verrier, a French nurse of some mysterious ill repute who tends to Laura when she stays the night at a hotel in Grissaint. Laura is by this time finally without family supervision, her grandfather having died from the shock of Chubinov's revelation, and her parents unable to get to her before the next day. The three people who undertake her protection do so without realizing that she is in danger from a terrorist, and the way in which each perceives her underlines her dilemma. Monsieur Barrault, a doctor who reveres the classics, insists on seeing Laura as a model of "Virgilian" womanhood "who, when the wind is no longer tempered to her femininity. . .remains feminine"; he "shut[s] her into a book because he liked her appearance in the same way he liked the book, and he had no eyes for her real troubles" (316). St. Gratien, also a doctor, and a more intelligent and complicated man than Barrault, is struck as well by Laura's beauty, yet realizes that something other than grief is troubling her. If Barrault represents a man completely believing of human stereotypes, St. Gratien is one who recognizes the possible lies behind them, but who likes them anyway. His lover (it is implied) is the feminist Madame Verrier (one of the reasons, no doubt, she is considered "inappropriate"), who delights in smashing pre-conceived ideas about women. But St. Gratien admits a liking for traditional femininity. "I adore frills, but the women I adore always detest them" (264). This honesty is refreshing, and it is possible that St. Gratien would believe Laura's story of Kamensky the double agent, but, as he sees her as a young woman best left to the care of her parents—like Barrault—she cannot bring herself to trust him.

Madame Verrier alone believes that Laura is in danger. But the danger Madame Verrier sees is Laura's sexuality, so clear to everyone but Laura herself, who sees her beautiful breasts merely as inconvenient breeders of cancer. While Tania wants to believe in a patriarchal world (partly because she holds it ace, beauty), and Susie uses the "male" game of hypocritical self-effacement to get what she wants, Madame Verrier bristles with anger toward the sexual status quo, and goes against it to protect women from the consequences of social and sexual intercourse.[12] As a result, though she is respected, she is considered an unsuitable companion for the supposedly sheltered and aristocratic Laura. Exactly what she does is never stated, but the implication is not only that she engages in non-marital sex with St. Gratien; she probably performs abortions, an act that breaks the written laws of God and men, and that specifically puts the life of women over that of children or men, their traditional concerns. The drunken landlord (yet another self-deceiving man) toasts her, saying that "if she withheld her aid from those hapless girls who call her blessed," they would face "death and despair followed by a life of shame," at which point St. Gratien cuts him off with, "It's time you and I left the ladies" (274), ironically trying to protect Laura from the woman who considers herself the greater protector. Mme. Verrier constantly points out double sexual standards and rejects Catholicism, both of which make her unusual in Laura's acquaintance, yet the young girl thinks it "impossible" that the nurse could be "a bad anything," and rather that she is "uncomfortably good" (241). Madame Verrier is the only person to see that Kamensky pretends meekness when he is in fact proud and powerful, but she too, without a gun, cannot protect Laura.

The most ironic symbol of Laura's new and frightening situation is the ball being held at the Grissaint hotel. As Laura listens to the adults worry about her apparent dilemma as unchaperoned maiden, and as she desperately calculates the moves most likely to save her life, an orchestra thumps downstairs while the town's highest social circle dances, and all around her sigh that it is a pity she is in mourning when she should be waltzing. The disparity between Laura's need for real protection and the chivalrous defense of her feminine vulnerability that the men manifest points up the uselessness of their attitudes in Laura's unknown new world. She remembers the pre-dance ballroom as a sardonic emblem of her old illusive identity as feminine and romantic subject and object.

> . . .the ballroom returned to what it had been, to what it always ought to be, flooded with undiluted light. . .white like the icing on a wedding cake, and the nun-like women tending the floor and the men with green baize aprons gentling the harp and setting up the music-stands. . .On the top of the great ladder the girl still wrote great O's on the highest pane of the window with her yellow duster, O, I love you! O, I adore you! O, come soon and save me! The young man at the foot of the ladder holding a sheet of music, covered with great O's, sang nothing but made more O's with his open mouth, O, I love you! O, I adore you! O, come soon and save me! (278)

Still, Laura does expect her father to come and save her, as do all of her Grissaint chaperones. The turning point of *The Birds Fall Down* occurs when Edward arrives and not only does not save her, but increases her danger by allowing Kamensky to be with them at all times. Irked at this interruption of his life, he notices his daughter and her state so little that she realizes he would never believe her while wrapped up in his sexual infatuation. In fact, he had not come sooner because he had been with Susie when Laura's desperate telegram was delivered. Stunned by this betrayal, Laura knows that "she had stopped loving her father," and she says aloud, "There shall be no more sea" (336), paraphrasing Revelation 21:1: "And I saw a new heaven and a new earth: for the first heaven and the first earth were passed away; and there was no more sea."[13] But this new world will not be for Laura a glorious new Jerusalem. By using the language of the Bible, a book dedicated to the belief that a masculine God will save and that He is good, she accentuates the tragedy of her dispossession: the loss of faith in men as loving guardians for women. Laura's grandfather is dead; her grandmother is ill and her mother is emotionally destroyed; she dares not trust the Grissaint people; Kamensky is plotting to kill her; and now her father is loyal only to his adulterous lover. Extending her distrust of men to a rejection of a deity, Laura later has "no hope that

God would answer her prayer and kill Kamensky" (370). Only her knowledge that she wants to live rather than to die guides her now.

The way that Laura can live is to kill Kamensky, and, though the bumbling Chubinov actually pulls the trigger, she engineers his murder. By killing him, she is daring to act on her own against the "male" threat to sanity and life that he represents. Kamensky, like Chubinov and Nikolai, operates according to an abstract ideology. He justifies his position as double agent with Hegelian philosophy, saying that the thesis, antithesis, and synthesis stand for, respectively, the czar's kingdom, the revolutionary movement, and the "third [that] will emerge which will be superior" (298), and that by working for both of the first two he will be able bring about the last. Laura sees this as ridiculous: "If you asked a child. . .or a navvy working on the road who couldn't read or write, they'd tell you that was wrong" (297). Because of his homicidal intentions, Laura is forced to use the violence she deplores and that Kamensky and his two political groups have fostered. She herself would never kill for selfish reasons masked as ideology, but he has necessitated it. Murder breeds murder.

West emphasizes the male connection with death and the continuing presence of female strength in spite of oppression with two symbols at the novel's end. Nikolai's coffin is covered with a pall made by an ancestor, a woman who "centuries ago, had been imprisoned for many years in a fortress in the marshes, because a lesser prince had accused the prince her husband of betraying a greater prince to the barbarians" (385). In spite of this absurd waste of her life, the woman, sewing with a needle made from a nail, created a "beautiful, inimitable" work of art from an old gown; using the resources at hand, she carried her spirit forward hundreds of years. Laura saves Chubinov's life by hiding the pistol with which he killed Kamensky in an orange shawl and putting it at her grandfather's feet in the coffin, where no one will find it. The dead Nikolai then is buried with two tokens of the feminine will-to-live.

Yet *The Birds Fall Down* does not end hopefully. The women and men of Laura's family separate: she and Tania plan to go to Russia, while Edward and Laura's two brothers will stay in England. The women's ironic expectations of a better life, the reader knows, will not be fulfilled in the turbulent pre-Revolutionary country they will find; nor will Laura escape the "dust of tedium" she sees as "the male world" (293) in a Communist country ruled by ideologues as brutal as the Tsar or Kamensky. Moreover, it seems likely that the men they leave behind will stay as they are and even thrive, while Laura and Tania will be forced to endure an even lesser life than the London existence they flee. Just as Edward inherited his father's house, so Laura's brothers—whose absence throughout the book perhaps emphasizes the lack of male support in the Rowan family and in the world at large—will probably become, after Eton, heirs to their father's hypocritical sphere. Edward and his sons lose little; Tania and Laura lose all.

But the greater implication is that they have all lost men like Nikolai and the world he and his kind sustained. Despite his obvious narrow-mindedness, and the way that he twists reasoning around to suit his purposes, Nikolai is the most admirable human being in the book. He, unlike Nicholas II, Kamensky/Gorin/Kaspar, Chubinov, or Edward, is consistent in his thoughts and deeds, and his masculinity is an affirmation of strength as much as it is a useless obsession with religious, social, and political structures. Nikolai *is* the "grand" father West seems to desire, a man who rules not always well and fairly, but nevertheless rules. A dream Laura has about him the night before her apocalyptic failure of father-love illustrates the kind of relationship Laura, and perhaps by extension West, wishes to have with a paternal figure in spite of the strongly critical attitude she also cannot help having toward such authority. In this dream, Nikolai raises to Laura's lips a piece of *marron glace*, at which point she feels "as if her constant dream of being an animal had come true, and she had been changed into [a] tame fawn kept by the children of the house" (307-8)). She thinks that if she could hold her breath, "or pass some other magical test, her grandfather would speak to her in animal language and that she might understand and answer in the same tongue." Putting down the fork "with a sorcerer's gesture," he gives her a "long, secret-sharing gaze," and Laura's "heart melt[s] with love" (308). The dream indicates a wish fulfillment for clearly defined, traditional sex roles: Nikolai (father and husband) and Laura (daughter and wife) playing the roles of master and subjugated but cherished pet, sorcerer and apprentice, teacher and student.[14]

At Nikolai's funeral, he is denied, in his disgrace, the reading of a "Book of Remembrance, in which there's written down the names of everyone united to a man by a bond of a certain strength, a certain good will. All his relatives, all his close friends, everybody whom he has helped, his blind, his lame, his idiots" (364-5). In this new world of male dominance without male guardianship, represented by the lax Edward and the murderous Russian revolutionaries, Nikolai's legacy of paternal "good will" is forgotten, as is the larger inheritance of general paternal responsibility. Chubinov may be a good man who takes action against evil, but he is also weak, shabby, and ridiculous; Laura cannot stop comparing his fragility with her massive and once-powerful grandfather. Chubinov will live out the rest of his life as an obscure teacher in England, hiding from murder charges and imagining that "the future" belongs to the revolutionary group opposed to Lenin, while Laura sees that "conspiracy was for him. . what cricket was for her fathers and her brothers. . .It was his kind of fun" (409). Even the good man is so caught up in "games" that he cannot see the practical consequences of his abstract theories. The women have no choice but to live on their own without fathers, brothers, or husbands, making their own choices and hoping that they can escape the death, physical or spiritual, that either patriarchy, English or Russian, might bring.

West never created a nearly perfect fictional father, as she did a nearly perfect son in Richard Quin. Her only trustworthy "fathers" are Mr. Morpurgo and Uncle Len of *This Real Night* and *Cousin Rosamund*, although Mr. Morpurgo's wife and children do not love him, and Len has no children, both factors pointing to the unlikelihood of successfully realized paternal relations. Together with Piers Aubrey—who has committed suicide by the time either makes an appearance as surrogate Aubrey father— they hold a triad of paternal qualities that, were they combined, would form West's ideal father. Mr. Morpurgo gives to the Aubrey women worldly knowledge, money, and an affection that amounts to worship. Len shelters them, and his wife and Aunt Lily, with physical strength, an unswerving confidence in his own traditionally masculine roles, and a sympathy for their lives as women that is unique in West's canon. He is especially protective of plain women, having a "tender concern for what would not be cherished" (*This Real Night*, 74). But Piers is mentally "great," with a greatness that grows in Rose's mind as the trilogy progresses: he represents, in spite of West's criticisms of it, the artistic and intellectual achievements of Western patriarchal culture. The Aubrey family remains loving to Piers's memory even while they are grateful for the absence of the trouble that inevitably accompanied him, and all agree they would give up anything—which includes, for Rose and Mary, their careers—if they could have him back. Having a father, even one so flawed as Piers, is better in its imperfection than living more peacefully but less happily without one.

Still, mothers are the ones in West's novels who hold together families and by extension lives, and generally their vigilance must make up for paternal negligence. Clare and Constance raise their children in spite of, rather than with the help of, their spouses; Marion Yaverland, for all the thwarted sexuality her relationship with Richard represents, has to take on the parts of father and mother, and she manages to bring up a son capable of great worldly success. In all of the lives of West's "good" mothers, and even in the lives of the "bad" ones, this vigilance means the sacrifice of their personal development or desires. West both adores and abhors this maternal immolation. The differences between the mothers in her first two novels and those in the *Cousin Rosamund* trilogy demonstrate in some ways her early socialist feminism, which emphasized the emptiness of women's parasitic lives, growing into her late conservatism, which glorifies male protection of women. They also exemplify her ruthless examination of both the positive and the negative sides of the famed maternal instinct.

One of the most maternal of West's characters is no longer a mother: Margaret of *The Return of the Soldier*. But she is the most obviously nurturing character West created, a woman whose life has been dedicated to other people. Ironically, Margaret's son died, and this is the great sorrow of her life. She moans to Jenny, "I want a child!" when she thinks, at the novel's emotional climax, that the world has "all gone so wrong" (176), and her child's death is a sign of the imbalance between life and death represented by World War I. Yet the fact that her care is given not to a child but to a man emphasizes the importance of this quality. Margaret is a symbol of goodness, which equals an "engenderment" of the best human qualities to which the male war is opposed; Chris's embrace of Margaret is a rejection of the "horrors" that "modern life brought forth" via "adventurous men [who] have too greatly changed the outward world which is life's engenderment" (63-4). He can hide from his memory of the male death wish, so perfectly embodied in World War I, in "the passion of her motherhood," strong enough to "bring God into the world" (172).

But as a person who cares most about the welfare of others, she knows that Chris must be made aware of the truth for his own sake and for the sake of the women who depend on him financially and emotionally, Jenny and Kitty. These two cling to the idea that the doctor will "cure" Chris with a sound science, but it is Margaret who comes to the doctor's aid and realizes that a memento of the son Chris and Kitty lost will restore Chris's adult memory. This highlights the complete lack of motherhood in Kitty, and thus her unwillingness to sacrifice her own wishes, when she tells the doctor that she "didn't think it mattered" (169) that they had had a child. Margaret sees, as even the Freudian psychiatrist cannot, what will bring Chris out of his willful, imaginary adolescence, because she does not follow any particular "method" but her instinct and her observations. This involves a definite sacrifice: once Chris remembers and acknowledges his marriage, Margaret's chance to be with him will be gone, and she will go back to her own marriage, which is also for her a maternal relationship, but without the sexual love she and Chris share. Still, it is what she must do. Jenny, who has neither husband nor child, believes that women desire to give this maternal love above all else, and that therefore Margaret has a blessed life in spite of her poverty and plainness. Seeing Chris asleep next to Margaret, she thinks that

> . . .it was the most significant as it was the loveliest attitude in the world. It means that the woman has gathered the soul of the man into her soul and is keeping it warm in love and peace so that his body

can rest quiet for a little time. That is a great thing for a woman to do.
I know there are things at least as great for those women whose
independent spirits can ride fearlessly and with interest outside the
home park of their personal relationships, but independence is not
the occupation of most of us. What we desire is greatness such as this
which had given sleep to the beloved. (144)

Margaret's personal connection with Chris makes her care so
effective. She, to go back to Gilligan's point that women see problems
contextually and relationally, sees the unique person and situation for
what it is, even though Chris's ailment can be termed "shell shock" and
he can therefore be lumped in with the many soldiers who suffered it.
She also, as a mother, believes in fathers; it is part of making him
drink "the wine of truth" (182) to see that his must be a paternal and
protective role, as hers must be one of sacrifice. Margaret is not a
problematic character, as *The Return of the Soldier*, though its language
and narrative viewpoint are subtle and complex, is not difficult to grasp.
Margaret is the good mother, as Chris must become again the good
soldier; she is eros, to which Chris returns after the thanatos of World
War I.

The Judge, however, is a problematic book, most particularly in the
character of Marion Yaverland. She is the most extreme example of
West's sacrificial, nurturing mothers, and also the one most damaged by
the father of her children and the fact of her motherhood. Marion, as an
unwed mother and thus a social pariah, suffers for her maternity in
many ways: by the marriage of her lover Harry Yaverland to another
woman, which means she gets no help raising Richard and no sexual
love; by the mental and physical abuse her neighbors heap upon her;
and by the rape she endures from the man she marries in a moment of
weakness brought on by this abuse, which causes her to have a son she
cannot love. But rather than reject motherhood altogether as a result of
these problems brought on by pregnancy and birth, she focuses all her
life and emotion on the first born. She is so wrapped up in her son
Richard's life and the circumstances which surrounded his conception
and delivery that she is a confirmed Westian "idiot" (unlike Clare
Aubrey or Margaret) who believes that "women are such dependent
things" (239) and that the "work of giving life" is a woman's "only
justification for existence" (254). The frequent descriptions of Marion's
body as "inert" but "powerful," the rich, beautiful clothing she wears,
her dramatic presence, and the restlessness that plagues her make ironic
her statement that women care only for personal relationships. It is
clear she has chosen this path of obsession with her son and her
abandonment by his father, and that she has enormous energy which
simply goes unused in her insistence that "thinking about subjects

unconnected with her family [was] as unwomanly as a thin voice or a flat chest" (340).

Ellen's mother Mrs. Melville, who has also been abandoned by the father of her child, is conversely quiet, economical, and "bird-like." She is truly dependent on her daughter, since Ellen supports them both, and Ellen sees her as the model of what a mother should be: "little, sweet, and moderate" (393). Ellen has grown strong partly as a result of her mother's lack of strength. But Richard, for all his physical prowess, is weak because of his mother's strength. Richard adores his mother, appreciating her adoration of him: "I tell you, mother, it's kept me going to think of the sacrifice you made for me" (338). Yet it is because of both their mothers that he and Ellen must finally separate. Richard kills Roger in a rage brought on by Marion's suicide, after Ellen has a vision of her mother's sacrifice:

'Tis I who made you do it. I thought of my poor mother and how she'd suffered through not making my father think of her first and last - and you were sitting there thinking of nothing but Marion - and I knew if you heard what Roger was saying about us you'd think of me. (427)

Richard exclaims to Ellen, "Between our mothers. . .If we could have lived our own lives!" (427).

But it is because of the fathers that these mothers have so aversely affected their children. In *The Judge*, West spares no man; it is a novel fueled by rage, written during the last years of West's involvement with Wells and in her first years of single motherhood. Here West seems to make an allegory of what might have happened to her had she not had a professional writing career to occupy her mind and time. Marion turns to maternal love because she has no sexual love to satisfy her intensely sensual nature, which makes Richard, out of guilt and fear that he will relive his father's abandonment, unable fully to love another woman. Ellen must suffer for her mother's unhappiness because her father made her mother unhappy: thus the subtitle, "Every mother is a judge who sentences the children for the sins of the father." Both Marion and Mrs. Melville are dead at the novel's end, killed by a disregard neither Richard nor Ellen can rectify, no matter how they act or agonize, but which will haunt them the rest of their lives, and will in fact make them relive the pattern of maternal sacrifice and paternal neglect. It seems only a full-blown tragedy, replete with two dead bodies at the end, will express adequately the mess Richard's and Ellen's fathers have made of their children's lives (and, implicitly, that Wells had made of West's by making her his mistress rather than his wife).

But what of the sexual energy between Richard and Marion? It is hard to miss. "[Richard] drew [Marion] into his arms. She tried to beat herself free and twisted her mouth away from his consoling kisses. .

presently she stretched out her hand and pressed back his seeking mouth" (339). Yet it is tempting to skip over it in analysis (as Wolfe, Deakin, and Orel all do), since it presents the reader with a tough puzzle. Why, when Marion is portrayed so obviously as a victim of male neglect and abuse, is she also such an unpleasant character? What is West doing by creating this Freudian melodrama of a son unable to get past his Oedipal conflict, whose mother must commit suicide in order to allow her son the freedom to love another woman, a son who must actually kill his brother, the only conceivable rival for his mother's love? Jane Miller sees *The Judge* as West's attempt at "the impossible": "it is, quite simply, Jocasta's story. . .[it provides] a woman's version of the dilemma posed but not faced by Freud in his Oedipus complex." The novel is often "shatteringly bad," Miller claims, because "it is not bearable to embody the rages and passions of a woman who takes the mother's legendary role literally" (97).[15]

I believe West here shows that the vaunted female role Patricia Meyer Spacks calls "taking care"—"the arduousness with which [a woman] trains herself, and is trained, for proper self-forgetfulness in the role of wife and mother"—can be as devastating as it can be life-enhancing.[16] Not only is the woman herself held back from a full life; her children can suffer from too much attention, from carrying too much of the weight of mother-love. West's use of Freud here works in two ways. First, she echoes his pessimistic conclusion that the family romance dooms all human beings to an impossible attempt to balance the id's incestuous desires with the superego that forbids them (another reason for the Wagnerian tragedy of *The Judge)*. Second, and more significant to my argument, the sexuality Freud sees between mothers and sons works here as the token of any improper relationship between mothers and children. Ellen's guilt is as burdensome as Richard's. If Marion has made herself conspicuous through a constant dramatic melancholy that Richard cannot ignore, and which he wants to mend with the masculine attention she does not receive from an appropriate man, Mrs. Melville's very self-effacement has caused Ellen to fear desperately the same fate, and to make her, like Richard, think she must make amends to her mother's memory. The tragedy that befalls the young couple is directly related to their mothers' overwhelming sacrifices. Ellen sees herself becoming less central in Richard's attention, and so fears becoming her mother; Richard hears Roger aiming accusations of "beastly lust" at himself and Ellen—exactly the crime of which Marion was considered guilty—and so, by killing Roger, kills all of the people who have tormented Marion. But this means separation from Ellen and the abandonment of their child: exactly the crime of which his father is guilty.

Marion Yaverland is weak, in spite of her powerful body and personality, to have allowed this mother-obsession to occur. West does not excuse her, in spite of the obvious sympathy with which she portrays Marion's passion and loneliness. The reader can only hope that Ellen Melville *is* choosing "the side of victory" (430), as she believes, when she decides to stay with the man she loves, and that she will somehow learn a way to raise her child outside the shadow of her sexual loneliness. Marion, in this case, may serve as a useful warning, as her own mother may. She may also be a preview of what Ellen will become. The dedication of a mother's life to her children will be positive or negative depending on the mother's character, but also on the father's actions. Richard and Ellen have a choice.

If motherhood brings out the worst in Marion, it brings out the best in Clare Aubrey. She is a mother who follows the pattern of received neglect and consequent sacrifice that Tania, Margaret, and Marion do, but her offspring do not come under threat of terrorists, die in infancy, or murder their siblings. Clare raises a mostly admirable slew of children. Not only this sets her apart from the rest of West's fictional mothers: she is also an artist who had a successful career before marriage and maternity.

In many ways the *Cousin Rosamund* trilogy—written during the 1950s and set in the first thirty-five years of the twentieth century—both rehearses and subverts conservative ideas about women's social and domestic roles that were in vogue after World War II. Just as they had during the first world war, women during the second were encouraged to work in place of men who had become soldiers. But, as Gilbert and Gubar point out, the propaganda encouraging women to join the war effort also stressed that they were only substitutes who would, and should, return home once the war was won, and that social ideologies "reified gender arrangements as rigidly as they had been demarcated in the Victorian period. . ." (*Volume 3,* 216). The British, exhausted and horrified by direct contact with battle, longed to return to the apparent safety of traditional families, and to reverse the falling birth rate that seemed to threaten the social and economic health of their country. Yet that same postwar economy had a need for women's work that conflicted with this glorification of the domestic homemaker. As historian Jane Lewis points out, the 1949 British Royal Commission on Population encouraged women to be both mothers and workers outside the home, even "express[ing] the view that there was nothing inherently wrong in the use of contraceptives"; yet simultaneously "the Ministry of Health was closing day nurseries, opened during the Second World War, on the grounds that stable family life required full-time mothers. . ." [17]

With Clare Aubrey, West appeases several sides of the conflict between work and motherhood within what Lewis calls "the familialist ideology of the 1950s" (178). Clare stays home with her children, which is hardly surprising given that she is a middle-class Edwardian mother, and based on West's own mother. But unlike Isabella Fairfield, Clare teaches her daughters to become professional musicians. Thus she works, but within the home; she earns no money, but she saves the expense of music teachers and prepares her children to enter the work force. Plus, she has four children rather than the three Isabella Fairfield had, and one is a son who will ultimately become a soldier, so she does her duty by a depleted British socioeconomic structure that might again face the threat of war.

Artistry is the greatest gift she passes on to her four children, the glue that holds the family together before and after Piers's death, and in this she differs from a traditionally imagined domestic mother, who would nurture and love her children but probably not educate them in a demanding artistic skill. In this Clare represents not just the real Isabella, who was a pianist (though none of her daughters became musicians); she offers a maternal artistic heritage to children whose father is usually absent, especially to her daughters who will literally inherit her vocation. In this vein, Margaret Diane Stetz diagnoses West's "female affiliation complex," which Gilbert and Gubar name as a preoccupation for all twentieth-century women writers. Stetz discusses West's recurrent adulation of painters in both her non-fiction and fiction as a strategy for identifying positive male role models, who offer "the possibility of a refuge, a realm of stillness, away from the sound of the critical voices of male writers and of her own angry responses"; and she connects West's use of music to this strategy.

> By moving outside the sphere of literature and into the realm of the other arts, she was able to locate models with whom she was not in direct competition. . .precursors who, in comparison with their literary equivalents, could stand as benign and welcoming fathers.[18]

Stetz's persuasive theory that West sought to avoid competition with male writers highlights a strong tension that runs throughout the *Cousin Rosamund* trilogy, between Rose's virtual worship of her mother's genius and her acknowledgment that Clare wishes to be subordinate to her husband. It is significant that music is the medium with which Clare expresses herself and teaches knowledge. Music does not consist of words; it is an expression of thought and emotion that need not impart an absolute meaning, but in fact suggests something unique to each hearer. Nevertheless, it follows its own rigid rules of form, and one can only perform it well with laboriously achieved skill, so that its creation or performance requires discipline and inborn ability.

An interpreter and not a composer, Clare does not "create" with her music, as Piers does with his writing, so she does not threaten his masculine and paternal territory. Neither is she trying to prove her point of view or effect social change, which are part of that same territory and aspects of Piers's journalism. But she constantly proves her aesthetic, physical, and academic mastery of music. For a woman in the late nineteenth century, Clare's musicianship is remarkable. While young aristocratic ladies had been encouraged to take up an instrument for centuries, she is a pianist good enough to tour professionally and to teach her daughters to become equally competent.

Moreover, her artistry is not in acting or dancing, areas in which women had traditionally excelled and in which a woman's body is her tool of expression. Mastering a musical instrument means leaving behind, in some sense, the awareness of the body other than the hands or the mouth or the feet, and certainly for an audience of classical music the focus of a concert is the sound itself rather than the sight of the performers. This is something singers cannot claim, since serious singing requires entire upper body coordination, and specifically highlights the fact that the sound is issuing from a human being. In Clare Aubrey's late Victorian and Edwardian days, women were usually singers if they were serious musicians. Patricia Meyer Spacks offers this explanation for why women's artistry was often limited to dancing, singing, and acting.

> [There is a] conflict between the yearning for artistic expression and the desire for relationship. . .[and] women are likely to experience it with special intensity. Feminine narcissism as traditionally defined centers on love for one's own body and involves the desire to attract men sexually. The artist's narcissism, on the other hand, connects itself with the sense of creative power, the need to express preceding the need to attract. . For a woman, the artist's power - assertive, insistent, dominating - combines uneasily with orthodox feminine modes of attraction. If she performs as a dancer, singer, actress, the potential incompatibility may be resolved: offering herself as an artistic product, she offers herself also as sexual being. (166)

Clare does not see herself as only a sexual being, and this is a precious legacy that she bequeaths to her daughters. The very problem with Cordelia's violin playing, as previously discussed, is the fact that she is only interested in presenting herself as a pretty girl, not in producing the music intended by the composer; Clare's despair over Cordelia's pathetic musicianship reflects the nearly religious feeling Clare has for music as an expression of truth and beauty, and her freedom from the desire to use music as a platform for herself. Rose recounts with pride the fierceness of her mother's musical integrity, and the ruthless honesty with which she handles her daughters' attempts at piano playing. Clare does not attempt to spare her daughters the most rigorous practice, since their femininity does not excuse lesser artistry; nor does she worry about being polite or kind, both ostensibly female and maternal qualities. She is, in her artistry, androgynous, even if within her marriage she performs traditionally feminine roles.

An extraordinary incident from *The Fountain Overflows* illustrates Clare's odd, admirable mixture of androgynous artistic sensibility and Victorian wifely piety. Piers commits adultery with the Lovegrove mayor's wife, though it is easy for the reader to miss the fact that this has happened, since Rose relates the episode as she experienced it when a child, and never directly says that her father was unfaithful to her mother. Clare receives two visits, one from the mayor and one from his wife, that upset her. The children assume that Piers must owe them money, and brace themselves for humiliation. But nothing much happens except that Clare suddenly sits down to read *Madame Bovary* from cover to cover, she and Piers argue frequently for the next few weeks, and they receive more visits from the mayor. Rose says little more about it, since Christmas, a wonderful and creative time for the Aubreys, overcomes the family tensions. The adult Rose's narrative voice winds up the mayor's wife episode with this brief explanation having more to do with the Aubreys' Christmas than with the devastating fact of her father's affair.

> By the first week in December Papa and Mamma were at work together sharing secrets and hiding things. . .I, who loved him too and can see him from a better distance, am sure that he had left the Mayoress of Lovegrove with an abruptness that broke the poor silly's heart, because his fingers were itching for the pleasure they were always given at this time of year, his imprisoned imagination insisted on its annual holiday. (54)

Rose forgives her father this ultimate breach because of his creative ability, aimed for once at giving his family pleasure. It is an oddly gentle forgiveness, given West's hatred for men's "insane sexual caprice" (*Judge*, 429). But more significantly, Clare's behavior illustrates her transcendent nature, rooted in an artistic empathy that sees beyond her individual experience. Instead of instinctively railing at her husband, she immediately understands the Mayor's wife as a type of Madame Bovary, a bored wife seeking excitement with a fascinating man like Piers, and she copes with her own jealousy by imagining her husband's lover's pain. Clare turns to art for solace, for the expression of the larger truth within Piers' infidelity. She also accepts that she must cope with knowledge of the affair and carry on with her marriage regardless; her strong love and sense of family duty overcome her individual agony.

Rose and Mary were not born with and never achieve, in Rose's opinion, the genius or ability of their mother, though Mary plays "like an angel, as if she came straight from heaven" (*Fountain Overflows*, 310). In fact, she is superior to her sister, something Rose must face before she goes to college and begins the exhaustive stretch of work that precedes her concert career. This sibling rivalry exaggerates Rose's fear of failure at the emotional close of *The Fountain Overflows*, but its strongest causes are both reverence for her mother and anxiety about her own inadequacy in light of her parents' energy and brilliance. Thinking that it is her "father and mother who existed" rather than she, Rose sees her accomplishment as that "which had been transmitted to me by my mother," something "pitifully diminished in the transmission, I was so much lesser a thing than she was" (312-3). Throughout her career, Rose hears her mother's voice urging her on to further work, greater realized expression; she imagines her mother wincing over performance errors as admirers and even peers would not. Even the "ruin to which [her] father dedicated himself" is "nearer salvation than [her] small safety could ever come." It is an "impossible task" to live "on the same scale as [her] mother and father" (313). To do that means to be an artist and a parent, and to take on, as Piers and Clare did, the responsibility of transmitting a tradition of sure sexual and artistic identity. Rose's anxiety of influence takes the form of thinking the past greater than the present or future can be. She does not imagine surpassing Piers or Clare.

Still, it is Rose who accomplishes what neither of her parents did: a consistently successful career that ensures economic stability and a definite place in society. In a sense, Clare has created in Rose (and Mary) the artist as career woman that she did not become when she chose to marry and have children. Part of the sisters' rejection of marriage involves rejecting their mother's life of sacrifice, even though that sacrifice is what enabled them to exist and to be musical artists. In this the *Cousin Rosamund* trilogy fits with Rachel Blau DuPlessis's description of the twentieth-century women's *Kunstlerroman*, in which a daughter "becomes an artist to extend, reveal, and elaborate her mother's often thwarted talents" (93). Rose and Mary also shun the masculine economic and sexual capriciousness their father constantly manifested and embrace the feminine group identity Clare has fostered in the Aubrey girls, Kate, Constance, and Rosamund. When Rose thinks at the end of *The Fountain Overflows* that she does "not want to grow up" (313), she is fearing, along with musical inferiority, connection with a world of men that has had little directly to do with her woman-centered family life. As Nina Auerbach describes it, such a "community of women" directly rebukes "the conventional ideal of a

solitary woman living for and through men, attaining citizenship in the
community of adulthood through masculine approval alone."[19]

But that fear is what Clare does not want Rose to feel. When Rose
wonders why Constance married Cousin Jock, Clare answers
immediately, though in a "voice thin as a wisp of mist, 'how could she
have got Rosamund if she hadn't married someone?'" (92). Though
aware of her own sacrifices in matrimony, Clare does not want the girls
not to marry or to be mothers. She is a true artist—as Rose is
eventually—but she is also a mother. The strength of her maternity
outlasts the strength of her art, though she manages to pass on the
latter with the former. Rose's artistic anxiety about Clare fuses with her
fear that she will not love as her mother did, and that she will be
unable, as Clare was, to put others before herself. This tension is at
least partly resolved in *Cousin Rosamund* by Rose's marriage to Oliver,
and with Rose's rescue of awkward but brilliant Avis from a loveless
life lit only by music. But, as Rose is middle-aged when she marries, it
seems unlikely that she will have children of her own, and so her fears
are at some level justified. She is the mirror opposite of Clare: she
achieves professional success, but not maternity. The Aubreys' story
does not answer directly the question of whether both can be achieved in
one life, but, significantly, none of these women do. Such a synthesis
therefore seems, if not impossible, at least very difficult, and unlikely.

The *Cousin Rosamund* trilogy is a testament to West's appreciation
of the parental influence in her life and art. The recreation of Isabella
Mackenzie Fairfield as Clare is a gift to her mother—Isabella
Mackenzie was probably not the superlative musician Clare is—as her
creation of Piers is both wish fulfillment and assuagement of old
pain—Charles Fairfield left Cissie earlier than Piers leaves Rose, and
the fictional character is more heroic than the real.[20] The novels also
offer representations of her archetypal parents: Clare as the nurturing,
teaching, life-affirming, always present mother; Piers as the brilliant,
creative, but death-desiring and ultimately absent father. Clare's love
flows toward her children and her husband, while Piers's love largely
goes out to the world in the form of political journalism and activism.
His defense of Queenie Phillips, which saves her life, and his
chaperonage of Aunt Lily prove him a man capable of the social
masculine protection West craves, and one able to manipulate the world
with his mind and will. Richard Quin inherits this, though none of
Piers's daughters do. The son will be a writer; he will speak in the
language of the patriarchy, and leave to his sisters the preservation of
the non-lingual art that has been passed on to them by their mother.

Since West was a writer, and not an actress as she (and countless
other young women) imagined at seventeen, her choice to give back, in
a sense, the written word to fathers, and by extension brothers, seems a

plea for her own femininity and maternity after a career of "masculine" journalism and a famously bad relationship with her own son. In the *Cousin Rosamund* trilogy, West recreates her life as an artist in a way that is non-threatening to male creativity: by making Rose an interpretive artist. Her autobiographical character, while voicing anxieties any artist might feel about great predecessors, does not, with her music, go out and make statements that criticize men and a man's world, as West did with her writing. She thus avoids what Elaine Showalter names as the "self-centeredness implicit in the act of writing [that] made this career an especially threatening one" for women (22). Instead, Rose summons beauty from music composed by men. And if in fact West believed that she did not exist and work at the superlative level of Charles Fairfield, in her autobiographical *Kunstlerroman* she sidesteps competition with her real father, and by extension the fathers of literature, philosophy, religion, and politics, by assuming instead her mother's career.

Plus, Rose's childless state perhaps indicates that West thought she would have been a better artist and person without having had a son. The sacrificial lives she imagines for Clare, Margaret, Rose, and Marion do not show the road West took. Her career, rightly or wrongly, took precedence over Anthony West, and West suffered criticism for not having put her child over her art. Bonnie Kime Scott reports that in a late interview West "offered the opinion that the world does not forgive a bad mother" (*Vol. 2,* 197). These fictional mothers may be an answer, both angry and appeasing, to those critical voices.

West also creates the son she never had, as she creates the mother she never was. Her bitter relationship with Anthony West was perhaps the greatest agony of her life, and her creation of Richard Quin in some sense rebukes her own son for his continuous, and publicly shared, sense of injury. Anthony West, in his 1955 novel *Heritage,* wrote his own autobiographical *Bildungsroman,* portraying his mother as a brilliant but selfish and melodramatic actress who neglects her sensitive son. *Heritage* was published as West was writing *The Fountain Overflows,* and it occasioned a spate of literary gossip that wounded West deeply. But West, rather than satirize her son in fiction directly as he had his mother, instead responded by showing Anthony all that he was not in Richard Quin. Anthony had never been a good student, and as a young man seemed something of a dilettante, attempting a career as a painter before turning to writing book reviews and fiction. Obviously Anthony would have been threatened by his famous parents' success, and in fact most of his early journalistic work was commissioned from contacts his mother supplied. Yet Richard Quin succeeds in everything he does, and specifically through connections he makes independently and outside the family's sphere. He inherits his two parents' best qualities, since he is both writer and musician, and thus he is the culmination of their abilities as well as the innovator who will forge new forms in the future. Anthony, on the other hand, was following the path his parents had trod, but with far less genius and originality. Perhaps more cuttingly, in *This Real Night* Richard Quin becomes a popular "man's man," a superb sportsman and an avid, skillful soldier. Anthony, conversely, was not athletic; nor was he willing to fight in World War II, implying to his mother that he would let other men do the fighting, an attitude that appalled the now hawkish Rebecca West.[21]

But Richard Quin's purpose in the *Cousin Rosamund* trilogy transcends West's implicit belittlement of Anthony. Not only does he seem, like Rosamund, irrefutable evidence of good in a universe rife with evil; he represents ideal masculinity, and a positive male superiority to and protectiveness toward women. The fact that he plays many instruments without steady practice, while his sisters play only one that they mastered after years of work, indicates his greater ability and wider artistic and intellectual reach, as Jock is a greater flautist than Clare is a pianist. But still West is pessimistic. Richard Quin's death in World War I cuts off his words. Jock's consuming negativity silences his music. Male ability, in the face of the overwhelming masculine death-embrace, will not overcome, even when women step aside and encourage men to have the more significant voice.

West's model of a good family in many ways copies the one Western culture has put forth as the ideal, what Gilbert and Gubar describe as Freud's "traditional middle-class family plot. . .the nuclear family dominated by a superegoistic father and sustained by a nurturing mother. . ." (*Vol. 3*, xv). West still grants the father the last word and superior intellectual abilities. But she wants him to use them responsibly; she wants him not to give up in the face of evil, as both Jock and Piers do, or to create elaborate abstract theories that ignore people and actual circumstances. And she wants fathers to love and to protect their daughters, as mothers do despite the world's cruelty: to connect, in Forster's phrase. But she is angry at them, with an anger that floods her novels and non-fiction. Her mothers give up too much in return for too little. The publication of *Family Memories* proves that the last thoughts West was having about fathers were not hopeful.

In her fiction, West illustrates the problems inherent in classic parental roles without advocating an absolute solution. Looking back to a time of definitely divided labor based on sex—from the 1890s through the 1930s—she shows how women were, and are, stifled by motherhood, but also that maternity can be a form of heroism that makes up for paternal weakness and passes on needed strength to a new generation. She deplores irresponsible fathers, yet she does not want to do away with patriarchal structures that perpetuate male dominance, because women then fall when they are removed. Those are the means by which things get done, she seems to say with such characters as Chris, Richard, Nikolai, and Piers. But just what the balance of nurture, labor, autonomy, and artistry should be for mothers and fathers is a Gordian knot she leaves tied and uncut.

When one looks at West's life, her support of women's and men's traditional paternal roles seems less convincing than the sweeping certainty of her fictional narrative voices might imply. West in fact took on her father's and not her mother's profession. Richard Quin could be the person she wanted to be as well as the man she wanted as a son or father or husband. Perhaps most tellingly, none of West's protagonists is a mother except Marion, a tragic woman whose fellow protagonist Ellen will take on her role in the tragedy. West's fiction, when studied in the context of her life and times, illustrates the complexity of affiliation for twentieth-century women, who have made tremendous gains in legal and professional equality, but still live within a world that rewards paternal authority and maternal sacrifice.

Notes

1. Carol Gilligan, *In a Different Voice: Psychological Theory and Women's Development* (Cambridge: Harvard University Press, 1982). Further references will be to this edition, identified by page numbers in the text.

2. Bonnie Kime Scott, in a discussion of *The Judge,* also points out that West "anticipat[es] the work of Carol Gilligan." See Volume II of *Refiguring Modernism*, 131.

3. See, for instance, Carol Tavris, *The Mismeasure of Women* (New York: Simon and Schuster, 1992), and Joanna Russ, *What Are We Fighting For?* (New York: St. Martin's Press, 1998).

4. Elaine Showalter in *A Literature of Their Own* discusses early twentieth-century novels by women as "anti-male, both in the sense that they attacked 'male' technology, law, and politics, and that they belittled masculine morality" (242). West certainly shares this sense, but by the time of World War II she had begun to see "male" technology as a necessary evil, and an aspect of the world men must not shirk as a result of being threatened by female equality.

5. Jane Marcus, "Rebecca West: A Voice of Authority." In *The Faith of a (Woman) Writer*, ed. Alice Kessler-Harris and William McBrien (Westport, Conn.: Greenwood Press, 1988): 237. This article praises the surety with which West tackles controversial subjects. "For seven decades Rebecca West's writing, fiction, essays, and literary and political criticism, has been a voice of female authority whose clear ringing tones have roused the faint-hearted feminists during doldrums and bounced off the barricades in times of struggle." Grouping her with George Sand, Mme. Stael, George Eliot, Harriet Beecher Stowe, Mary Wollstonecraft, Olive Schreiner, and Virginia

Woolf, Marcus applauds the "moral imperative in these voices of female authority, the political criticism of patriarchy and capitalism, [which] is the backbone of their artistic bodies."

6. For instance, in "Charlotte Bronte," West says, "Tolstoy is as fully sentimental a writer as Charlotte Bronte. In *War and Peace, Anna Karenina,* and *Resurrection,* he pushes his characters about with the greatest conceivable brusqueness in order to prove his thesis, and exhorts his readers to accept his interpretations of their movements. He even admits in *What is Art?* that he thinks this the proper way for the artist to behave. . [T]his use of art to prove what man already knows is a shameful betrayal of the mission of art to tell man more than he knows. . .He attempts to influence his readers in favour of a thesis dependent on the primitive sense of guilt, and the need for expiation by the endurance and infliction of suffering. . . (*Celebration,* 436).

7. "My Father" is one of the bitterest statements West made about Charles Fairfield and about men in general. She reviles Fairfield for being "continually and frenetically unfaithful to [her] mother, who was in love with him. . .[he] had a taste, which showed him to be either a sexual maniac or to be idiotically rooted in the eighteenth century, for having sexual relationships with the women [her] mother employed, as servants or governesses, and with prostitutes" (203). But the short essay ends with an affectionate childhood story in which she embraces him and is and "swung up into his tobacco-ish warmth" (208).

8. See *A Celebration,* xvii, and Carl Rollyson, *The Literary Legacy of Rebecca West,* 211.

9. Sister Mary Margarita Orlich and Loretta Stec both discuss *The Birds Fall Down* in their dissertations.

10. Rebecca West, *The Birds Fall Down* (New York: Popular Library, 1966): 9. Further references will be to this edition, identified by page numbers in the text.

11. Kamensky is based on the infamous Yevno-Meyer Fishelevich Azef, the leader of a strong Russian terrorist organization in the early twentieth century who was eventually identified as an active police spy and exposed as a double agent. His downfall led to Lenin's ascendancy.

12. Loretta Stec reads Madame Verrier as representing a "faint feminist hope" within a pessimistic novel: "[She] suggests that female friendship, comradeship, and cooperation are indeed possible," and that this character undercuts West's vision of the "sense of the futility of progress, (or nostalgia), a belief in the unchangeability of human nature" that is "at odds with her feminism and the possibility for progress, especially political progress" (240-1). Madame Verrier at least attempts change in spite of her bleak view of human nature.

13. This apocalyptic phrase had powerful meaning for West; it appears again in *Cousin Rosamund,* when Kate quotes it to Rose after meeting Rosamund's repellent husband for the first time. This emphasizes the enormity of their loss when Rosamund cleaves to him instead of the Aubrey family and their circle.

14. During West's analysis with Mary Wilshere in 1927, West "recovered" various memories of possible sexual abuse from her father that

in later life she discredited as "latent highly disguised sexual fantasy." One
of her recurring images at this time, which she called an "animal fantasy,"
was of her father urinating in a grove as naturally and openly as an animal,
juxtaposed with Lettie's censoring face. Musing on the way "animals were
free from the taboos of sex," West concluded, "if my father and I were
animals we would be free to enjoy each other" (Rollyson 115). The memory
of this fantasy may have inspired Laura's dream of her grandfather and
herself as animals.

15. Shirley Peterson reads *The Judge* as "an inviting allegory of the
women's movement in its immediate postsuffrage phase as it sought a
modern identity in the overwhelming shadow of presuffrage feminism."
Marion, the representative of the "mothers" of the suffrage movement, is
for Ellen "the site of conflicting desires and realities related to the
'liberated' woman," and Ellen learns from Marion's experience "how
strenuously patriarchy seeks to divide the sexual woman from the mother
woman." As I do, Peterson sees Ellen's fate as potentially tragic, since
"feminists handed down the patriarchal sexual code that ensured
condemnation of the sexually deviant woman," and Ellen's exile with
Richard "suggests imprisonment rather than escape. . . ." "Modernism,
Single Motherhood, and the Discourse of Women's Liberation in Rebecca
West's *The Judge*." In *Unmanning Modernism: Gendered Re-Readings,* ed.
Elizabeth Jane Harrison and Shirley Peterson (Knoxville: University of
Tennessee Press, 1997): 105-116.

16. Patricia Meyer Spacks, *The Female Imagination* (New York: Alfred
A. Knopf, 1975): 87. Further references will be to this edition, identified by
page numbers in the text.

17. Jane Lewis, "Myrdal, Klein, *Women's Two Roles* and Postwar
Feminism 1945-1960." In *British Feminism in the 1920s,* ed. Harold L.
Smith (Amherst: University of Massachusetts Press, 1990): 178-9.

18. Margaret Diane Stetz, "Rebecca West and the Visual Arts," *Tulsa
Studies in Women's Literature* 8:1 (1989), 43-4. In a discussion of *Harriet
Hume,* Bonnie Kime Scott also claims that "[m]usical accomplishment and
self-expression could be considered another tradition in female modernism"
(*Vol. 2,* 141).

19. Nina Auerbach, *Communities of Women: An Idea in Fiction*
(Cambridge: Harvard University Press, 1978): 3.

20. In the *Family Memories* chapter called "My Relations with Music,"
West writes, "My defence has been the capacity for pure pleasure inherited
from my father and mother. The pleasure with which he used to paint water-
colours, rather in the Lear manner, and talk of historical and political
matters, say the philosophy of Burke, which made him glow; the pleasure
with which she played Schumann's *Carnaval,* and looked at the mellow brick
and creamy stone of Hampton Court or the Georgian houses round Ham; that
pleasure was my perpetual anaesthetic and stimulant, and because of it I have
not had such a bad life after all" (220).

21. See Rollyson *Rebecca West: A Life,* 197.

Chapter 4

Marriage and Martyrs

I realized that when Christ met the woman of Samaria, He was grieved because she had had five husbands. But it never occurred to me the reason for his grief was that she had led a riotous life of self-indulgence and immorality. I thought that He was angry because she had thrown happiness away by taking a husband, which of course meant that she became poor and had to do work that spoiled her beautiful hands and had to wear ugly clothes and generally destroy herself, and then had not realized her good fortune when her husband died or went away, but had taken another one. And to go on doing this five times over would of course make Christ very angry. It was like going bankrupt five times, or being sent to prison five times for an offense one could easily avoid committing: a perverse revisitation of squalor. "I Regard Marriage with Fear and Horror"

The goddess who is the most potent embodiment of good in this group of immortals [Catherine Linton in *Wuthering Heights*] consorts with the embodiment of evil, loving it, for love does not disdain evil - but it destroys her. *The Court and the Castle*

Reviewing Victoria Glendinning's biography of Rebecca West, Samuel Hynes records a sentence that puzzles and disturbs him, from the first page of West's then unpublished memoirs *Family Memories* (which she later put near the end). "I was never able to lead the life of a writer because of these two overriding factors, my sexual life, or rather death, and my politics" (*Family Memories*, 223; Hynes, 48). That is a strong statement, but it is characteristic of the intense tone West takes when discussing personal disappointments. Hynes wonders, "What did she mean by sexual death? The end of her sexual activities? That's sad enough. Or that her whole sexual life had been a death? That's a good deal sadder." Glendinning prefaces this sentence with the statement that "Rebecca West would have liked to be loved as a woman by a man who knew her 'distressing multiplicity' and remained unshaken. She never resolved the general problem of men and women. . ." (250). That is a great understatement. West grew more bitter in her pronouncements about men as she grew older, and by the time of *Family Memories*, she

110   *Paradoxical   Feminism*

saw all of her romantic relationships as failed and believed that her work was tainted by this failure: "My work might have been as important as either [my marriage or my politics] if it had not been condemned to exist in limbo" (223) due to this "sexual death."[1]

Whether or not West's sexual life was a "death," as she believed, she constantly probes in her novels the problems that plague the intimate relationships of men and women, especially in the context of marriage. The fact that her own marriage was sexually barren after the first five years must have contributed to her pessimistic thinking about sexual happiness and fidelity in marriage, as her position as Wells's mistress and her father's affairs gave her strongly negative opinions about adulterous sex.[2] Neither of her two primary sexual relationships was satisfactory. Wells, said West, "devoured [her] youth and nagged and bullied [her]" (Glendinning, 192), and though Henry was sweet and outwardly devoted, he had a series of extramarital affairs that West discovered after his death. He was, moreover, "a very inconvenient husband for a woman writer" (Glendinning, 249), one who had no strong work life of his own to occupy his time and mind, and a man who was apparently slow and pedantic in his speech and thought. As mentioned previously, Hynes comments on the strangeness of this marriage, as do others. It seems a generally accepted fact that West married for a security she never really achieved; many of her letters record her dissatisfaction with Henry.[3]

But she insisted on loyalty in marriage, and never separated from Andrews though she complained often of his eccentricity and flirtations. West's feud with Anthony really began when he separated from his wife and planned to marry another woman. Though he reconciled with Kitty, his first wife, at that time, he later divorced her and married a girl in her teens. Rebecca West refused to see her grandchildren by Lily, this second wife, and ultimately broke with her once-adored grandson Edmund, Kitty's child, because he too divorced and remarried. She had, as Glendinning says, a "terror of broken marriages in the family and of men's 'abandoning' women" (259), obviously formed from her father's desertion and her sense that men are as sexually inconsistent as wild animals.

West's tragic sense of marriage, tied as well to her criticism of men as overly abstract, impersonal thinkers, shows up early in her career. In the 1925 article "I Regard Marriage with Fear and Horror," West claims that she wants "more than anything else in the world to know the truth about everything," yet that her views on marriage are immutably tainted by the negativity in her own parents' marriage.[4]

> Indeed, it is not that I do not like men. I like them very much. . .But nevertheless I feel marriage, the entry into a permanent and public and State-aided alliance with a man, as the rashest conceivable act. .

This is a pity, because intellectually I am now convinced of the
desirability of the institution of marriage. . [since] marriage is of use
for riveting the fact of paternity to the male mind. . .[it helps him to]
imagin[e] his child in relation to the world rather than to himself.
[and] turn it into a social triumph in the world that is based on the
family system. . .[A woman] will, therefore, if she is a conscientious
person, realize that it is her duty to submit to the institution of
marriage, since only by its agency can the man's primary duty of
fatherhood and his secondary way of thinking be reconciled. (210)

That obligation to "duty" appears repeatedly in her novels, accompanied
by the simultaneous "fear and horror" West so passionately relates.
Critics often quote a sentence from *The Judge* as a summary of Westian
sexual pessimism. When Ellen waits at the novel's end for Richard to
make love to her for the first time, she thinks that "though life at its
beginning was lovely as a corn of wheat, it was ground down to flour
that must make bitter bread between two human tendencies: the insane
sexual caprice of men, the no less mad excessive steadfastness of
women" (429). Here West grants the two sexes a seemingly equal
weight of guilt in making the "bitter bread" of sexual relationships. But
her novels focus on male culpability more often than female, even
though they show women knowingly going into and staying in
marriages that will entail suffering.

Many of West's fictional wives are martyrs for their husbands (or, in
a few cases, lovers) and the general "cause" of their marriages. These
wives are not only the sacrificing mothers I have discussed, but they are
admirable women who try to "save" flawed, even evil, but brilliant men
from the fate of unrealized potential or undefined disaster. In doing so,
these women often leave their own lives unfulfilled or unhappy, yet
they win an almost saint-like battle for the forces of good over the
forces of evil: a Manichaean fight for light over darkness. Their
victories involve the familiar surrender of a woman's life to that of a
man's, but not because of traditional pressures so much as a courageous
decision by the woman to perform this personal quest. West has a
heroic vision of life, describing it frequently in terms of conquerors and
martyrs and cowards and the brave. The marriages in her novels,
especially the later ones, are as much battles for men's and women's
right and wrong roles, sexual and otherwise, as they are in D.H.
Lawrence's, though in her case the soldiers are women. She writes, in
"Woman as Artist and Thinker," that "women express in life a force
which is opposed to the force that [men] themselves represent."[5] She
wants husbands to be as strong as she wants fathers to be, and part of
what her wives attempt is to goad men into that strength and to a
defiance of their dark inclinations.

But West does not advocate male supremacy in marriage for the same reasons Lawrence does. They share a belief in strong gender boundaries and essential sexual characteristics, both having a dualistic sense of life and of human beings; West thinks that women and men see different "bricks" in the universe.[6] Both see sexuality as life-affirming, the "secret web of nakedness" that kept the earth "from being naked of people, chilly with lack of love and life, a barren top spinning to no purpose" (*Cousin Rosamund*, 235); and both argue for marital fidelity. Yet West, though she grants husbands dominance, does not wish to focus on men as the rightful recipients of sexual pleasure, as subduers of the destructive female will, or as powerful tribe members who will leave their wives to tend the home so that they may pursue great philosophical and political futures. West sees women as the saviors of men, and part of what they need to be saved from is the celebration of pure masculinity that Lawrence desires (in some of his writing). Masculinity without femininity results in a drive toward death, West believes; it is women's work to temper it.

Still, this martyrdom is not usually joyous. At some level, Lawrence's fiction fulfills personal fantasies about his masculine sexuality: he creates male characters with his physical characteristics, whom he grants hypnotic erotic power and who have relationships with women that he wished to have. His triumphant men can achieve their desired roles through sheer will, often without compromising their distinct ideologies. West does something similar, yet with significant differences. She reveals the pain of her own fears by creating women with the same problems she felt she had in sexual relationships, then by imagining what they could do, usually in the way of building up their men, to remedy those problems. Lawrence feared impotence; West feared that she made men impotent with her intellectual and artistic achievements. Lawrence invented men who could not, or would not, be conquered by women; West invented women who could, but chose not to, conquer men. Her female characters are what she was not: dominated, and in love with their dominators. Usually they are as aware as West would have been that in accepting such relationships, they forfeit some honesty and much opportunity. But the love for a man, and the moral sense that selfishness is the worst sin, win out.

West, like Lawrence, creates in her novels a myth: in her case, that of the female martyr for the male hero who needs her help to realize his destiny, to be sexually fulfilled, and to stay sane. Within this myth there is plenty of anger at women's subordination and treatment. West believes that men are threatened by feminine sexuality, so sexually vibrant wives are cheated on for less threatening women, and sensual lovers are scorned for cold wives. She sees women as victimized by their own maternal, pitying tendencies, since men will take advantage of women's kindness and persuade them to stay in relationships that are destructive. But West also excuses some male behavior. She creates fictional men who are overburdened by social, political, and economical demands and who then collapse, mentally or physically, under the strain: "great men" whose sexual relationships suffer for understandable causes. And she shows, finally, one good marriage in *Cousin Rosamund*—that of Rose and Oliver. Their relationship is a serious, and more consistently successful, version of the mock-marriage between Harriet Hume and Arnold Condorex. The *Cousin Rosamund* trilogy also contains two characters (that West considers) nearly perfect in their sexual personifications, Rosamund and Richard Quin. This chapter explores West's fictional marriages: how and why they work and do not work, what constitutes "correct" sexual identity, and the myth of martyrdom in which she enfolds most of her wives.

Sunflower—drafted, interestingly, in roughly the same period as "I Regard Marriage with Fear and Horror"—shows no actual marriages firsthand, but it presents most of West's ideas about the problems in long-term sexual relationships. It is also, as I have said, an exaggerated version of West's own desires for male domination and a traditionally "passive" female life centered on a man, a home, and children. What is odd about Sybil's desire for domination is not just that it comes from Rebecca West the feminist, but that Sybil has already been so mentally (if not physically) dominated by Essington that one cannot help but wonder why she wants more of the same when this relationship makes her feel like a "trapped rat" (1). Sybil's world, for all her fame, is small, and there are few characters in this unfinished novel, particularly women; Essington "loathe[s]" his "Sunflower" having friends, and she has "almost none left" (20). The only other woman who appears more than a few times is Etta, Pitt's sister, who is also dominated by a "great" man, and who sees Essington's treatment of Sybil for what it is since she suffers the same from her brother. Her parallel existence of subordination emphasizes Sybil's and hints at less than benevolent qualities in this man so worshipped by the actress. Significantly, and paradoxically, *Sunflower* shows its protagonist longing for a state the novel insistently illustrates as unfair.

An incident in the first chapter serves as an example. Sybil's car breaks down in the afternoon, stranding her and her chauffeur in the country and affording her free time away from work and Essington that she rarely gets. Exhilarated, she visits a courtroom and witnesses an old woman named Alice Hester on trial for bigamy. She seems to Sybil a representative of fecund, traditional femininity, a natural giver, "a very good old woman" who makes one think "enviously of how much she would have done for one if one had had the luck to belong to her": "She was like a barn full of grain" (29). The oddity of her presence in the prisoner's dock is not lost on anyone in the courtroom, and as she tells her story, all are sympathetic. When young, Alice married a poor agricultural laborer who drank and abused her, and by whom she had ten children. He tried to make this family go into a workhouse when the strain of supporting them seemed too much, and when she refused, he locked her and the children out of the house one night when drunk and disappeared by the next morning (as another overburdened laborer, Walter Morel, locks out Mrs. Morel early in *Sons and Lovers*, possibly a deliberate allusion). A young ploughman who worked at the same farm as Alice's husband offered to move with her and the children to a different district and to say that he had married her as a widow, an offer Alice gratefully accepted. They had a child of their own together, "and all was nice and decent for forty years" (33). Eventually he became ill and needed a stomach operation, a procedure he did not expect to live through. His strongest wish was to marry Alice before he died, and though she knew "quite well that it was not right to do it" since her lawful husband was still alive, she felt compelled to it since her "man want[ed] it so bad" (33). This man did indeed die after the marriage and the operation, so Alice was guilty of bigamy for only a few days. But unfortunately, her sister's grandson was staying with them and witnessed the bogus ceremony; he turned Alice into the police.

The most striking thing about the story, besides its plot, is Alice's charity toward all the principal players. It was not her husband's fault, she insists, that he drank and "knock[ed] her] and the children about so that it could not be borne" (32), because he came from a bad home and had had an "outlandish" upbringing, and because their cottage was a poor place and they had only twelve shillings a week. Tom, the sister's grandson, is excused as well for his laziness and meanness: "'Tis not his fault. His mother was frightened by a ferret when he was on the way" (33). The man who asked of Alice that she risk being arrested for bigamy by marrying him (for she knew that the boy was following them to the registry) could not be disappointed: "with my man set on marrying me, what could I do?" (33). She even forgives the policeman who performed the arrest, for she "knew it was right he should take me to the station" (33). Alice keeps asking what else she could have done in order to avoid either breaking the law or displeasing another person, "as if she really wanted an answer"; she feels that life had forced her to these decisions, but she would rather blame herself. Sybil imagines that Alice "was willing to clear God's character at the expense of her own" (34), as if this woman were out to shoulder all the responsibility in the universe and to forgive all representatives of masculine authority right up the hierarchical ladder.

But Alice is innocent of anything but a technical crime—specifically, and ironically, related to treachery in marriage—and her willing acceptance of punishment makes her an unconscious martyr for her husbands, both of whom are guiltier, in some sense, than she. She has not attempted personal gain in either liaison. The breakup of her first marriage was not her fault, as having ten children, one assumes, was not necessarily her desire. Alice opposes her husband, Amos Bullen, only because she will not allow her children to endure life in a workhouse. She goes with Stallibrass, the laborer who takes her in, for the sake of her children's support, and she "marries" him to make him happy. Amazingly, while living with Stallibrass she has even been sending Bullen, in the workhouse where he ends up, money for little extras, "baccy and that" (33). She will inherit nothing from Stallibrass though she is now his wife. It is she who will be indicted for the crimes her husbands forced upon her, but she would rather take the punishment herself than see one of them suffer it. Alice is almost a caricature of unselfish virtue, but Sybil views her hungrily, as if she is Demeter or an icon of a specifically feminine religion that opposes and triumphs over masculine ideas and faith.

> Looking at this old woman made her feel as she sometimes did in church when she looked up at the cross over the altar; only this feeling did not run up and lose itself in the empty sky. Looking at Alice Hester one looked down, towards the ground, and one's feelings seemed to run along the earth, to delve into it, to shoot up into the light, triumphant. . .Religion was like everything that men made. It was all very fine but it didn't work. . .It has to be tethered to people's attention by pretty services with incense and vestments and music; by creeds that men can argue about without coming to any conclusion that has to be acted on. . .What men do is thin as paper, dry as dust. But this other thing. . .Without being reinforced by being talked about, since it could not be put into words, it had survived for seventy years within this body that had never been beautiful, that had been starved and chilled, vexed with rough clothing, hurt by blows, deformed and torn by baby and baby, laid waste altogether by age. And it had worked. How it had worked! (34-35)

Sybil's worship of Alice Hester, then, includes an appreciation of her martyrdom: the life force that overcomes male injustice but supports men, and that cleaves to earth-bound "feminine" processes in spite of those who would interrupt them. It comforts Sybil to realize that Alice cannot read or write, since ignorance seems to make an alliance between them; Sybil thinks almost gratefully, "So she also was stupid" (36). The difference between Sybil and Alice, thinks the former, is that Alice would always know what to do in any human situation because "she was inspired" (36), unlike Sybil, whose acting is famously uninspired. Men, and the role-playing that they necessitate, always stand between Sybil and her "natural" self.

But Sybil behaves to Essington, and to other men, in a manner not unlike Alice's. She sacrifices her own wishes to please him. Even staying with him she does out of pity and intimidation rather than the desire to be his lover; every time she threatens to leave, he breaks down like a child and cries in her arms, begging her not to give him up, until she gives in out of sheer kindness. Consequently, she suffers the stigmatization of being a mistress while being deprived of her main objectives, marriage and children. Yet he is a "great man," and this makes Sybil think his behavior and her martyrdom justified, the way Alice excuses her husband his abuse because of the pressures of his hard work. That Pitt would be any different from Essington is not clear, and in fact seems unlikely. "The point of the novel was to be," writes Glendinning in an afterword to *Sunflower,* "that great men—such as Wells [Essington] or Beaverbrook [Pitt]—spelled death to a woman's sexual and domestic happiness and personal autonomy" (275). She quotes West's notes on "The Theme of the Book."

> I. Women have remained close to the primitive type because doing the same job - wifehood and motherhood. Men have departed from the primitive type because they are doing utterly different jobs.
> II. The type of civilisation men have produced demands great men - greatness that presses too hardly on the men. They are bound to buckle under the strain. (276)

Sybil wonders what the alternative to such "greatness" is for men. "What was it then that a man ought to try to be?" (50). She concocts a pastoral fantasy starring herself and Pitt as a possible answer, one that brings Pitt back to the "primitive" in the way she has supposedly retained in spite of her career and childlessness. Imagining him to be a pre-modern man who has not been forced into duality—"He seemed to have been created before the human soul had split itself up into these subdivisions" (48)—Sybil dreams of Pitt as the essence of ancient masculinity in "an age when words were not yet important" (49). Her recurring image, obviously drawn from ideas of Native American life, pictures her standing next to a fire in a wood by a lake as Pitt drives a canoe full of food for her and their children toward her. He is a "man with strong arms, with broad shoulders, who crie[s] to her across the water, a round-mouthed cry without words. . ." (49). This imagined Pitt would have only to worry about the getting of food and shelter for his family, not complicated businesses and political enemies and alliances as the real man does. He would not sacrifice his relationship with the woman who loves him for these pressures. This vision leads back, again, to "I Regard Marriage with Fear and Horror," where West claims that men's spiritual separation from their roles as husbands and fathers can be traced to the loss of a patriarchal agricultural society: the mere "decorous performance of routine" in modern industrial society weakens their positive, nurturing "primitive characteristics" (210).[7]

But Sybil's vision is only that; its unreal nature becomes evident when she must give comfort to Pitt the way she gives it to Essington, for decidedly modern troubles. Pitt, when he is distressed, becomes as unaware of her as Essington can be. Sybil's reaction to her new love is the same: she wants to give him comfort, she wants to give him her life as a way of compensating for the theft of his life by the strain of being a "great man." When they declare their love, Pitt asks, "You understand, Sunflower, I want you to give me your whole life? Would you do that for me?" She asks back, "amazed, 'Why, what else would I do with it?'" (259-260). The reader has seen the result of Sunflower giving her "whole life" to Essington, and despite West's intention of elevating Sybil's potential relationship with Pitt over her past disasters with Essington, the basic connection seems bound to be the same. Sybil will sublimate her own desires in order to build him up; she will be so convinced of his superiority and importance that she will martyr herself for the cause of Pitt's burdensome greatness.

Sybil's belief that what men do is "dry as dust" conflicts with her apparent belief that men's "greatness" excuses their childish needs and tantrums, and illustrates again West's consistently punitive way of ceding men their traditional superiority. If she grants men political and intellectual dominance with such characters as Pitt and Essington, she undercuts their portraits so acidly that their "greatness" can only become ironic. Sybil's sacrifice therefore seems wasteful rather than admirable, and male "greatness" inevitably diminishes when it must be sustained by such sacrifice. "The Abiding Vision" from *The Harsh Voice* has a similar theme in its story of two women who lose beauty, health, and individuality taking care of an American businessman. But in it West clearly intends to criticize the cultural tradition of female self-abnegation that creates the twin martyrdoms of wife Lulah and mistress Lily for the decidedly ungreat Sam Hartley, who at the story's end is hungering for a new girl to dedicate herself to him. The narrator of "There is no Conversation," also from *The Harsh Voice*, sees her two marriages as service to bad and good men, not as choices she made for herself. She seeks from solid Nancy Sarle the assurance that Nancy ruined Etienne de Sevenac out of love, as if this could convince the narrator that her ten years as his wife was somehow justified: "I wanted her to tell me that she too had found it possible to love a cad. . .that some circumstance connected with this anguished sacrifice of my best years to a cheap and empty man made all of it worthwhile" (128-129).

About her current marriage she seems curiously dispassionate. It has "been building up a tranquil home for people who are among the salt of the earth" (129), but not much else. Living for others has left her empty.

Sunflower's emptiness comes not only from her isolation as Essington's mistress, but from the knowledge that he treats her badly while he treats his wife well. She believes he does this in part to strengthen his control over her, and because he cannot show kindness to a woman he desires sexually.

> It was [a] sort of prudent investment he had made in his wife, Mabel, whom he had selected as the woman he was good to. He had given her everything material she could want, that fine quiet house in the country which he visited politely and did not rush into to upset, and a great deal of money. . .he wrote to her every other day when he was away, not scratching letters saying that he had been thinking over her last performance (for one thing, the lucky woman did not have to give any) and it was so stupid that he would have to leave her, but friendly letters suggesting ways by which she might get her gentle pleasures out of life; then, since he could not enjoy being the lover of a woman to whom he was kind, he turned to his mistress and could enjoy illimitably his relationship with her because he could make her life a misery, and always argue that that must be her fault, since he was a kind man to women, and could prove it by his relations with his wife. (153-154)

These thoughts, Sybil believes, make Essington "utterly inhuman," and a "monster." Yet she still forgives him, thinking that "he did not mean it," but that his "false religion of thought" (154) compels him to act this way. Of course, Mabel too probably suffers from this imbalance in her relationship with the great man. Essington may be kind to her, but he does not (apparently) make love to her; and whether or not this is a mutually satisfying arrangement is never made clear. What is clear is that Essington divides his loyalties absurdly between the two women, one representative of sexuality and thus inferiority, the other of economic responsibility and respectability but therefore not eroticism. This theme—men's social and legal sacrifice of the sexual to the non-sexual woman, which coexists with omnipresent images of women as desirable objects—recurs in much of her work, and connects to Western culture's distinction between sacred and profane love.

Nicola Beauman, analyzing portrayals of marriage in women's novels from 1914-39, observes this division, and traces it to early awareness and appropriation of Freud. Using Mrs. Dalloway as an example of a wife who is "not an object of sexual desire for her husband," she claims that

[t]his concept held sway not only in fiction but also in upper- and middle-class life. In Freud's 1912 paper "The Most Prevalent Form of Degradation in Erotic Life," he argued that very few cultured people can achieve an ideal fusion of tenderness and sensuality, and that this manifests itself in a lack of sexual desire for women who inspire affection - in other words the well-brought-up wife. (125)

Harriet Hume's Arnold Condorex manifests this inability to fuse "tenderness and sensuality." From the book's first page he views sex as a punishable act, something mysterious and secret to be hidden from unseen spies. We first meet Harriet and Arnold scurrying like mice down from her bedroom in the afternoon, whispering "as if they feared to awaken sleepers," though soon Arnold is swaggering "back into the daylight, challenging it to punish one for having been where one had been," claiming that "Kensington. . .has been waiting for us all the time! It has been threatening us! . . .It is saying it will get us yet!" (7). They see a family going out for a summer walk—two fat parents and two fat children—and then Arnold changes the afternoon's imagined menace from the undefined penalty for enjoying extramarital sex to the specific dullness of married life. "It is threatening us that some day we will spend Saturday afternoons not at all as we do now, that instead we will go and take tea with Grandmamma. . ." (8-9). The message is clear: sexual pleasure will not coexist with matrimonial domesticity.

It is just at this point—when Arnold is forewarning Harriet, if unconsciously, that she will not always shine in his life as she does now, whether she is mistress or wife—that Harriet first hears Arnold's thoughts in her own mind, as if her ability comes with the necessity to protect herself. Later that same day she receives, via this same clairvoyance, blatant information on Arnold's marital ambitions.

[H]e wondered how soon he might chance on some undesired woman [who]. . .could be quickly got and would be a stairway to better things. The plain daughter of a Privy Councillor had been his thought, which had been expanded into a consideration of what ways he might use. . .to enjoy Harriet till the last safe moment and then disembarrass himself of her. (55)

Such a preference for the less beautiful woman over the more beautiful not only goes against Harriet's moral and aesthetic views, as the narrator has just explained them; she considers that she has been a "giver" to Arnold, both by telling him a story (about the Dudley sisters) and by sharing her body. This is important, since it "is the special hardship of women that it is their destiny to make gifts, and that the quality of their giving is decided by the quality shown by those who do the taking" (55-56). Harriet is willing to give to Arnold anything he wants so long as his desires remain as purely motivated as her own, but she will not knowingly be, unlike Sybil, the mistress sacrificed to the wife who embodies his ambitions. By making love with him when he entertains such thoughts, she feels she has made herself "easy"; but now, with psychic power, she will not make the same mistake. Arnold's excuse—"A man must rise in the world!" (56)—does not excuse him.

Arnold's subsequent marriage to a woman even more beautiful than Harriet, but much less lovable (she is the daughter of a rich, important statesman, and possessed of little personality and less intelligence) eventually proves the truth of Harriet's earlier observation: "Write me down. . . as all that Arnold Condorex rejected" (93). But his wife, while outwardly perfect for an ambitious MP, finally seems physically repulsive to him, "limp as an anchovie" (138), and Arnold (one assumes) shuns her sexually, fulfilling his earlier playful prophecy about boredom in marriage. Though Harriet does not become Arnold's lover again until their union after (apparent) physical death, they remain in sporadic touch, mostly because Harriet comes to Arnold, like Sybil to Essington, out of pity and concern for his problems as a statesman. But there is more to it. Arnold and Harriet are as clearly "meant" for one another as lovers in a fairy tale. The irony of Arnold's intent to destroy his "opposite" before she destroys him is that Harriet is his salvation, a fact emphasized by their heaven-like alliance at the novel's end. She will not martyr her earthly life for him, choosing to lose his sexual love rather than exist as an illicit sweetheart, but she will die in order to be with him in the right way: as his first sexual *and* matrimonial choice. Harriet will even forgive his initial intent to murder her, so strongly does she want to marry him.

Yet they *are* "opposites." Though West mocks the exaggerated femininity of Harriet Hume and the way the insistently masculine Arnold Condorex sees her as ethereal, insubstantial, intuitive—all the qualities Harriet both accentuates and belittles in herself—the two are nevertheless secure and even "correct" in their sexual identities as West presents them. Part of Arnold's mental journey to the point where he can love Harriet as she deserves, which includes sexual desire not separate from legal and economic union, is to accept his feminine opposite and to stop trying to make her life as unpleasant as possible, as Essington, Sunflower believes, chooses to make their life a hell instead of a heaven. Harriet makes this journey possible by pitting her feminine faith and love against his masculine hatred. She teaches Arnold that he has to conquer his dislike for Harriet as a woman before he can love her as a woman, and that he must accept her strong sexuality (Harriet apparently has many lovers before and after Arnold) as a part of her makeup. He also must stop blaming her for his self-induced troubles, another of Essington's tricks.

Harriet even leads Arnold to believe that his conquering masculine sexuality has won her, as her femininity has redeemed him. In a humorous passage, she loses her protective ability to read his thoughts (calling them a "gross pretension to innocency" and "a plaguy gift") at the moment he points his phallic "pistol" at her: "[You] spurred me to consider our true positions in the universe" (275). They agree that both of their qualities are needed in the world instead of the dominance of one over the other, though Harriet's artist/woman preoccupations will be less "potent" than Arnold's political and male actions.

> "Why, what was the use of me being so innocent in this g-g-garden," she bleated into her handkerchief, "when I had no power to impose my state on the rest of society? I may have been innocent, but I was also impotent. . .I should be churlish if I blamed those who have the power I lacked, and went out into the world, and did what they could or what they knew to govern it. Humanity would be unbearably lackadaisical if there were none but my kind alive. 'Tis the sturdy desire you have to shape the random elements of our existence into coherent patterns that is the very pith and marrow of mankind. . .Did you not see to the building of bridges, the teaching of children, the suppression of riot and bloodshed?" (266-7)

Arnold grants the importance as well of Harriet's role, both as an artist and a woman, which is "contemplating the eternal beauties" (267); but Harriet still claims that the end of this, if it is one's only occupation, is "smugness, and stagnation, and sterility!" (268). As the book closes, she busies herself happily with "housewifery" (276), seemingly done forever with being a concert pianist and ready to be Arnold's dedicated lover and servant. Arnold claims that Harriet will be enough for him in this new death/life, relieved that he need not make the house "a palace" or his wife "an empress" (284). Both have relinquished their particular obsessions once their "true positions in the universe" are adhered to and enjoyed.

Written in the 1920s during the era of "high" modernism, *Harriet Hume* is West's most overtly modernist work of fiction in its focus on character and psychology rather than plot, its heavy use of myth, its stream-of-consciousness depiction of Arnold's mind, and its lushly poetic language. It explores more explicitly than any of her novels the "sex antagonism" she frequently depicted and deplored, and in its style and subject she comes the closest to emulating Virginia Woolf than she does anywhere else in her canon. Rollyson points out that while West was working on *Harriet Hume,* she "realized that Virginia Woolf in *Orlando* was grappling with the same set of issues" (*Literary Legacy,*

67): in part, the constructedness of gender that Harriet both mocks and encourages, and that she tries to teach Arnold to see.

Yet again, perhaps West's novel explores, and then deliberately rejects, the separate room for women that Woolf advocates in *A Room of One's Own*—which came out a year before *Harriet Hume*—and that by emulating Woolf's fiction style to make, in some ways, the opposite point, West was making this clear. Showalter's description of the "female aesthetics"—Woolf, Dorothy Richardson, and Katherine Mansfield—could then function as an articulation of West's criticisms. In these feminist modernist writers' subversions of traditional expository narrative, Showalter argues, their "deliberate female aesthetic. . .transformed the feminine code of self-sacrifice into an annihilation of the narrative self" (33). *Harriet Hume* could in some ways be a parody of this very "annihilation," in its narrative focus on Arnold rather than Harriet, which emphasizes the emphatic mystery of Harriet's mind. Moreover, Showalter claims that these "female aestheticists"

> saw the world as mystically and totally polarized by sex. . female sensibility took on a sacred quality, and its exercise became a holy, exhausting, and ultimately self-destructive rite, since women's receptivity led inevitably to suicidal vulnerability. (33)

Harriet's willingness to commit suicide for Arnold fits this definition of a peculiarly female mindset, as the deliberate duality of male and female throughout the novel supports this sense of a polarized world, and Harriet's clairvoyance represents such a "sacred" feminine sensibility. But Showalter also defines their "sexual ethic" as androgyny, which "provided an escape from confrontation with the body" (33); and Harriet's strong sensuality and adoration of masculine power obviously rejects an androgynous viewpoint. Moreover, her desire to join with Arnold rather than stay isolated in her garden home with her music and flowers indicates that "a room of her own" no longer satisfies her desires. While the two sexes are clearly different, West implies, they need, and want, each other. West ultimately rejects the "separate but equal" viewpoint.

Nevertheless, though *Harriet Hume* is a light-hearted novel, West's pessimism about marriage is evident there. Only in fantasy (the book's subtitle is "A London Fantasy"), or only in a life not on this earth, can the two opposites, man and woman, share "A Very Happy Eternity" (288). It is also hard to believe that Harriet has really made a good choice in giving up her life and artistry to live with Arnold, though he does seem better off without his wife Ginevra (who matches *Villete's* Ginevra Fanshawe for shallowness) and his ill-gotten, deceitful political career. Arnold gives up a bad life for a good afterlife; Harriet loses her satisfying and meaningful existence as a musician for an eternity of "housewifery."

Harriet Hume, published in 1929, was written before West's marriage and after her relationships with Wells and Beaverbrook. Glendinning and Rollyson both name the chapter that covers this period "Sunflower," to connect the sexual loneliness and isolation West was feeling and was blaming on her literary success with her desire, like Sunflower's, for marital love and security. West wrote to her sister Winnie, "[Men] sit and gaze at me with adoration at parties and go away and talk about me rapturously as the most marvellous woman on earth—but they refrain from taking any steps about it whatsoever. . .It's obvious that men are terrified of me." Claiming that she "loathes life" without a man, West continues, "I can't bear to feel that I will presently have to build up a position in the world simply by dominance, when I could have done it if anybody had let me simply by being a human being" (Glendinning, 117-8).

Harriet, like her fellow pianist Clare Aubrey, does what West often imagined in her fiction but never did; she gives up her career so that a man will not be threatened by her "dominance." But she makes the story specifically an allegory—the only one she wrote—as if she could not imagine Harriet's and Arnold's happiness as a realizable reality: as if Arnold, as threatened man, would never really lose his sex-antagonism and be kind to the woman he desires sexually, or that Harriet, as successful woman, would never really relinquish her new artistic power to build him up.

Though West originally intended *Harriet Hume* to be a novel about feminism, H.G. Wells liked it partly because he approved what he saw as its theme of women's secondariness.[8] It was, interestingly, West's favorite among her novels.[9] It may be that, though Rose Aubrey is West's most autobiographical character, Harriet is the closest thing to a wishful self that she created. Many write of West as having been beautiful, especially when young, but she was not delicately built, consistently impeccable in her dress, or deferential to men, all of which contribute to making Harriet the essence of femininity.[10] Sunflower is supposed to be one of the world's most beautiful women, but she is untalented, and thus too unlike the brilliant West to be her fictional alter ego. Harriet combines beauty with great artistic perception and ability, as West did, but she is an expert, literally clairvoyant, at pleasing men, a talent West often felt she did not possess. *Harriet Hume*'s "happy" ending reflects West's desire to experience a sexually and emotionally fulfilling marriage, but also her belief that such a marriage is possible only when a woman has deliberately assumed a secondary position.

The Aubreys' cousin Rosamund is the more mature West's more realistic invention of what she considers an ideally feminine woman. She is of central importance in the trilogy that bears her name. From early in *The Fountain Overflows* to the end of the unfinished *Cousin Rosamund*, she represents to the Aubreys a continuity and stability that withstands poverty, treacherous fathers, several deaths, and a world war (in fact both world wars in West's original plan), to name some of what the family endures. Rose and Mary look to Rosamund as if she is a saint who can guide them through life as through a maze, and West intended for her—and her male counterpart, their brother Richard Quin—to stand for "all that their art did not give them," which is "in fact, religion."[11] Rosamund is West's female martyr incarnate: Rose and Mary were meant, in the unwritten fourth volume of the *Cousin Rosamund* trilogy, to discover that "Rosamund is a woman who died in Belsen Camp, and as they look back through the past they realise that all she did was planned to the one moment described by [a] witness, when she appears as doing a deed of unique mercy" (294).

What particularly needs explaining about the past is Rosamund's heretofore inexplicable marriage to a crass and dishonest Middle Eastern billionaire whom she clearly does not love, a union that dismays her relatives and creates a distance between Rosamund and the Aubreys that never before existed. It appears to the world that Rosamund has married Nestor Ganymedios for his money, but the people close to her cannot believe this, since she has never done a selfish thing. *Cousin Rosamund* is a novel about marriage, and most of it satisfactory, which makes its treatment there unique in West's fiction. Four of the main characters get married, three of whom are unlikely candidates for the altar and who seem to marry, as Rosamund says of Nancy Phillips's fiance, the only person he or she could possibly have married (*Cousin Rosamund*, 17). That the exception is Rosamund, whose beauty, youth, and goodness make her appear destined for and deserving of great love, is significant. Part of Rosamund's martyrdom is to be with a man who takes her from what is most important to her: the tremendous nurturing she gives as a nurse and as a woman.

Rosamund is, like Margaret in *The Return of the Soldier*, a woman who thrives on caring for others. Her ability to do so amounts to a kind of genius. Also like Margaret, but unlike Mary and Rose, she has no ambition other than to be allowed to do this caring. To explain to her cousins what nursing means to her, Rosamund calls it her "music," but she lacks their desperate desire for a career. Instead she excels in the traditionally feminine occupations of sewing and gardening—in contrast, the Aubrey women are incapable of successfully growing plants—and she seems content just to exist rather than to strive for difficult ends: "Her talk was as colourless as water, she never said anything funny. But it was as pleasant to listen to her as to lean over a bridge and watch a clear stream running by" (*Fountain Overflows*, 81). She is "natural" in a way that Richard Quin alone can match. He teases her that she can beat him at chess only because "she thinks with her skin," since "she hasn't got a mind" but "does quite well without it" (*This Real Night*, 18).

Yet Rosamund is an expert at soothing unhappy people by finding exactly what they need at a particular moment and giving it to them, similar to the way Woolf's Mrs. Ramsay handles men and children. When Cordelia is recovering from a botched suicide attempt brought on by the brutal rejection of a famous violin teacher—a rejection that accentuates her difference from her musically capable sisters—Rosamund nurses her back to physical and mental health by turning Cordelia's attention to the "feminine" occupation of sewing at which she may excel. Rosamund distracts Richard Quin from his grieving over Piers's death by taking down her gorgeous blonde hair and reminding him of the sensuous joy and beauty that she represents and in which he revels. Perhaps the most important thing she does is to tell Clare Aubrey how worried Rose and Mary are about how they will afford their music colleges. This convinces Clare to sell the original Lawrence and Gainsborough portraits she owns and had told Piers were copies; Rosamund both soothes Clare's conscience when her aunt feels guilty about this necessary deception, and brings in the money that will further her cousins' careers. In one action, she accomplishes the bettering of (at least) three lives.

Rosamund seems to be shy—she stammers and blushes—but she is the most certain, of all the women in her extended family, of what she believes and the most skillful in her chosen expertise. Though she usually seems acquiescently feminine and awkwardly reticent, she is, interestingly, the most sure and articulate of them all in her criticisms of men. Rose hates much of what her father Piers does, but she worships him nevertheless, commenting, "Temperamentally I was born to acquiesce in patriarchy" (*Fountain Overflows*, 245). Rosamund will obey and cater to her father Jock, but she will calmly, even acidly, dissect his foibles, without raging over them as Rose does but also not longing madly for him to be what he is not. She applies her inborn logic, which helps her to win chess games, to the behavior of "papas." When Rose claims that her mamma says "that men have quite different sorts of minds, not better but different, and can do work we cannot," Rosamund replies,

Oh, I am not talking of their work. . .it is all the states they get into. Your Papa goes on and on about the world falling into ruin. But what would that mean but that a whole lot of people are going to live as he has made you and your Mamma live? And if my Papa is so sad because

life is terrible, why does he do so little to make it less terrible for my
Mamma and me? If he feels so horrified at the thought of people
getting cancer, might it not occur to him that Mamma and I are just
as likely to get cancer as anybody else and let us have a little
gaiety?. . .[T]he world must be getting worse, if they say so. . .So
life is not so hard as it is going to be when we are grown up. But our
Papas are doing very well in the present. Someone always saves your
Papa at the last moment, and my Papa makes lots of money. But as
for you and me, and Cordelia and Mary and Richard Quin, all the
trouble the Papas foresee will come down on us. It is we who will
have to bear the hardships and do heroic things. (*Fountain
Overflows*, 245-6)

   Part of Rosamund's "natural," and innately feminine, quality is this
clear vision of what problems consist of and which are worth help, even
when   they   concern   the   apparently   unreachable   lives   and
accomplishments of adult men.[12] She uses this ability to aid others in
their emotions and actions. Rosamund's willingness to do something to
help others, besides involvement in art, sets her apart from all of her
cousins except Richard Quin; but she is also the most ruthless analyst
of social and personal problems in the family. She is capable as well of
accepting "any physical fact" (*This Real Night*, 5) according to Rose,
who is disgusted by menstruation as Rosamund is not.
   So Rosamund is a paradox in herself; Rose thinks, "Everything
about her was very contradictory" (*Fountain Overflows*, 291). Though
she has conventionally, if even negatively, feminine aspects—a great
beauty whose initial impact on others is definitely physical, a woman
who supposedly is not smart or talented, a person who appears slow and
mostly interested in sensual pleasures—she is also a human being of
enormous power and surety. Part of that power is deception, a trait also
unhappily assigned to women, but Rosamund uses it always for
unselfish reasons, again unlike Rose or her sisters. In fact, her female
counterpart in the *Cousin Rosamund* trilogy is Rose, whose similar but
different name points up her role as Rosamund's antithesis and obverse.
Rose is brilliant but thorny, a singular person who acts and thinks for
herself and who lives in a solitary world of artistic endeavor. Rosamund
is literally of and for the world as she works for others in a hospital and
within her family; she is outwardly less accomplished than Rose, but
she is ultimately superior, as her superlative name implies.
   Most importantly, Rosamund does not threaten men, as even her
placid mother did as a young woman—Clare says that "men were afraid
of" Constance (*Fountain Overflows*, 92)—and as many of the other
female characters in the trilogy do. Clare has "inconvenient genius and
integrity," and Piers fell in love with her not because of it, but "in spite
of" it (*Fountain Overflows*, 54). Rose and Mary, as professional

musicians, are directly competitive with most of the men they meet; they receive marriage proposals made only in anger. Queenie Phillips literally murders her man. Part of Rosamund's cleverness as a woman (and as a saint) is to hide her power behind apparent stupidity and uncertainty—hence the blushes and stammers, the "blind look" she feigns when she wants to appear as if she does not understand that she is not to interfere or to hear—and her rich, natural beauty works effectively as a mask of femininity, even as an icon of ideal woman: "by simply existing, by simply having the face and body that she had, she conveyed a meaning of a sort that [Rose] found in music" (*Fountain Overflows*, 134). Rosamund does confine her activities to "woman's work," but she is potent within that sphere in some measure because she does so confine herself. Though Rosamund is naturally protective herself, she is also skillful at making men feel her apparent need for their protection and care, never hiding her fear or discomfort from them but rather accentuating it to build their confidence. Rose notes that when their doctor asked Rosamund if something hurt, "she opened her large blue-grey eyes very wide and answered, 'Oh yes, it does,' and it was as if she were making him a present by her confession of pain; and he always behaved gratefully, as if she had given him something nice" (*This Real Night*, 94). She gets men to behave as she believes they should by behaving as she thinks they believe she should.

Rosamund's male counterpart is Richard Quin. (The *Cousin Rosamund* trilogy, like all of West's fiction, is full of deliberate duality: each of the main characters has his or her opposite, usually someone whose very connection to another emphasizes their reversals.) He is as manly as she is womanly, and Rose reflects so often and so insistently on his secure, definite masculinity that clearly West intends him to be a paragon of his sex. Much of his maleness is in line with a customary "boys will be boys" attitude. He is good at math, and enjoys it in a way that none of his sisters do. He is excellent in any game or sport, especially those involving balls, and his room in the house at Lovegrove is hung with "his boxing-gloves and his fencing foils, his rackets and bats" (*This Real Night*, 209). When Richard Quin enters the British army at the start of World War I, he likes it, becoming "more of a man, and more deeply infatuated with some mastered technique" (*This Real Night*, 219) with each visit home. But most significantly, he is a protector of women, as Rosamund is a protector of both sexes. Richard Quin believes that "nobody should keep demons if they have a wife and children. That's the last truth, there's nothing behind that one. If I live to be a hundred I shall never find out that that isn't true." He speaks out against his beloved father only in reference to Piers's failure as a provider, claiming that "he would beat [Piers], beat him savagely for

leaving us. . .without making sure that Mamma and [the] girls had
anything to live on when he had gone" (*This Real Night*, 114).

Yet the desire to beat someone is completely unlike Richard Quin,
who "hate[s] all violence" (*Fountain Overflows*, 112), and this is what
sets him apart from the other men the Aubrey women have known: he
is a force for life, not death. Though he is "so male that he had no
reason to be irked by the sexual division," he lacks the "masculine
vinegar" that drives men to want to make women unhappy and to fight
with each other over land, abstract ideas, honor, old grudges. Instead of
creating discord, he shields the women of his world from it. "With his
maleness, this other element, the difference of every cell in his body
from every cell in ours, he was protecting us," Rose gloats (*This Real
Night*, 193). Thus, in Richard Quin West creates her perfect man. Not
only is he the best of the Aubrey children (and so superior, specifically,
to girls), as Rose repeatedly informs the reader; he is a symbol of
"correct" and positive masculinity, killed by the masculine folly of
World War I. Richard Quin, like Harriet's and Arnold's happy marriage,
is not capable of surviving in the modern "real" world, "this real night"
of confused sexual identities and triumphant violence.

The Dog and Duck, the Thames inn where the Aubreys find a refuge
from London, is an Eden-like retreat from this modern world, a place in
which, in Westian terms, "men are men and women are women." Uncle
Len, its proprietor, is another male protector and another man who is
absorbed in properly masculine interests: science, math, horses, the
business of his hotel. His wife Milly cooks and sews as if by nature;
her friend the barmaid, Aunt Lily, is a happy server of men. The Dog
and Duck, with its uncomplicated gender boundaries, is therefore an
appropriate setting for two of the courtships in *Cousin Rosamund*,
those of Queenie and Mr. Bates, and Nancy and Oswald. The inn also
seems to be a place of healing and resolution, since these two marriages
make amends, in a sense, for past damage in all four lives. As such,
they represent the way Rose comes to believe that sexual love and
marriage can be for a woman something other than misplaced
martyrdom for a great but tragically flawed man. At the beginning of
This Real Night she is "determined not to marry," since her mother

> had committed herself to [her] marriage without knowing what it was
> going to cost her. If we who had seen her pay the price condemned
> ourselves to such misery, even for the same reward, there would be
> something suicidal about it, and that would be contrary to the desire
> to go on living which was her chief characteristic.
>   Indeed, marriage was to us a descent into a crypt where, by the
> tremulous light of smoking torches, there was celebrated a glorious
> rite of a sacrificial nature. Of course it was beautiful, we saw that. But

we meant to stay in the sunlight, and we knew no end which we could serve by offering ourselves up as a sacrifice. (6)

The imagery here recalls Proserpine's violent abduction into the underworld, and so emphasizes not just the sacrifice of a woman's autonomy, but her enforced subordination to a man she has not chosen, and the "hell" of living with the king of death: a reference suited to Piers Aubrey, in spite of his brilliance.

Both Queenie Phillips and Mr. Bates had suffered marriages of a sacrificial nature—though not to spouses of genius like Clare—and both had chosen poorly. Mr. Phillips was a well off but crude and tasteless man, if kindly, who could not begin to match the energy of his wife. Rose calls "excessive" her sense of Queenie's "life and reality" (133), and comments on Queenie's intense hunger for something her life has not given her, a desire so strong that she committed murder for it. She is "inconveniently important and unique" (139) although she has lived most of her life either as a Victorian housewife or a prison inmate. Mr. Bates shares with her a dramatic presence. Once an ironmonger, he is an evangelist for a religious sect called the "Heavenly Hostages," and this calling suits his wild-eyed, fanatic personality and appearance. His "life and reality" are as intense as Queenie's, and his marriage almost as disastrous: Mrs. Bates was an alcoholic whose drunkenness marred and haunted her husband's and son's lives, so that Nancy and Oswald both live under the stigma of famously bad mothers, and both Queenie and Mr. Bates remember disappointing partners.

Specifically their marriages were, in the conventional sense, sexual role reversals. Queenie was stronger than Mr. Phillips, and her murder of him takes that dominance to its farthest limit. As Uncle Len says, "Phillips was a good chap, but soft, who didn't know how to keep her down" (225). In fact, in Queenie West reconfigures the classic murderess of popular Victorian "sensation fiction," in Showalter's term, which articulates their readers' and writers' fantasies "of protest and escape" from "their roles as daughters, wives, and mothers" (158-9). Queenie imagines that she can flee her unhappy marriage through murder, and her extreme solution emphasizes just how strongly she felt her married life to be a prison that could not contain or utilize her "importance" and "uniqueness." It also shows her inability to distinguish between the private fantasies these novels offer her—in her first appearance at Nancy's birthday party, Queenie is looking for her "new Elinor Glyn" (*Fountain Overflows,* 140)[13]—and the truth of murder's evil. In her portrait West both sympathizes with the reality of such unfulfilled women, and yet says that living a fiction will not do, that it lies outside "the wine of truth." Murder breaks the immutable moral laws that give goodness ascendancy over evil in the universe, goodness represented most powerfully by Clare, Rosamund, and Richard

Quin and that Rose senses to be fighting with evil throughout the
Cousin Rosamund trilogy.

Moreover, the problem was not with the man, but with the
marriage. Queenie has been waiting for a man to rule her, as Mr. Bates
has been waiting for a personal, and sexual, subject. The first Mrs.
Bates was weak in her addiction, but powerful in her ability to
undermine anything her husband might have achieved in any
community by making a public fool of herself. But at first sight, Bates
recognizes that Queenie's needs complement his own. He initially
infuriates Queenie, as if she rightly spots a kind of adversary—"What's
the old bugger think he's playing at?" (218)—but she immediately, and
humbly, submits to his demand to know if she is the "great sinner"
about whom he has heard. After their eyes have "burned" into each
other's, Mr. Bates roars, "Come with me and I will deliver you bound
and gagged to the mercy of the Lord God" (219), possessively laying
his arm across her shoulders.

Comic as this scene is, its imagery of subjugation is unmistakable.
Uncle Len and Mr. Morpurgo, who have themselves been involved in
happy and unhappy sexual relationships (as Rose, who witnesses the
scene, has not yet been), recognize that the attraction between Queenie
and Bates is erotic, and that sexuality is what has been missing from
this new couple's separate lives. Mr. Morpurgo is "awed" by Mr.
Bates's capture of Queenie—this time, a positive re-enactment of Pluto
and Proserpine—and Rose recognizes it as "something that guaranteed
the safety of both" her and Queenie (219), and then as a "law" that had
been established and "would be maintained" (223). That law is sexual
love. "There is no substitute for sex" (230), says Mr. Morpurgo to
Rose as they discuss Queenie and Bates and as Rose prepares to see
Oliver and to face sexual desire for the first time in her life.

The marriage of Oswald and Nancy has been a very different
preparation for Rose's own. If Queenie and Bates represent passion,
their children stand for the domestic happiness of ordinary people.
Nancy will tend the house and bear and raise children while Oswald
works as a teacher in the appropriately masculine subject of science. In
the midst of extraordinary family and friends, neither is a remarkable
person: Oswald is argumentative and stupidly pedantic, not in fact a
talented scientist, and Nancy is colorless and unaccomplished. Yet the
description of their wedding and its anticipation is a prose
epithalamion—"it would be impossible to paint it justly without
recourse to such symbolic devices as court painters used in celebrating
royal weddings" (28)—and Rose imagines them, in their decidedly
humble and unoriginal home, as "classical. . .idyllic, they might have
been outside time" (99). Oswald, unlike his father, cannot "bear" the
idea of sex. He must hide behind its scientific reality rather than admit

the importance of that which embarrasses him, while Mr. Morpurgo names it "the lowest note" in the scale of male-female relationships, but without which "there is no use in any relationship between a man and a woman" (230). Still, he and Nancy are as happy in their conventional, even prudish, marriage as their parents are in their sex-based union.

The marriage of Rose and Oliver, toward which these different but lesser marriages in *Cousin Rosamund* have been leading, is the culmination of domestic happiness, sexual attraction, and professional fulfillment that no other Westian characters experience. Oliver, while not flawless, manages to be a total man in a way that Piers, Jock, Uncle Len, Mr. Morpurgo, Oswald, and any of Rose's past suitors are not: a brilliant artist and a man secure in his masculine sexuality, he is not overcome by the male death-wish, nor is he full of condescension toward and dislike for women. And unlike many of the men Rose encounters in post World War I society, he is decidedly heterosexual. *Cousin Rosamund* surpasses *Sunflower* and *The Thinking Reed* in its condemnation of homosexuality; it is part of the novel's glorification of gratified marital love between a "real" woman and a "real" man. Rose calls "silly" the "fashion" in Paris of the twenties for "men [to love] men and women [to love] women," claiming that they do so "not because there was a real confusion in their flesh, such as Mary and [she] often noted in those with whom [they] worked," but "because a homosexual relationship must be nonsense in one way, since there can be no children, and it can be made more nonsensical still" (4). The outrageously rude, rich young people Rose and Oliver encounter at Lady Mortlake's are primarily homosexual men. Lady Treddinick, a long-time friend and supporter of the Aubrey sisters, suffers from a scandal that reveals one of her sons to be homosexual, but the blame for his sexual choice seems to lie at least in part with her own improperly masculine persona. Her eventual suicide emphasizes West's view of homosexuality as tragically wrong.

Rose herself has suffered some confusion about her femininity. A composer in Paris tells her, as she rehearses her independently formed interpretation of his concerto, that she is "*trop male pour [son] frele oeuvre*" (3). Rose is not offended by this remark; she sees it as "adventitious aid" (7) of the sort Mary has not necessarily needed in her greater artistry. But even Mary, Rose thinks, is not "strong" enough, as a woman, to play the Emperor Concerto without the help of her sheer genius. In fact, Rose tends to see musicians through gendered glasses. She imagines a male violinist's expression while playing as that "of a woman tending domestic apparatus such as a sewing machine or a mangle," though she precedes this idea with the assurance that "he was entirely masculine" (153). She has known Oliver since late childhood, but her first sexual considerations of him come as appreciations of his masculinity, as if these offset his possibly effeminate status as musician: "I noticed the jut of his shoulders, for they were not broad, yet he held them as men with broad shoulders do" (183). After Oliver has told her the cathartic story of his late wife's adultery with the horrible genius Jasperl, she is pleased by the way he lifts her "gently but so strongly," and remarks that he "look[s] after women so well that he might have been an American," and that she "was foolish ever to have suspected that he was homosexual" (196).

It is Oliver's masculinity itself, however, that Rose must learn to accept before she can love him. Conditioned to thinking of men as treacherous, and used to a predominantly female circle, Rose reacts to her budding sexual desire with physical repulsion, seeing sex as "pollution" that "spoils women to the destruction of their essence" (203). She clings like a child to the people she has always known, becoming hysterical over the loss of her parents, brother, and cousin, and furious at the idea that she must ever change from being the person who is utterly dependent upon and fulfilled by them. Even wishing to give up music in order to remain untouched by the world—as her sister Mary will indeed do—she rejects her previously cherished belief that "music is an answer to the pit" of despair: "I do not want to make that answer anymore" (215). Yet it is Oliver's music that convinces her to risk sexual love, music that is an emblem of his masculine force, now "the answer" Rose is seeking. Just as Mr. Bates is strong enough to capture and hold Queenie, Oliver's genius is greater than Rose's, and so is powerful enough to make her desire him.

> . . .I asked myself what I, who played Mozart so well, by comparison with nearly every other pianist, was doing bothering myself with this man who insisted on spending his life composing so much less well than Mozart. . .I was gritting my teeth at hearing this [Mozart] tune not even allowed to be difficult in its own subtle way, as it was poked out of the keyboard, when Oliver broke off and repeated with a delicacy which I had not believed within his powers, the first four bars of the movement, in which the tune is first presented in all its prettiness. The third time he played it he achieved a certain colour of tone in the second bar which somehow solved the problem and established it on the level of classical dignity. I had never thought of this effect. Why had I never thought of it? Because I had a lower order of musical intelligence than he had. I might be a better pianist than he was a composer but to be a creative artist with any valid title to the name is a better thing than to be an interpreter. He was much my superior, and I tingled with pleasure. (232-233)

With the characterization of Oliver (and Richard Quin), West glorifies traditional masculinity in a way that she does nowhere else in her fiction. The working out of abstract thought becomes admirable instead of overdone, when Oliver does it rather than Arnold Condorex or Kamensky; Mr. Morpurgo, Uncle Len, and Oliver delight in mathematical and scientific puzzles and games while Rose, Lily, and Milly serve the men tea. Kate and Miss Beevor enjoy taking care of Oliver's clothes, thrilled to have a man around the house, and Rose conjectures that part of the "domesticated vital principle" is the presence of male power, "this unpredictable, extravagant, violent thing that was tamed enough to live in a house" (251). Repeatedly Rose stresses her new fulfillment, a revelation akin to music's beauty and the perception of divinity.

> I was amazed at lovemaking. It was so strange to come, when I was nearly middle-aged, on the knowledge that there was another state of being than any I had known, and that it was the state normal for humanity, that I was a minority who did not know it. . .It was fantastic that nobody should speak of what pervaded life and determined it, yet it was inevitable, for language could not describe it. (234)

Yet it seems that Rose must lose almost everyone else she loves in order to have Oliver, just as she feared before marriage, as if the price of her ecstasy in sexual love is the end of her old and extremely important relationships. The theme of love as irrefutable human law runs throughout *Cousin Rosamund;* its strictures include the rightness and inevitability of this marriage-induced sacrifice. Rosamund insists that Nancy must go with Oswald regardless of what her friends and family may think of him, and Rosamund herself deliberately cuts off communication with the Aubreys and their circle once she has mysteriously married, knowing that her husband and her past are incompatible. By the time of her marriage, Rose has lost Piers, Richard Quin, Clare, and Rosamund, but a seemingly indestructible tie is severed when Mary recoils from Rose's new life with Oliver. Two aspects of marriage particularly repulse Mary, specifically the ones Rose sees as its foundation: the lack of safety in relinquished solitude, and sex. By choosing to cut herself off from all but those she has known, asexually, since childhood, Mary chooses a "sanctity" that Rose believes evil: "I knew from my mother that such sanctity was evil, was too safe, it meant coming to an end instead of working perpetually, as she and Richard Quin were now at work. In this Mary was, suddenly, on my father's side" (239). By denying sexual love, Mary misses "the archetype of pleasure, the primal model" of joy, that which shows "how extraordinary existence was, how stupendous its contrast with nothingness" (249). Although Mary's art is greater than Rose's—partly because, like the Lady of Shalott, Mary allows almost nothing else into her room of her own (she even moves to a tower once Rose marries)—Rose's life is ultimately greater than Mary's.

Rose deliberately opposes (what would have been modernist) literature's "heavy broadside against marriage" (252) and its idea that "an arrangement that had become irksome" should simply be cancelled. The most stable of Rose's intimates show their approval for whatever sacrifices she must make for marriage. Uncle Len tells her that she is "better off. It's more natural to be married, no matter who you are," but that she will "have to fall in with Oliver's ways, and if they aren't ours, well, we heard you take your vows. . .and if keeping them means we don't see so much of you, there'll be no hard feelings." Aunt Milly chimes in that "in the long run it's worth it" (254).

The great mystery of *Cousin Rosamund*, however, remains Rosamund's marriage to Nestor Ganymedios, a bridegroom who seems utterly undeserving of the sacrifice of Rosamund's career and family. Its solution lies partly in Oliver's explanation of why Celia, his first wife, was drawn to the equally repulsive Jasperl. Celia's story and character obviously parallel Rosamund's; Rose thinks constantly of her cousin as she listens to Oliver's narrative about his dead wife. Celia, an opera singer, was a woman of beauty and great talent who lost her vocation ("She sang quite without genius for the last four years of her life" [186]) and her marriage to an adoring, sane husband when she chose to be the lover of an evil but brilliant composer, a man who had already ruined other women's lives in a similar fashion. Oliver claims that "it seemed to her a law of nature that she should do anything that [Jasperl] told her to do" (187), and Oliver initially saw this state as "madness," in part because he believed then that Jasperl's music was worthless. Jasperl's "constant aim" is only "to hurt people" (187), so when Celia committed suicide over his rejection, Oliver believed her love only a "disease" from which she suffered.

But Oliver discovered after Celia's death that Jasperl's work was great in a way that he believed his own was not, and this solves "the mystery of Celia's love for [Jasperl]" (189).

> He was her destiny, the martyrdom to which her cruel God called her, it is possible that when she came face to face with him she followed him as an early Christian saint might follow a bishop whom she knew was to lead her to the stake, the grid, the lions of the arena. (190)

Celia's genius was not only for music; she had "a genius for love," and Jasperl's "state was a challenge to her. She had to win his soul from Satan. She went to him as to a battlefield" (192). Surely this is the reason Rosamund marries Nestor Ganymedios.

West did not finish Rosamund's life in full novel form, but the groundwork for what was to be the key to her unhappy marriage and concentration camp martyrdom is put down here. For Celia and Rosamund, the ultimate meaning in life lies in losing what is most personally precious in trying to save a man from evil. Celia's effort to free Jasperl's genius so that it might produce great works of art is understandable, though just what Rosamund was to do for Ganymedios, or in Belsen camp, will never be known (though, again, it fits with the trilogy's overall theme of the human necessity to fight evil with good). But the Westian myth of martyrdom in marriage, whether a legal or illicit union, is as explicit in their stories as it gets.

Like her attitudes toward motherhood, money, women's careers, and women's beauty and vulnerability, West's ideas about marriage cannot be put neatly into a folder and labeled one thing or another. Though she envisions joy for Rose and Oliver, for Queenie and Mr. Bates, and for Nancy and Oswald, the majority of her fictional marriages are so flawed that divorce seems a better option than the gritty endurance of Constance, Chris Baldry, Mrs. Melville, Tania Rowan, Mabel Essington, or Arnold Condorex, to name a few. Of course, there are some divorces in West's fiction, most notably those in "Life Sentence" and "There is no Conversation" from *The Harsh Voice*. But in the first story, the odd denouement shows that Josie's and Corrie's divorce was in fact a terrible mistake; in the second, the narrator is not purged by her escape from Etienne de Sevenac, but obsessed by his continuing existence. West never imagines a successful marital breakup, only widows and widowers released by their partners' deaths into some sort of peace or new life.

It seems clear that at some level West is both vilifying and defending her father, Charles Fairfield, in all these fictional husbands and lovers who have genius but not reliability, a passion for justice but not thoughtfulness. Clare Aubrey, modeled on West's mother, is her most admirable martyr in marriage: a woman who never loses faith in or patience with her husband in spite of his compulsive gambling, and who supports him in pursuing what achievements his brilliance warrants and his sickness allows. Isabelle Sallafranque almost leaves her husband Marc for the reasons Clare might leave Piers, yet she pulls back at the last minute, convinced that her love for him is more important than liberty from his faults. For both Clare and Isabelle, a strong consideration is the welfare of present and future children. But even stronger is their belief that their best lives lie with these men, even though both had the option not to marry at all, unlike Victorian heroines doomed to act in only the marriage plot. Maybe West is justifying her own marriage; maybe she is rewriting the history of her parents' lives together in order to make sense of her father's desertion and her mother's love for him.

There is another possible answer to why West creates these sacrificing wives, other than for the obvious reason that their stories are representative of lives real women have led and lead. As a woman known and berated for feminist ideas early and late, she could be trying to give men the story she thinks they want to hear as a way of making herself more desirable sexually and socially. Her sense of being isolated from complete emotional and sexual fulfillment in marriage, or in other love relationships, was strong enough to motivate these plots that almost present apologies for feminine aggression and ambition and which put men back at the center of a woman's life. As I have stressed, West's characters live out what she did not—marriage to a dominating man and the final surrender of intellectual and artistic goals to that man. Perhaps she thought that this life would include a deep joy that hers lacked. Or maybe she wanted to write of the successful marriages she saw, and these were the patterns she actually observed. Or maybe she wished to gain male approval she never received.

But whatever the reason, West makes clear in her fiction that, rightly or wrongly, she believes the happiest marriages exist when husbands are motivated by wives who are devoted to them. Women can find strength in themselves, she thinks; men need the help of dedicated women. So even though she assigns the greatest political, artistic, or intellectual feats to men, she bestows on women the final credit for those deeds. It is another example of her paradoxical feminism: let men do the work that gives them the most visible power and glory, she says, but admit that women are behind them, just as the old saying goes.

Notes

1. Along these same lines, Glendinning quotes part of a letter from West to the Elizabethan scholar A.L. Rowse. (Hynes, in his review, also quotes it.) "I have never been able to write with anything more than the left hand of my mind; the right hand has always been engaged in something to do with personal relationships." Glendinning quotes more, saying that nevertheless, West "felt that her left hand's power, 'as much as it has,' was due to 'its knowledge of what [her] right hand is doing'" (193). Here is an example of West granting human connection, the talent she accords women, ultimate importance.

2. To corroborate this point, Glendinning quotes an unpublished notebook now housed at the University of Tulsa. "He [Henry] had appeared to find me attractive until that moment. The breach was sudden, no warning. I attempted to question him about it; he would not reply. I could not believe how he was repudiating me" (192).

3. Glendinning and Rollyson are both careful to point out that there was much affection between them as well. Glendinning mentions in her preface that West liked to talk "affectionately" about her late husband during the time of the biographer's acquaintance with West.

4. Rebecca West, "I Regard Marriage with Fear and Horror," *Hearst's International Cosmopolitan* November 1925: 210. Further references will be identified by page numbers in the text.

5. Rebecca West,. "Woman as Artist and Thinker." In *Woman's Coming of Age*, ed. Samuel D. Schmalhausen (New York: Horace Liveright, Inc., 1931): 378.

6. "Woman as Artist and Thinker": 381.

7. See Stec, Chapters 2 and 3 of her dissertation, for a thorough analysis of what she calls West's "nostalgic repetition-compulsion about primitive gender roles" in *Sunflower* and *Black Lamb and Grey Falcon.*

8. Glendinning writes that Wells's correspondence with Arnold Bennett "makes it clear that [Wells] saw the novel's theme as proving, unintentionally, their shared belief in the essential 'secondariness' of women" (134).

9. Glendinning, 135.

10. In *Black Lamb and Grey Falcon,* West calls her own figure a "sturdy pack-horse build" (776). Virginia Woolf commented a few times on what she considered West's shabbiness. Woolf wrote to her sister Vanessa Bell, on May 25, 1928, that "Rebecca. . .[is] no beauty. She is a cross between a charwoman and a gipsy, but as tenacious as a terrier, with flashing eyes, very shabby, rather dirty nails, immense vitality, bad taste, suspicion of intellectuals, and great intelligence." (Nigel Nicolson, ed., *The Letters of Virginia Woolf*, Vol. 3, Hogarth Press, 1977): 501. In her diary entry of December 17, 1932, she calls West "rather rubbed about the thorax" (131).

11. See Victoria Glendinning's afterword to *Cousin Rosamund,* 291. The following quote in the text also comes from this afterword.

12. In *Black Lamb and Grey Falcon* West writes,

If there is one certain difference between the sexes it is that men lack all sense of objective reality and have a purely pragmatic attitude to knowledge. A fact does not begin to be for a man until he has calculated its probable usefulness to him. If he thinks it will serve his purposes, then he will recognize it; but if it is unwelcome to him, then he will deny it.

She uses as an example the idea of the human soul, about which nothing can be proved.

[N]othing is more debatable for any of us than whether it is a good or a bad thing that our souls should have come to be. That life is preferable to death is a conviction firmly held by our bowels and muscles, but the mind has never convincingly proved it to the mind. Women, however, do not greatly trouble about this, since we have been born and we shall die, and even if the essence of our existence should be evil there is at least a term set to it. Therefore, women feel they can allow themselves to enjoy the material framework of existence for what it is worth. With men it cannot be so. Full of uncertainty, they sweat with fear lest all be for the worst. Hence the dichotomy that has been often observed in homes for the aged: the old women, even those who in their time have known prosperity, do not greatly distress themselves because in their last days they must eat the bread of charity, and they accept what pleasure can be drawn from sunny weather, a warm fire, a bag of sweets; but the old men are perpetually enraged. (678)

Rosamund and Jock certainly fit these descriptions of male and female temperaments.

13. Elinor Glyn, 1864-1943, was a popular novelist in Edwardian England.

Epilogue

Magic

[As] I passed one of the nuns [I] remarked, as I had done before, that the rank and file of the female religious order present an unpleasing appearance because they have assumed the expression of credulity natural and inevitable to men, who find it difficult to live without the help of philosophical systems which far outrun ascertained facts, but [which is] wholly unsuitable to women, who are born with a faith in the unrevealed mystery of life and can therefore afford to be sceptics. *Black Lamb and Grey Falcon*

Previous chapters in this study explore the strong anger Rebecca West displays toward men and patriarchal structures and old restricting images of women perpetuated by society and art, and the ways that she rebels against women's lack of support and choice in artistic and professional careers. Yet they also illustrate how she blames not necessarily the framework of male domination for many women's unhappiness, but rather the irresponsible male relations of women in general and fathers and husbands in particular who do not uphold that framework. From this comes her scorn for "unmanly" men and homosexuals as representatives of "incorrect" masculinity: men who are not protective of women. Each chapter ends with the idea that Rebecca West seems, in the final analysis, to retell old stories in her novels that might be deemed masculine narratives in spite of strong feminist themes. She implies that women are better off as wives, mothers, and homemakers than they are as professionals or artists; that men should be given ultimate possession of the written word; that some women should relinquish their autonomy and desires in order to save great, or even ordinary, men from their evil inclinations; that the best mothers are sacrificing saints.

I have claimed that West used her fiction to relieve the guilt and anxiety she may have felt over her literary success—which made men impotent with her, she believed, or at least uninterested in her sexually—by rewriting her own life in terms more acceptable to a patriarchal society. That is at best only a theory; but I think it a plausible explanation for why she blatantly contradicts her own feminist anger with these plots of woman's-conflict-resolved-in-traditional-marriage, and woman as self-effacing martyr. Much of West's fiction exemplifies what Carolyn Heilbrun calls, in *Reinventing Womanhood*, a woman "unable to imagine [herself] as both ambitious and female," a woman writer who has "failed to imagine autonomous women characters."[1]

Still, it is impossible to dismiss as ultimately reactionary West's ideas about gender and "proper" sexual identity without taking into account her female characters' consistent subversion of male hegemony. West's women always rebel in *some* way against their "feminine" fates and the man's world that has created them. Even the insistence that men guard and keep the women in their lives comes from a rebellion against what West sees as the existing masculine status quo: a society that creates dependent women and then fails to provide their support. That this rebellion takes the form of the desire to have *more* male supervision is surprising (though directly related to her father's desertion); but it is still a tactic of revolt.

One of the most interesting subversive tactics West invokes in her novels against a male-dominated world is female magic, a strategy that connects her with cultural lore about women throughout recorded history and in virtually every known civilization. Though her fiction is largely realistic, it contains many allusions to magic. In general, the ability to tap into the supernatural works as empowerment for West's women: as personal fulfillment, as protection against patriarchal laws and customs, and as revenge against male oppression. It is for them a peculiarly female way of communicating, a language: a way of perceiving truth, and a means of connecting with what one wants, whether it be freedom, admiration, knowledge, or solace. Moreover, female magic often results in a corruption of male power.

The most obvious example is Harriet Hume. Though she is the ideally feminine woman in traditionally male terms—physically delicate and beautiful, sexually and socially submissive, delightfully muddled about the "real world"—she has the power literally to read Arnold Condorex's mind, which effectively destroys his ability to function in his consummately masculine world. Bonnie Kime Scott, in *The Gender of Modernism*, calls Harriet and other of West's fictional characters "Cassandralike" (564). Certainly Arnold does not believe Harriet's prophecies any more than the Trojans believed Cassandra. Though *Harriet Hume*'s ending belongs more to Gilbert and Sullivan than to epic tragedy (as Jane Marcus points out)[2], the consequences for Arnold, his political and physical demise, are (initially) as disastrous for him as they were for the soldiers who did not believe Cassandra's warning that the giant horse was full of armed enemies. Harriet may surrender her independent artistic life and space in order to live with Arnold, but not until she has equally annihilated his smugly superior life as a privileged imperialistic Englishman. In the novel's first pages, Arnold thinks that he "dislike[s] above all things women who laid claim to occult gifts," particularly because it means a woman will claim to remember having been an "Egyptian princess" who "kept [her] own pyramid" (9). This thought lays the groundwork for Arnold's eventual hatred of Harriet's power as his equal "opposite," when he thinks she should be instead his subordinate.

Magical powers and perception show up with surprising regularity in the otherwise realistic *Cousin Rosamund* trilogy. There is an autobiographical element to this. West, according to Glendinning, believed herself psychic, so much so that "[d]uring the Second World War, she seemed to sense when there were going to be air raids on London with such accuracy. . .that people observing her movements thought she must be a German spy." The poltergeist in *The Fountain Overflows* is based on one she claimed had "manifested itself in the house of her despised cousin Tom Mackenzie, who himself attended spiritualist seances." West wrote in 1962, "The supernatural keeps pounding at my door," including occasional poltergeists that in her old age she believed were working against her.[3]

The supernatural presence in the *Cousin Rosamund* trilogy, perhaps because it is closer to her own life, is somewhat more representative of West's paradoxical feminist thinking than in *Harriet Hume*. These manifestations of the supernatural are shunned by the "good" female characters such as Clare, Constance, and Rose as chaotic, "dirty," and dangerous, rather than embraced as the shield against hypocrisy that telepathy is for Harriet. The juxtaposition of "good" magic versus "bad" magic is a persistent theme: the light and dark universes Moira Ferguson accurately names as part of West's consistently dualistic vision. This battle represents what Margaret Diane Stetz names as West's most persistent philosophical preoccupation: whether the universe is good or bad.[4] West, through the voices of the Aubrey women, seems to eschew the use of otherworldly communion for personal gain; one might say that she goes along with the Christian, and arguably male, ban against magic as the opposite of the good that creates and maintains the correct order of the universe. But she erodes her own intent by showing the ways that women's magic succeeds for them as individual gratification or as retaliation for restrictions placed on them by a man's world.

In the *Cousin Rosamund* trilogy, as in *Harriet Hume*, this magic specifically takes the form of clairvoyance: several of the female characters have the ability to see future events and to read minds. I suggest that these powers are symbolic of traditional "feminine intuition," and that by granting her fictional women this gift, West is both acquiescing in and assaulting patriarchal culture. Admitting its existence, and supposedly agreeing that it is a stronger force in women than the ability or desire to run the world, to create new art, or to advance scientific knowledge, West also shows that feminine intuition has evolved to a high art in itself, and one whose end will as often as not be male ruin. This advanced evolution possibly occurred because intuition was one of the few mental powers granted women in their marginalized intellectual lives. As it was supposedly born into them and was not something they could learn or control by usurping male education or professions, it was perceived as unthreatening, even life-enhancing, and was allowed to develop unchecked. Consequently, it became not only an amusing talent; it became a way for women to go beyond their margins and influence their lives and the lives of those around them. But something so intangible as second sight (a phrase that implies inferiority) could not be counted a real accomplishment like amassing money or controlling governments. So while women's communication with otherworldliness perhaps emphasizes their connection with some profound truth and with the past—claims that men might make about artistic achievement or cultural development—it also symbolizes their secondary status in this world. And that secondariness, as West perhaps unconsciously emphasizes, has engendered rage that seeks retribution.

The Aubrey household contains no fewer than four female seers. The mother, Clare, is known to have "second sight": on a South African beach, while looking out on "a blank sea" (*Fountain Overflows*, 40), she has a vision of a steamer in flames and rowboats going toward the shore, and twenty-four hours later it happens just as she had seen. Rose thinks of her as a "sybil who knows more than philosophers and mathematicians" and as a "wonder-working fetish" (*This Real Night*, 78). Cordelia, though the least artistic of the Aubrey children, is clairvoyant, yet she is "at odds" with "her gift, neither controlling it nor yielding to it" (*This Real Night*, 206). Rose proves her telepathic ability by correctly guessing the numbers in children's minds at a birthday party. She is also, along with Clare, capable of seeing ghosts, as the remarkable night scene in the stable at Lovegrove illustrates, when mother and daughter feel the presence of horses long dead.[5] And Kate, the Aubreys' devoted servant, comes to them under threat of arrest for having told fortunes to sailors' wives; she and her mother would fill a bucket with water and claim to see in it what had happened to the women's husbands' ships on the sea.

Kate's involvement with the supernatural effectively illustrates the alternating pattern of power and impotence that the other women experience. Clare tells Rose that "in Kate's family the women have always done this thing," and though she does not elaborate farther than to say that at that time "people did not understand" the potential wickedness of tampering in what she terms the "dirty" supernatural (*Fountain Overflows*, 92), it is not difficult to understand why the women would attempt such knowledge. Left at home alone with rare and possibly unreliable sources of information, women would be desperate to find out whether their family's support would continue or cease with their husbands' (or other male relatives') good or bad fortunes at sea. They would also be curious, no doubt, about the adventures their menfolk were having in faraway places as they tended the home and the children. Imagining that they viewed their brothers', fathers', sons', or husbands' lives in a bucket would be a way for women to live vicariously the seagoing life their sex prohibited. Kate is frequently likened to a sailor, and Rose mentions several times that Kate would have been one if she had been a man. Kate and her mother both surround themselves with nautical objects, and follow passionately the consistently maritime careers of their male family members. When Kate's brother visits the Aubreys one Christmas, Rose remarks upon his unsailorly, almost fragile appearance; the implicit comparison with his sister seems to point out the injustice of the prohibition against female sailors, and the larger prohibition against women as anything but nurturers, servants, or limited artists.

Still, the fact that Kate can see the future (and it seems we are meant to believe that she really can) gives her an unmistakable force. It is a proven way to make money, not only for Kate, but for women traditionally. Telling the future functions as a kind of language that women use and seek as a way of understanding a world they often do not understand; it seems a method improbable in a world of masculine rationality, but trenchant in an alternative female universe where marginal methods of communication and artistry have been the norm. Bonnie Kime Scott points out West's "unique responses and strategies" in the "underexplored regions of female sub-culture."[6] Kate and her mother, though they are bastions of Edwardian working-class respectability in most ways, are representatives of such a sub-culture: women traditionally scoffed at and feared as witches and seance-holders. Though they may genuinely have a message that could save a life or avert disaster, they are usually ignored. Kate's near-arrest illustrates, in fact, a male taboo against female magic (or power); the fact that Kate so often sees a man's death indicates a buried wish for the end of such male control and explains why men might prohibit it. They perhaps subconsciously understand this ritual of feminine fulfillment.

Rose's life as an artist represents another kind of taboo. As previously discussed, she and her twin sister Mary are shunned throughout their school days for the fact that they are pursuing professional performing careers instead of perfecting the customary domestic feminine graces. When Rose attends a birthday party at the home of one of her rich schoolmates, the children are asked to perform for each other. Although Rose is already an exceptional pianist, she chooses not to play, but to do a thought-reading trick in which she guesses, always correctly, the number in a child's mind. Immediately she is showered with respect and admiration, even to the point of gaining the attention of a grown-up—Queenie Phillips, the mother of the birthday girl—who begins wooing her with candy in an attempt to find out how Rose reads minds. When Queenie asks Rose if she can tell fortunes, Rose lies and says that she can, believing Queenie "stupid" to think that because Rose could see numbers in another's head, she could also "knock down the walls between the present and the future" (*Fountain Overflows*, 202).

But if Rose sees thought-reading as a way of gaining the popularity and acceptance her musical ability does not give her, Queenie grasps at this seeming magic as proof that all rules can be broken. She had played successfully by Victorian patriarchal rules: she used her good looks to get a rich husband, and now spent her days literally eating bon-bons around the house or shopping for expensive clothes. But Queenie does not love her husband and is not gratified by motherhood, and, being a strong, spirited woman, she is wildly frustrated by her domestic cage. Exactly what Queenie wants from Rose's potential prophesy is never articulated: perhaps she hoped Rose could tell her when her husband would die naturally and leave her free, or whether she would get away with homicide. Rose does not tell Queenie's fortune, but Queenie poisons her husband anyway. When the news comes that Mr. Phillips has died, Rose has an image of Queenie as a tarot card, and Clare and Constance know instantly that Queenie has killed him, and that she was inspired by Rose's ability to break what had seemed to Queenie indestructible laws. The dreadful use she makes of this knowledge means that she exchanges the imprisonment of her marriage for the real confinement of jail, but she does accomplish two things: she escapes her husband and his house, and, however unjustly, rids the world of a man. Once again female clairvoyance means male demise.

Clare and Constance abhor the use of their own, their children's, or Kate's magical abilities, considering them literally powers of evil to be controlled. In what is one of the most interesting (and surely the oddest) of scenes in *The Fountain Overflows*, Rose and Clare arrive unannounced at Constance's house to find that a poltergeist is waging incessant war against her and her daughter Rosamund. The poltergeist's weapons and methods seem unmistakably male: a phallic poker flies straight at Clare and Rose as soon as they knock, a heavy piece of furniture is easily toppled. Comically, it particularly sets out to undo all the housework Constance and Rosamund might do, as if it is the consciously spiteful spirit of the domestic male. Rosamund comments that it never actually hurts the women, it "just break[s] things and spoil[s] things, so that we have to spend our lives mending and washing" (108).

The poltergeist, in fact, is representative of Constance's brilliantly talented but hateful husband Jock, the classic death-embracing Westian man who wastes his time and ample salary on bogus societies for supernatural and psychical research instead of developing his musical genius or enjoying his wife and daughter. Jock is, as the poltergeist shows, bad magic of the kind Clare and Constance despise, and they oppose him with their good magic: once Clare, Constance, Rose, and Rosamund are all in one room together, the poltergeist gives up its battle. Jock's alleged research into the occult, which apparently consists mostly of going to spurious seance circles, may stand for a kind of inappropriate usurpation of a feminine world: his dislike of women—a trait West frequently attributes to men in general—goes so far that he wants to dominate even their subculture of supernatural communication. Interestingly, this feminine magic is a power not encompassed in Christianity. When Rose remembers that the Bible mentions "two or three gathered together" as a power against evil and wonders if the four women ought to have said the Lord's Prayer in front of the poltergeist, Clare, who believes in an unspecified God of goodness for whom she tirelessly battles, sighs that "it's not so easy as all that" (126). Even Christ, the ultimate savior of western patriarchal culture, cannot save the women from Jock's masculine malevolence; they must rely on the alternative powers they have developed as sheer survival tactics. (In fact, Clare conspicuously wins the battle with Jock; as she dies in the harrowing and beautiful final pages of *This Real Night,* he stands outside her window and mourns.)

Nevertheless, Rose deplores magic with escalating intensity for the rest of her life after the Queenie incident, considering herself a "murderess by proxy," and even that Queenie had done the killing for her (*Cousin Rosamund,* 217). Mary and Rose leave the beloved Aubrey house in Lovegrove after their mother's death because they believe it "could have seduced [them] into the practice of magic" (*Cousin Rosamund,* 1). In her strongest condemnation of magic in the entire trilogy, Rose remembers in *Cousin Rosamund* that when she

> had raised a paper from the ground and held it in mid-air by supernatural means. . .Richard Quin had turned from [her] and wept when [she] made him watch [her] at this trick, and had grown sick and nearly died. For he had been a saint. . .whose repulsion from evil had been absolute; and at that time [she] had been evil. (131)

This passage is representative of West's paradoxical attitude toward female magical powers. Granting her brother superiority over her—Richard Quin is, in fact, the most deliberately admirable character West created—Rose hates the memory of a female power used to thwart his male will. Yet Rose continues to use tropes of the supernatural to describe Rosamund's, Clare's, and even Richard Quin's admirable ability to communicate: she calls them "conjurors" on several occasions, and persists in seeing their influence as "good magic" and wickedness as "bad magic." Try as she might, Rose cannot ignore her own occult perceptions and magical abilities, probably meant by West to represent a seduction to evil. But I believe their presence also demonstrates West's desire to depict the struggle between alternative feminine powers and male authority, and the ambivalence she felt toward granting men the final victory.

This ambivalence underlies all of the speculations about women and men in her fiction. In *Black Lamb and Grey Falcon*, West muses on the apparent contradiction in the fact that the poem which gave her magnum opus its name, which "above all other works of art celebrated [an] appetite for sacrificial self-immolation," is one that the Yugoslavian people in 1941 loved to recite, though "there was no one who would have bought his personal salvation by consenting to the subjugation of his people, and no one who would not have preferred to be victorious over the Nazis if that had been possible" (1145). She ties this in to an idea about artistic motivation.

> Yet the poem sounded in their ears as a prophecy fulfilled in their action, a blessing given across the ages by omniscience perfectly aware of what it was blessing behind the curve of time, and indeed none who loved them could read it now without a piercing sense of appositeness. It applies; and the secret of its application lies in the complex nature of all profound works of art. An artist is goaded into creation on this level by his need to resolve some important conflict, to find out where the truth lies among divergent opinions on a vital issue. His work, therefore, is often a palimpsest on which are superimposed several incompatible views about his subject; and it may be that which is expressed with the greatest intensity, which his deeper nature finds the truest, is not that which has determined the narrative form he has given to it. The poem of the Tsar Lazar and the grey falcon tells a story which celebrates the death-wish; but its hidden meaning pulses with life. (1145)

This is illustrative, and proleptic, of the "several incompatible views" West expresses about feminism and sex roles in her novels, especially the later ones. That which is expressed with the greatest intensity—to my mind, her feminist anger—is not that which has determined the narrative form given to it—plots which reiterate women's subordination, and which emphasize their relations with men as the determining forces in their lives. West struggled with where the truth lay among her own, and the Western world's, divergent opinions on the vital issues of women's autonomy and equality with men. That she does not provide a watertight vision of feminist belief fulfilled and maintained will perhaps always make her unpopular with some, yet it also proves the ferocity of the opposition she must have encountered. The evidence of her struggles is unmistakable; and for Rebecca West to have struggled as magnificently as she did attests her courage, and proves that she was willing to explore, in the name of truth in art, all of the contradictions of being a human being and a woman.

Notes

1. See Carolyn Heilbrun, *Reinventing Womanhood* (New York: Norton, 1979): 34 and 71.

2. See Jane Marcus, "A Wilderness of One's Own: Feminist Fantasy Novels of the Twenties: Rebecca West and Sylvia Townsend Warner," 146.

3. See Glendinning, 73, and Rollyson, 379.

4. See Margaret Diane Stetz, "Rebecca West and the Visual Arts," *Tulsa Studies in Women's Literature* 8:1 (1989): 46. Stetz takes this phrase from *The Court and the Castle* (6).

5. West's sister Winnie remembered the stamping of the long-dead horses at Streatham Place, and apparently Lettie was also "preoccupied with the supernatural." See Rollyson, 315, and Glendinning, 73.

6. See Bonnie Kime Scott, "The Strange Necessity of Rebecca West." In *Women Reading Women's Writing*. Ed. Sue Roe (Brighton: Harvester, 1987): 269.

Bibliography

Auerbach, Nina. *Communities of Women*. Cambridge: Harvard University Press, 1978.

Beauman, Nicola. *A Very Great Profession: The Woman's Novel 1914-39*. London: Virago Press, 1983.

Bell, Pearl K. "Duchess of Letters." Review of *This Real Night* by Rebecca West. *The New Republic* 22 April, 1985: 33-36.

Briggs, Austin. "Rebecca West vs. James Joyce, Samuel Beckett, and William Carlos Williams." In *Joyce in the Hibernian Metropolis*. Ed. Morris Beja and David Norris. Columbus: Ohio State University Press, 1996. 83-102.

Brownstein, Rachel M. *Becoming a Heroine: Reading About Women in Novels*. New York: The Viking Press, 1982.

Butler, Judith. "Variations on Sex and Gender: Beauvoir, Wittig and Foucault." In *Modern Literary Theory: A Reader*. Ed. Philip Rice and Patricia Waugh. New York: Routledge, Chapman, and Hall, 1996. 145-59.

_____. "Contingent Foundations: Feminism and the Question of 'Postmodernism.'" In *Feminists Theorize the Political*. Ed. Judith Butler and Joan W. Scott. New York: Routledge, 1992. 3-21.

Clarke, Ann Jennifer. "Know This is Your War: British Women Writers and the Two World Wars." Ph.D. diss: State University of New York at Stonybrook, 1989.

Colquitt, Clare. "A Call to Arms: Rebecca West's Assault on the Limits of 'Gerda's Empire' in *Black Lamb and Grey Falcon*." *South Atlantic Review* 51.2 (1986): 77-91.

150 *Paradoxical Feminism*

Conrad, Joseph. *Under Western Eyes* [1911]. New York: Penguin, 1984.

Crooks, Robert C. "The Eternal Moment: Paralysis and Stasis in Modern British Fiction." Ph.D. diss: Tufts University, 1989.

Deakin, Motley. *Rebecca West*. Boston: Twayne Publishers, G.K. Hall and Co., 1980.

_____. "Rebecca West: A Supplement to Hutchinson's Preliminary List." *Bulletin of Bibliography* 39: 2 (June 1982): 52-8.

de Beauvoir, Simone. *The Second Sex* [1949]. New York: Alfred A. Knopf, 1971.

DuPlessis, Rachel Blau. *Writing Beyond the Ending: Narrative Strategies of Twentieth-Century Women Writers*. Bloomington: Indiana University Press, 1985.

Ellmann, Mary. *Thinking About Women*. New York: Harcourt, Brace, and World, 1968.

Evans, Faith. Introduction to *Family Memories: An Autobiographical Journey* [1987]. Ed. Faith Evans. New York: Penguin, 1989. 1-12.

Ezell, Margaret J.M. *Writing Women's Literary History*. Baltimore and London: The Johns Hopkins University Press, 1993.

Faulkner, Peter. *Modernism*. New York: Methuen, 1977.

Ferguson, Moira. "Feminist Manicheanism: Rebecca West's Unique Fusion." *Minnesota Review* 15: 53-60.

Ford, Ford Madox. *The Good Soldier* [1915]. New York: Vintage, 1955.

Forster, E.M. *Howard's End* . New York: Vintage, 1921.

Fraiman, Susan. *Unbecoming Women: British Women Writers and the Novel of Development*. New York: Columbia University Press, 1993.

Freud, Sigmund. *The Freud Reader.* Ed. Peter Gay. New York: Norton, 1989.

Fromm, Gloria G. "Rebecca West: The Fictions of Fact and the Facts of Fiction." *The New Criterion,* January 1991: 44-53.

Gilbert, Sandra M., and Susan Gubar. *The Madwoman in the Attic.* New Haven: Yale University Press, 1979.

_____. *No Man's Land: The Place of the Woman Writer in the Twentieth Century. Vol. 1: The War of the Words.* New Haven: Yale University Press, 1988. *Vol. 2: Sexchanges.* New Haven: Yale University Press, 1989. *Vol. 3: Letters From the Front.* New Haven: Yale University Press, 1994.

Gilligan, Carol. *In a Different Voice.* Cambridge: Harvard University Press, 1982.

Glendinning, Victoria. "Afterword." *Sunflower* by Rebecca West. New York: Penguin, 1986. 268-76.

_____. *Rebecca West: A Life.* New York: Fawcett Columbine, 1987.

_____. "A Woman for Our Century." *The New Republic* 11 April, 1983: 28-32.

Goldsworthy, Vesna. "*Black Lamb and Grey Falcon:* Rebecca West's Journey Through the Balkans." *Women: A Cultural Review* 8:1 (Spring 1997): 1-11.

Hammond, J.R. *H.G. Wells and Rebecca West.* New York: St. Martin's Press, 1991.

Hardwick, Elizabeth. *Seduction and Betrayal: Women and Literature.* New York: Random House, 1974.

Hardy, Thomas. *Tess of the D'Urbervilles* [1891]. New York: Bantam, 1992.

Hargrove, Anne C., and Maurine Magliocco, ed. *Portraits of Marriage in Literature.* Western Illinois Press: 1984.

Heilbrun, Carolyn. *Toward a Recognition of Androgyny: Aspects of Male and Female in Literature.* New York: Knopf, 1973.

_____. *Reinventing Womanhood.* New York: Norton, 1979.

_____. *Writing a Woman's Life.* New York: Norton, 1988.

Huf, Linda. *A Portrait of the Artist as a Young Woman: The Writer as Heroine in American Literature.* New York: Frederick Ungar Publishing Co., 1983.

Hutchinson, G. Evelyn. *A Preliminary List of the Writings of Rebecca West: 1912-1951.* New Haven: Yale University Press, 1957.

Humm, Maggie. *The Dictionary of Feminist Theory.* Columbus: Ohio State University Press, 1990.

Hynes, Samuel. "The Wild West." Review of *Rebecca West: A Life,* by Victoria Glendinning. *The New Republic* 19 October 1987: 46-49.

_____. "Introduction: In Communion With Reality." *Rebecca West: A Celebration.* Ed. Samuel Hynes. New York: The Viking Press, 1977. ix-xviii.

Irigiray, Luce. "This Sex Which Is Not One." In *Feminists Theorize the Political.* Ed. Judith Butler and Joan W. Scott. New York: Routledge, 1992. 248-76.

James, Henry. *The Portrait of a Lady* [1881]. New York: Penguin, 1981.

_____. *The Princess Cassamassima* [1886]. New York: Penguin, 1985.

Jones, Suzanne. Introduction to *Writing the Woman Artist: Essays on Poetics, Politics, and Portraiture.* Ed. Suzanne W. Jones. Philadelphia: University of Pennsylvania Press, 1991. 1-19.

Joyce, James. *Dubliners* [1914]. New York: Penguin, 1985.

_____. *A Portrait of the Artist as a Young Man* [1915]. New York: Penguin, 1983.

Kaplan, Sydney Janet. *Feminine Consciousness in the Modern British Novel.* Urbana, Chicago, London: University of Illinois Press, 1975.

Kent, Susan Kingsley. "Gender Reconstruction After the First World War." In *British Feminism in the Twentieth Century.* Ed. Harold L. Smith. Amherst: University of Massachusetts Press, 1990. 66-83.

Klein, Melanie. *Envy and Gratitude: A Study of Unconscious Sources.* New York: Basic Books, Inc., 1957.

Land, Hilary. "Eleanor Rathbone and the Economy of the Family." In *British Feminism in the Twentieth Century.* Ed. Harold L. Smith. Amherst: University of Massachusetts Press, 1990. 104-23.

Lawrence, D.H. *The Complete Short Stories, Volume 2.* New York: Penguin, 1984.

_____. *The Rainbow* [1915]. New York: Penguin, 1984.

_____. *Sons and Lovers* [1913]. New York: Penguin, 1983.

_____. *Women in Love* [1916]. New York: Penguin, 1983.

Lawrence, Shirley. "Rebecca West: Battle-Axe and Silver Pen." *Simone de Beauvoir Studies* 10 (1993): 151-57.

Levin, Gerald. *Sigmund Freud.* Boston: Twayne Publishers, 1975.

Lewis, Jane. "Myrdal, Klein, *Women's Two Roles* and Postwar Feminism." In *British Feminism in the Twentieth Century.* Ed. Harold L. Smith. Amherst: University of Massachusetts Press, 1990. 167-88.

_____. *Women in England 1870-1950.* Bloomington: Indiana University Press, 1984.

Marcus, Jane. "Acting Out." Review of *Sunflower* by Rebecca West. *The Nation* 4 April, 1987: 487-90.

_____. "Rebecca West: A Voice of Authority." In *The Faith of a (Woman) Writer.* Ed. Alice Kessler-Harris and William McBrien. Westport, Conn.: Greenwood Press, 1988. 237-46.

_____. *Virginia Woolf and the Languages of Patriarchy*. Bloomington: Indiana University Press, 1987.

_____. "A Wilderness of One's Own: Feminist Fantasy Novels of the Twenties: Rebecca West and Sylvia Townsend Warner." In *Women Writers and the City: Essays in Feminist Literary Criticism*. Ed. Susan Merrill Squier. Knoxville: The University of Tennessee Press, 1984. 134-60.

_____. "A Speaking Sphinx." *Tulsa Studies in Women's Literature* 2.2 (1983): 151-54.

Meredith, George. *The Ordeal of Richard Feverel* [1859]. Toronto: Dover, 1983.

Meyers, Judith Marie. "'Comrade Twin': Brothers and Doubles in the World War I Prose of May Sinclair, Katherine Anne Porter, Vera Brittain, Rebecca West, and Virginia Woolf." Ph.D. diss: The University of Washington, 1985.

Miles, Rosalind. *The Female Form: Women Writers and the Conquest of the Novel*. New York: Routledge and Kegan Paul, Inc., 1987.

Miller, Jane. *Women Writing About Men*. London: Virago, 1986.

Miller, Nancy K., ed. *The Poetics of Gender*. New York: Columbia University Press, 1986.

Moers, Ellen. *Literary Women*. New York: Doubleday, 1976.

Nicholson, Nigel, ed. *The Letters of Virginia Woolf, Volume 3*. New York: Hogarth Press, 1977.

Orel, Harold. *The Literary Achievement of Rebecca West*. London: Macmillan, 1986.

Orlich, Sister Mary Margarita. *The Novels of Rebecca West: A Complex Unity*. Ph.D. diss: The University of Notre Dame, 1966.

Peterson, Shirley. "Modernism, Single Motherhood, and the Discourse of Women's Liberation in Rebecca West's *The Judge*." In *Unmanning Modernism: Gendered Re-Readings*. Ed. Elizabeth

Jane Harrison and Shirley Peterson. Knoxville: University of Tennessee Press, 1997. 105-16.

Pringle, Alexandra. Introduction to *The Harsh Voice,* by Rebecca West. New York: The Dial Press, 1981. vii-xiii.

Pugh, Martin. "Domesticity and the Decline of Feminism, 1930-1950." In *British Feminism in the Twentieth Century.* Ed. Harold L. Smith. Amherst: University of Massachusetts Press, 1990. 144-64.

Ray, Gordon N. *H.G. Wells and Rebecca West.* New Haven: Yale University Press, 1974.

Ray, Philip E. "*The Judge* Reexamined: Rebecca West's Underrated Gothic Romance." *English Literature in Transition* 31.3 (1988): 297-307.

Redd, Tony Neil. "Rebecca West: Master of Reality." Ph.D. diss: The University of South Carolina, 1972.

Richardson, Samuel. *Clarissa* [1748]. Abr. George Sherburn. Boston: Houghton Mifflin, 1962.

Rollyson, Carl. "Rebecca West and the FBI." *The New Criterion,* February 1998: 12-22.

_____. *Rebecca West: A Life.* New York: Scribner, 1996.

_____. *The Literary Legacy of Rebecca West.* San Francisco: International Scholars Publications, 1998.

Scialabba, George. "Woman of the Years." Review of *Rebecca West: A Life,* by Carl Rollyson. *Boston Globe* 17 Nov., 1996: N15, 18.

Scott, Bonnie Kime. "Rebecca West." In *The Gender of Modernism: A Critical Anthology.* Ed. Bonnie Kime Scott. Bloomington: Indiana University Press, 1990. 560-69.

_____. "Refiguring the Binary, Breaking the Cycle: Rebecca West as Feminist Modernist." *Twentieth Century Literature* 37:2 (Summer 1991): 169-91.

_____. *Refiguring Modernism. Volume 1: The Women of 1928.*
Volume 2: Postmodern Feminist Readings of Woolf, West, and
Barnes. Bloomington: Indiana University Press, 1995.

_____. "The Strange Necessity of Rebecca West." In *Women Reading*
Women's Writing. Ed. Sue Roe. Brighton: Harvester, 1987. 263-
86.

Showalter, Elaine. *A Literature of Their Own: British Women*
Novelists From Bronte to Lessing. Princeton: Princeton
University Press, 1977.

Smith, Harold L. "British Feminism in the 1920s." In *British*
Feminism in the Twentieth Century. Ed. Harold L. Smith.
Amherst: University of Massachusetts Press, 1990. 47-65.

Spacks, Patricia Meyer. *The Female Imagination.* New York: Avon,
1972.

Spender, Dale. *There's Always Been A Women's Movement This*
Century. London: Pandora Press, 1983.

_____. *Time and Tide Wait for No Man.* London: Pandora Press, 1984.

Stec, Loretta. "Writing Treason: Rebecca West's Contradictory Career."
Ph.D. diss: Rutgers University, 1993.

_____. "Female Sacrifice: Gender and Nostalgic Nationalism in
Rebecca West's *Black Lamb and Grey Falcon.*" In *Narratives of*
Nostalgia, Gender, and Nationalism. Ed. Jean Pickering and
Suzanne Kehde. New York: New York University Press, 1997.
138-58.

Steinem, Gloria. "Women in the Dark: Of Sex Goddesses, Abuse, and
Dreams," *Ms.* January/February 1991: 35-37.

Stetz, Margaret Diane. "Drinking 'The Wine of Truth': Philosophical
Change in West's *The Return of the Soldier.*" *Arizona Quarterly*
43.1 (1987): 63-78.

_____. "Rebecca West and the Visual Arts." *Tulsa Studies in Women's*
Literature 8.1 (1989): 43-62.

_____. "Rebecca West's Criticism: Alliance, Tradition, Modernism." In *Rereading Modernism: New Directions in Feminist Criticism.* Ed. Lisa Rado. New York: Garland Publishing, Inc., 1994. 41-66.

_____. "Rebecca West's 'Elegy': Women's Laughter and Loss." *Journal of Modern Literature* 18:4 (Fall 1993): 369-80.

Stewart, Grace. *A New Mythos: The Novel of the Artist as Heroine 1877-1977.* Montreal: Eden Press Women's Publications, 1979.

Stokes, John. "'A Woman of Genius': Rebecca West at the Theatre." In *The Edwardian Theatre.* Ed. Michael R. Booth and Joel H. Kaplan. Cambridge: Cambridge University Press, 1996. 185-200.

Teachout, Terry. "A Liberated Woman." *The New Criterion* 6.5 (1988): 13-21.

Thomas, Sue. "Rebecca West's Second Thoughts on Feminism." *Genders* 13 (Spring 1992): 90-107.

Ulanov, Ann and Barry. *Cinderella and Her Sisters: The Envied and the Envying.* Philadelphia: The Westminster Press, 1983.

Urie, Dale Marie. "Rebecca West: A Worthy Legacy." Ph.D. diss.: The University of North Texas, 1989.

Weldon, Fay. *Rebecca West.* Harmondsworth: Penguin, 1985.

Wells, H.G. *Marriage* [1912]. London: Hogarth Press, 1986.

_____. *Tono-Bungay* [1908]. Lincoln: University of Nebraska Press, 1978.

West, Anthony. *Heritage* [1955]. New York: Washington Square Press, 1984.

West, Rebecca. *The Birds Fall Down.* New York: Popular Library, 1966.

_____. *Black Lamb and Grey Falcon: A Journey through Yugoslavia* [1941]. New York: Penguin, 1994.

_____. "Charlotte Bronte" [1932]. In *Rebecca West: A Celebration* [1977]. Ed. Samuel Hynes. New York: Penguin, 1978. 429-38.

_____. *Cousin Rosamund* [1985]. New York: Penguin, 1987.

_____. *The Court and the Castle: Some treatments of a recurrent theme* [1957]. New Haven: Yale Paperbound, 1961.

_____. "Elegy." In *The Legion Book.* Ed. Captain H. Cotton Minchin. London: Cassell and Company Ltd., 1929: 178-86.

_____. *Ending in Earnest: A Literary Log.* Garden City, New York: Doubleday, Doran & Co., 1931.

_____. *Family Memories: An Autobiographical Journey* [1987]. Ed. Faith Evans. New York: Penguin, 1989.

_____. *The Fountain Overflows.* New York: The Viking Press, 1956.

_____. *Harriet Hume: A London Fantasy* [1929]. New York: The Dial Press, 1980.

_____. *The Harsh Voice: Four Short Novels* [1935]. Harmondsworth, Middlesex: Penguin, 1956.

_____. *Henry James.* New York: Henry Holt, 1916.

_____. "I Believe." In *I Believe.* Ed. W.H. Auden. London: Geõrge Allen & Unwin Ltd., 1940.

_____. "I Regard Marriage with Fear and Horror." *Hearst's International,* November 1923: 67, 207-209.

_____. *The Judge* [1922]. New York: The Dial Press, 1980.

_____. *A Letter to a Grandfather* (an essay; "Hogarth Letters Series," no. 7). London: Leonard & Virginia Woolf at the Hogarth Press, 1933.

_____. *The Meaning of Treason* [1947]. London: Macmillan & Co., 1949.

_____. "My Religion." In *My Religion.* Ed. Arnold Bennett. New York: D. Appleton and Company, 1926: 19-25.

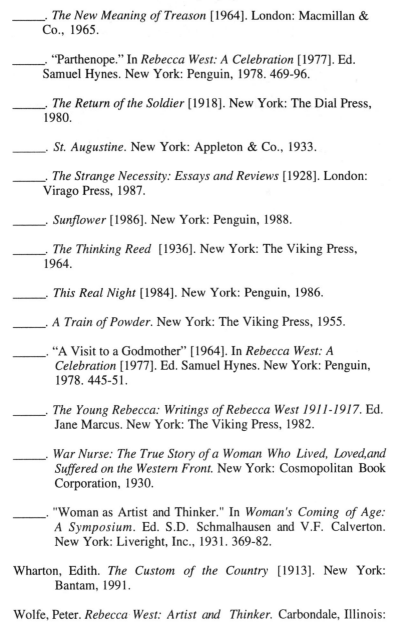

_____. *The New Meaning of Treason* [1964]. London: Macmillan & Co., 1965.

_____. "Parthenope." In *Rebecca West: A Celebration* [1977]. Ed. Samuel Hynes. New York: Penguin, 1978. 469-96.

_____. *The Return of the Soldier* [1918]. New York: The Dial Press, 1980.

_____. *St. Augustine.* New York: Appleton & Co., 1933.

_____. *The Strange Necessity: Essays and Reviews* [1928]. London: Virago Press, 1987.

_____. *Sunflower* [1986]. New York: Penguin, 1988.

_____. *The Thinking Reed* [1936]. New York: The Viking Press, 1964.

_____. *This Real Night* [1984]. New York: Penguin, 1986.

_____. *A Train of Powder.* New York: The Viking Press, 1955.

_____. "A Visit to a Godmother" [1964]. In *Rebecca West: A Celebration* [1977]. Ed. Samuel Hynes. New York: Penguin, 1978. 445-51.

_____. *The Young Rebecca: Writings of Rebecca West 1911-1917.* Ed. Jane Marcus. New York: The Viking Press, 1982.

_____. *War Nurse: The True Story of a Woman Who Lived, Loved,and Suffered on the Western Front.* New York: Cosmopolitan Book Corporation, 1930.

_____. "Woman as Artist and Thinker." In *Woman's Coming of Age: A Symposium.* Ed. S.D. Schmalhausen and V.F. Calverton. New York: Liveright, Inc., 1931. 369-82.

Wharton, Edith. *The Custom of the Country* [1913]. New York: Bantam, 1991.

Wolfe, Peter. *Rebecca West: Artist and Thinker.* Carbondale, Illinois: Southern Illinois University Press, 1971.

Paradoxical   Feminism

Woolf, Virginia. *The Diary of Virginia Woolf, Volume IV.* Ed. Anne
Oliver Bell. New York: Harcourt Brace Jovanovich, 1977.

_____. *Jacob's Room* [1922]. New York: Harcourt Brace Jovanovich,
1950.

_____. *Mrs. Dalloway* [1925]. New York: Harcourt Brace Jovanovich,
1953.

_____. *A Room of One's Own* [1929]. New York: Harcourt, Brace,
Jovanovich, 1957.

_____. *To the Lighthouse* [1927]. New York: Harcourt Brace
Jovanovich, 1981.

_____. *The Years* [1937]. New York: Harcourt Brace Jovanovich, 1965.

INDEX

as "great men," 29, 84-85,
91-92, 113-20
irresponsibility of, xviii,
33-34, 67, 84-91, 127
loss of primitive in, 22, 116-
17
as "lunatics," 25, 47, 75-92,
110-11, 115, 118, 128, 133,
137-38
in marriage, 4-36, 65-71, 87,
109-36, 144 *See also*
marriage
as protectors, 91-92, 126-
28, 132, 139-40
sexuality of, 22-32, 47, 48,
111-36
as sons, 94-97, 102-104,
127
violence of, 11-13, 15-17,
19-20, 45-47, 77-90, 93,
104, 128
as workers, 8-17, 21-36, 98-
105, 127-36
Meredith, George, 11, 50
Miller, Jane, 49-50, 96
Milton, John, 64
Minerva, 60
Modernism, 121-22, 134
Monkey Island, 11, 37
Monroe, Marilyn, 58
mothers, motherhood, 4, 6, 20,
48-49, 76, 92-105, 135
See also Women
Mozart, 132
Mrs. Dalloway, 118-19
music, 98-100, 131-34
Nation, The, xii
Nazis, 20
New Meaning of Treason, The,
77
Newsweek, xi
Nicholas II, 84, 86, 90-91
O'Brien, Norah, 41-42
Ordeal of Richard Feverel, The,
11, 50
Orel, Harold, 19, 72, 83, 96
Orlando, 121-22
Orlich, Sister Mary Margarita,
23-24, 106n9

Pascal, Blaise, 14
pastoral, the, 16, 23, 42, 52, 55
Paul, Saint, 79-80
Peterson, Shirley, 107n15
Piaget, Jean, 75
Portrait of a Lady, The, 14,
37n12
Postmodernism, xvii, 70
Pre-Raphaelites, The, 41-42, 52
Pringle, Alexandra, 25
Profumo Scandal, The, 60-61
Proserpine, 129-130
Ray, Philip E., 43-44
Return of the Soldier, The, 8-14,
25, 80, 93-94, 97, 105, 124,
135
Revelation, 89, 106n13
Reynolds, Sir Joshua, 54
Rhondda, Lady, 5
Richardson, Dorothy, 122
Rollyson, Carl, xii, 1-3, 7, 13,
77, 82, 121, 123
Room of One's Own, A, 122
Rosmersholm, 3
Rossetti, D.G., 42
Russia, 83-92
"Salt of the Earth, The," 26-27,
38n20, 66
Scott, Bonnie Kime, xii, 3, 66,
103, 105n2, 107n18, 140,
143
sex antagonism, 20, 55, 121,
123
sexuality, *see* men, women
Shakespeare, William, 80
Shaw, George Bernard, 3
"Short Life of a Saint, The," 66
Showalter, Elaine, xix, 35, 63,
103, 105n4, 122, 129
Siddal, Elizabeth, 42
Smith, Harold L., 6
soap operas, 58
Sons and Lovers, 114
Spacks, Patricia Meyer, 96, 99
Stalin, Joseph, 77
Stec, Loretta, xii, 6, 77-78,
106n12, 137
Steinem, Gloria, 58-59

as parasites, 4, 9, 12, 15, 18,
56-57, 65, 92
promiscuity of, 17-19, 56-57
sexuality of, 20, 24, 29-32,
47-48, 88, 99, 110-36
"stupidity" of, 58-60, 125-
27, 144
vulnerability of, xviii, 23,
45-48, 87-89, 122
as workers, 4-5, 18, 21-36,
47, 97-105, 124-139
Woolf, Virginia, xvii, xxin16,
8, 13, 61, 63, 118-19, 121-
22, 125, 137n10
World War I, 5-6, 8, 11-12, 20,
26, 32, 93, 104, 124, 128,
131
World War II, 77-78, 97, 124,
135, 141
"World's Worst Failure, The,"
71
Wuthering Heights, 109
Years, The, 61
Young Rebecca, The, xv